Boycie & Beyond

By the same author:
Being Boycie

Boycie & Beyond

Part Two of
an Autobiography

by

John Challis

First published in Great Britain in September 2012

By Wigmore Books Ltd

ISBN 978-0-9569061-1-3

Wigmore Books Ltd
Wigmore Abbey
Leintwardine
SY7 0NB

Printed in Great Britain by the MPG Books Group, Bodmin and King's Lynn

This book is dedicated to the men and women of the RNLI at the Lizard Lifeboat Station, the volunteers and crew of 'the most southerly'

Acknowledgements
I'd like to thank the usual gang for their help in getting this book to the press:
My (quite) patient wife Carol, Peter Burden, Damian Russell, Celestria Noel and Martin Ellis

FOREWORD
Sue Holderness

I read *Being Boycie* eagerly, from cover to cover. Having now spent nearly thirty years on and off working with John, I was rather surprised that I didn't enter his 210-page autobiography until page 210. Well it just goes to show what a rich and varied life he has led. All those wives! Still I am proud to say that my marriage to John – strictly professional and on stage – has lasted longer than any of the others. We hit it off from day one and fifty or so episodes later, I can honestly say that I've enjoyed every minute of it. Our first episode together was entitled *Sleeping Dogs Lie*. Well, John has bravely decided to wake the dogs up and reveal much of his extraordinary life. In this second part of his autobiography you will learn more about *Only Fools & Horses* which was a joy from start to finish, but the biggest thrill for me and John was when John Sullivan decided to write the spin-off *The Green, Green Grass*. What fun we had! We discovered that we enjoy working together as much on the stage as on screen and I hope our professional paths will cross frequently in the future. Of one thing I am confident, our friendship is here to stay.

The Story So Far...

In the previous volume of my memoirs, *Being Boycie*, I charted the choppy seas of the first forty-two years of my life – my happy, if lonely childhood, an iffy academic career, an almost accidental introduction to the actor's life and my early experiences on stage.

By 1966 I was married for the first time and working with the Royal Shakepeare Company in Stratford-on-Avon.

By 1976 I was no longer married, I had toured an English farce across South Africa, fallen in love half a dozen times and played *Scorby* in a six-part *Dr Who* story with Tom Baker.

In 1979 I went to the US to tour two plays with the great British playwright Tom Stoppard, fell in love with America and two American women, and came back to London to play a short role in the second episode of a new English sitcom, *Only Fools & Horses*, and to marry for the second time.

By 1985 *Only Fools & Horses* was established as a major British sitcom, and Boycie as a key character in it. Lennard Pearce, who played *Grandad*,had sadly died and Buster Merryfield had entered the cast as *Uncle Albert*.

Another new member joined the cast in March 1985, *Boycie's* wife, *Marlene...*

Chapter 1
A New Wife for Boycie

In March, 1985, watched by 18.7 million viewers, *Marlene Boyce*, played by Sue Holderness, was introduced to the cast of *Only Fools & Horses*. An episode in the fourth season, *Sleeping Dogs Lie*, showed *Boycie* and *Marlene* together for the first time in a television marriage that was to last an astonishing twenty-four years. It became one of the classic shows of all the series. Although *Marlene* had often been referred to in earlier episodes – usually with a dirty wink from *Del Boy* – as someone who'd spread her favours around, this was the first time John Sullivan had given her flesh.

Sue Holderness slotted into the part of *Marlene* as if she'd been in our show from the start. She was an experienced and versatile actress (or actor, as the *Guardian* would call her) who'd been seen in a lot of popular TV series, in *The Avengers* and an early Rowan Atkinson show.

Sue was feisty, funny and very quick to establish her character. I soon found we had a good chemistry on set and I was delighted when I discovered she was married to a friend of mine, Mark Piper, whom I hadn't seen since we'd worked together twenty years before at the Theatre Royal, Windsor. His mother, the famously forthright Joan Riley, had been directing for a season while my first wife, Carol Robertson, was stage-managing there. Now Mark himself was directing plays, as well as running the Windsor theatre.

In fact *Boycie* and *Marlene* appear only briefly in their first episode together, when, at the beginning of the show, *Del Boy* persuades them that he can look after their new Great Dane puppy, *Duke*,while they are away on holiday.

When *Rodney's* trying to get the dog out of the van to take him for a walk, he sees that *Duke* is behaving very dozily. He finds *Del*, and they decide to take the animal to the vet. They are worried the dog may have eaten some reheated pork leftovers for breakfast; the vet concludes that the dog has probably got salmonella poisoning.

Back home, they discover that *Uncle Albert* had eaten the other half of the pork joint, so they race off to hospital with him. After a few nasty tests, *Albert* turns out to be fine, but *Del Boy* discovers that

A New Wife for Boycie

Rodney has been giving *Albert's* sleeping pills to *Duke*, and the dog's vitamin supplements to *Albert* – all great Sullivan material, with *Del's* line at the end: 'Albert's been on the *Bob Martins*.'

After that, I had a short appearance in the next episode, *Watching the Girls Go By*, without *Marlene*. I guessed John Sullivan (the writer) and Ray Butt (producer) were going to mull over her appearance and decide whether or not to ask her back. This must have depended to some extent on how important they planned to make *Boycie* in subsequent shows, especially as, by now, *Only Fools* was getting such impressive viewing numbers and looked set for a long life, in TV terms. The show had already run for four years, and frankly I really doubt that even John and Ray dreamed that fresh episodes would still be appearing – albeit as Christmas Specials – in 2003, which was still eighteen years away. In the meantime, I had a nine-month break from the show before making the 1985 Christmas special, *To Hull and Back*.

Between acting jobs I couldn't resist a little tinkering on the fringes of the antique trade, as I'd done some years before when I'd worked in Portobello Road. This time I was helping my girlfriend, the actress Sabina Franklyn, and her mama, Margo, or 'Moo Moo', as we affectionately knew her. By the time I met her Margo Johns was a delicate little thing. She had been quite beautiful in her day and a talented actress. But Sabina's father, Bill *'Schh... You Know Who'* Franklyn, had left her thirteen years before, when Sabina was only eight, and she'd not been persuaded back into marriage with anyone else. She'd never found anyone to replace Bill, she said, and her acting career had dwindled with her confidence. She had a pretty two-up two-down terrace house in Westfields Avenue, in that picturesque part of Barnes known as Little Chelsea, from where she eked out a living by using her fine eye for antique porcelain and *bric-a-brac*.

She lived there like a small, eccentric bird in her tiny home, which was cluttered to the brim. Every possible space was filled with objects of taste that she'd bought but failed to sell because she'd paid just a little too much; antiques or *bric-a-brac* seem to be as price-sensitive to the punters as a litre of diesel.

There's little room for sentiment in the antiques trade, which was really too tough and grubby for her. I found it quite heart-rending sometimes to see Margo scuttling into the lion's den of Covent Garden market at the crack of dawn with battered cardboard boxes full of newspaper-wrapped stock, which she'd spent hours finding, choosing and ineptly haggling over. Every weekend or so we would help her hump a carload of *objets* to an antiques fair somewhere in the home counties, where we would often hang around to help chivvy the punters and keep her spirits up when the dealers came round, picking up pieces of precious porcelain or silver, peering at them, fingering them like spuds on a costermonger's barrow, and sniggering nastily when told the price. If Margo had inadvertently underpriced something good, it would be snatched up immediately by some rapacious dealer for the Bond Street trade, or re-surface on another stall a few minutes later at twice the price; indeed it could change hands a few times among other traders before it left the building in the grasp of a genuine punter at five or six times Margo's original price.

Sabina had inherited her mother's eye but she was much tougher and harder at buying and selling. I would do a little dealing myself from time to time, pottering around at the fairs trying to indentify stuff that looked underpriced, which I'd then sell for more at another, better-located fair. On one occasion, I spotted and bought a handsome Georgian mahogany writing-box that looked cheap. I'd learned that there were a lot of collectors for these potentially decorative objects, which needed only to be placed on a guest-room side table to suggest life in an era of Bennets and Darcys.

After it had been displayed at a few fairs, and dismissed roundly by a number of hard-nosed, impolite dealers (wearing bowties/fake tans/half-moon spectacles) whom I wouldn't have trusted with my last biro, as being neither Georgian nor mahogany, but a twentieth-century fake in some Indonesian hardwood, I pounced on the next interested punter. 'Is it eighteenth century?' he asked, looking a little uncertainly at the ticket that said so.

'Oh yes, indeed,' I said, in my most authoritative manner, hoping desperately that he wouldn't recognise my *Only Fools* persona.

As he walked away clutching the thing, having purchased it at slightly less than I'd paid, I added under my breath, to satisfy my conscience, 'At least... the tree it's made from was eighteenth century, or even older.'

A New Wife for Boycie

Sabina and I had met working at the National Theatre at the Olivier, in my second outing with the company. This wasn't an entirely wonderful experience, although, of course, I'd loved the first time I'd been with the NT, a few years earlier in Stoppard's *On the Razzle*. But I couldn't deny that it had been terrific once again to be in a piece by one of our greatest writers and there was nothing wrong with being asked back after that by the director, Peter Wood, to be in his production of *The Rivals* in the nation's premier theatre company.

But I would have felt I was making more progress if I'd been given a nice meaty leading role in a contemporary blockbuster, rather than a minor part in a classic play, which must have been produced several hundred times since Sheridan wrote it in 1775, and while I was glad to be back, I admit to being disappointed not to have ratcheted myself a few rungs further up the ladder.

I'd heard – and, while it may not be true, it was still discouraging – that the casting director, Gillian Diamond, had expressed a thought in an unguarded moment in front of people who shouldn't have been present: 'Darling, there are three categories of actor at the National – stars, TV names, and shit.'

I wasn't a star and I wasn't a TV name, so I knew where this left me in her eyes. Not surprisingly, after *The Rivals*, I turned down the next job I was offered by Michael Rudman, an important director, in *The Last of Mrs Cheyney*, in which I was asked to play the butler. 'The sort of character that vanishes into the wallpaper,' was how Michael described it. That didn't sound much fun, after all the hilarity and energy of *Razzle* and *The Rivals*. I felt, rather as I had fifteen years before at the RSC, that they'd like me to stick around, they could use me, but without guaranteeing me any chunky parts. So, trying to keep my tail up and proud, I took my leave. Of course, from a public perspective, I suppose my career looked on a good course: *Only Fools* was unquestionably doing well; all the doubts after Series 1 had been swept away by subsequent ratings, and I felt pretty bullish about *Boycie* becoming bigger in the show, but by instinct and in essence, I was a live performance actor, and this was what I always wanted to do. It was very tantalizing to have been on the fringes of theatrical glory with the National without really drinking from the cup myself.

Within the confines of the television world Sabina was pretty successful. The show she'd been in, *Keep it in the Family*, with Robert Glenister and Stacy Dorning, had done well. She and Stacy had become friends and they kept in touch. Stacy's father, Robert Dorning, was a good old actor, whom I admired as a great character man. It's sad but, I suppose, inevitable, that as most actors age – unless they are very special indeed – they become what are known in the trade as 'character bags'... or they stop working altogether.

This was a fate to which Sabina's father, Bill Franklyn, refused to submit. He was a well-established and popular actor, who still insisted on playing dashing boulevardiers, leading men, who appeared implausibly with a succession of younger women in a weary cycle of drawing-room comedies and edgeless thrillers. Other well-known cads and seducers have recognised the inevitable and adopted a strategy, like moustachioed Leslie Phillips. He had goosed, winked at and drawled '*Hello...*' to a hundred screen bimbos, but he'd reached a point where he decided to turn down all the caddish roles while he waited (a long time) for a real part to turn up. When it did (in *The Cherry Orchard* in the West End), he was able to reinvent himself as a character actor and this gave his career a new lease of life. Bill Franklyn, on the other hand, had decided that the character bag was not for him – possibly because he knew it was outside his range – and the jobs melted away.

I well remembered Oliver Fisher, an old trouper I'd worked with when I was twenty and in the Penguin Players in Bexhill, telling me, '*You'll* have to wait at least until you're forty before you get the sort of recognition you deserve.'

I was forty-three, and I reflected ruefully that most of the recognition I was getting was in the saloon bar of the Coach & Horses in Barnes High Street.

Sabina, on the other hand, was getting a lot of recognition, at least from Joe Public, when she starred in another very popular sitcom, *Full House*, with Christopher Strauli, Brian Capron and Natalie Forbes.

By the time the cherry trees were blossoming along the avenues in spring 1985, I had my feet well under Sabina's table in Barnes, quite contentedly, as far as that's possible for two people in our profession. I was keeping fairly busy with several TV jobs besides my *Only Fools* activity. These weren't just your derisory 'coughs and spits', although they weren't major roles, either.

In Irish stand-up Jimmy Cricket's *And There's More*, for instance, I was a psychopathic Mexican bandit, and in a *Storyboard*pilot, *King & Castle* I played a rather pathetic villain called *Billy Cato*. I had a shock – and a good laugh – when I saw myself for the first time running on screen. Being fairly knocked-kneed, my calves were splayed out like a lizard's on hot rocks; it seemed only right that *Billy Cato* should have been caught, tortured and embedded forever in the concrete piles of the Hammersmith flyover.

I also had a brief reunion with Warren Mitchell, with whom I'd worked in my first ever feature movie, *Where Has Poor Mickey Gone*, over twenty years before. In this particular episode of *In Sickness and in Health*, I was a copper trying to keep *Alf Garnett* under control after a perceived slight to his beloved West Ham United. The scene was filmed, curiously enough, at QPR's ground at Loftus Road, just around the corner from the BBC's Wood Lane Television Centre – excusable parsimony, I thought.

I reflected ruefully that my career in feature films since that first outing could not be said to have blossomed. Apart from a few odd bit parts (and a brief meeting with Jack Palance) there had been nothing and no siren calls from Hollywood.

However, I was becoming aware that *Boycie* was being noticed in the streets more often, with all the benefits and perils that can bring.

As a result of this minor fame, I suspect, I was asked by Sabina's father, Bill, to turn out regularly for a charity cricket team he captained – these days it would be known as a 'celebrity' team. I didn't mind as I loved cricket, although opportunities to play had been sporadic over the years. As it turned out, I could still connect with the ball – quite vigorously sometimes – and race up and down the wicket with my knock knees or snaffle the odd catch in the deep. In Bill's team pure enjoyment of the game was a little marred by never knowing if we were trying to win, lose or draw. Quite often we would find ourselves in a good position to win, only to be deterred by frantic (and ill-disguised) signals from the pavilion to, 'Slow it down' and 'Give 'em a chance,' with the result that we usually ended up achieving a tactful loss.

The team, the Sargentmen, had been formed to honour the

memory of orchestral conductor Sir Malcolm Sargent and support the Malcolm Sargent Cancer Care for Children, which had been founded in his name a year after his own death from pancreatic cancer in 1967.

A number of actors have made good use of their celebrity to promote charities, most notably, that *grand farceur*, Brian Rix, who was a leading supporter and chairman of Mencap. His daughter, Louisa was married to another member of the Sargentmen, Jonathan Coy, a well-thought of actor with a waspish sense of humour and perhaps best known for his long-running parts in *Rumpole* and *Hornblower*.

Brian Rix had often employed Sabina's grandfather, Leo Franklyn, in the nonstop string of farces he produced at the Whitehall Theatre – legendary home of English Farce, with all its trouser-dropping, arch suggestiveness and *double-entendres*. As a result, Sabina and Louisa had been friends since they were toddlers, while Jonathan was a regular big hitter on our team.

An unexpected member of the team was Bob Peck, taciturn northerner, regular RSC player and star of *Edge of Darkness*,the hugely successful British TV drama which was running at the time. Less widely seen, he played *Amos*, the twins' father in the beautiful and moving film of Bruce Chatwin's *On the Black Hill*, set in the Welsh Marches, which I came to know and love when I moved there in the late '90s.

Despite the inevitable backbiting and bitching that goes on among any group of assorted actors, these cricket matches were memorable for the particular quality of quaint Englishness that the game can evoke. I remember especially idyllic days spent in the wonderfully picturesque surroundings of the cricket ground at Nettlebed in the Chilterns – a setting no film designer could ever have created – along with the distinctive soft clunk of hard leather sweetly struck by willow, and the smattering of applause over the insect hum and the breeze in the beeches, as the ball rolled on to pass through and demolish a carefully prepared picnic of egg-and-cress sandwiches. And a later batsman, having sought to put out his cigarette before walking out to the crease, calls out his guard to the umpire, only to find smoke spiralling up from his now smouldering pads, and a moment later he is hopping around frantically trying to put out the flames licking up towards his groin, while the umpire calls to the scorer in the pavilion: 'Batsman out. Caught fire!'

On another Sunday, on another pitch, a ball was hit for six, and landed in the back of a passing lorry, not to be seen again until the driver found it back at his depot, sixty miles away. But he remembered where he'd been and returned it – the longest hit in the history of cricket, we guessed.

Another of our better batsmen was Jonathan Kydd, a versatile and ubiquitous actor, an *acapella* singer and voice-over artist of distinctive dressing habits. If and when he turned up (which tended to depend on the quality of tea likely to be on offer) he would be wearing a striped cricket blazer of ancient provenance and a Harlequin cap, while carrying a battered old leather cricket bag, and looking like someone from Douglas Jardine's famous '30s England cricket side.

There was a palpable tension between him and Bill Franklyn. The old actor obviously felt that Jonathan should show more respect for his captain and senior, while Jonathan made it clear he didn't think much of Bill's autocratic style and insistence on bowling too many overs from an increasingly arthritic run up.

The trouble for Bill was that Jonathan, for all his cavalier disdain for a captain's authority, was a class act, quite capable of winning a game on his own by his maverick batting.

More in harmony with Franklyn was his great old chum, Francis Matthews, who sometimes came to watch our matches. A quality actor and old-school charmer, Francis was well known in the business for his Cary Grant impressions, while I, as I may have told you before, fancied my own James Stewart. On occasion, sitting outside the pavilion, we would pass a very enjoyable half hour creating conversations between our two heroes, while Bill Franklyn looked on with a cocked eyebrow, trying not to laugh.

I soon learned that Bill was very competitive on and off the cricket pitch. It happened that I was still doing a lot of useful work in the voice-over studios, which he considered very much his own territory, not without justification. His voice had a wonderful, distinct fruity timbre, blended with a hint of sophisticated irony, that was always a pleasure to hear. However, by way of conversation and unaware of his strong territorial instincts, I would sometimes attempt to compare notes with him. He was unforthcoming and evidently sceptical. He asked Sabina when I wasn't with them if she was sure I wasn't making it all up, because, he said: '*I've* never heard him.'

Sabina assured him that I was often busy doing voice-overs.

'Is he?' Bill asked doubtfully. 'How many does he do a week? I never see him waiting in the studios.'

The following winter, I thought of him sitting comfortably ensconced in a warm London studio, smoothly purveying encouragement about 'Schh... YouKnow Who', as I walked up a bleak hillside in the Pennines above Burnley. I was there as a nasty, long-haired villain for an episode of *Juliet Bravo*, in which Simon Williams, a long way from Eaton Place and his usual comfort zone, played a slippery and nefarious *Mr Big*. The scene was given an extra chill by a north wind howling across the moor, so cold that the diesel in the coach had frozen.

My character was posted as a lookout, while plans were hatched for a hostage-taking robbery. At the appropriate moment, I was to walk about fifty yards and deliver a few pearls of wisdom about the feasibility of the scheme. I arrived at my mark in time and opened my mouth to speak. With a shock, I found that one side of my face had completely frozen, as if in preparation for a painful molar extraction. The only sounds that emerged, 'Erurrfblair I greffur', seeped into the polar atmosphere and seemed to drop and shatter in a million pieces at my feet.

Opposite me, Simon, with pointed features pinched tight by the frost, looked even more uncomfortable.

Why, I thought, did we take these jobs?

After two appearances as a rotter in very early episodes of *Howard's Way*, which went on to fill the BBC's Sunday night schedule for the next five years, I was back with Ray Butt, John Sullivan and the gang, making the 1985 *Only Fools* Christmas special and first feature-length episode, *To Hull & Back*. Coincidentally my main co-player in this, Tony Anholt, had come in to *Howard's Way* a few episodes after mine, as *Charles Frere*, lover to *Lynne Howard*, played by Tracey Childs.

To Hull and Back, like all subsequent *Only Fools* Christmas shows, was more lavish in production terms than a normal episode. It was filmed entirely on location, with even a bit of foreign travel – if you call Holland foreign – though *Boycie* never got to go there. It was also one of the few episodes with no studio work, therefore with no live audience, with the result that at 90 minutes, it looks more like a movie than a TV episode.

It worked very well, with a broadcast audience on Christmas Day of nearly 17 million, and subsequently became one of the show's all-time favourites. It was one of John Sullivan's great stories: complex, convoluted, and self-parodying.

Boycie has a dodgy chum, with whom he does a few deals, but who hasn't appeared before. He is an urbane villain of vaguely 'Arab' origins called *Abdul*, played, with his matinée idol good looks slightly darkened, by Tony Anholt. Tony had a number of issues to deal with. He was having great success as *Charles Frere* in *Howard's Way*, perhaps in part due to his embarking almost immediately on an affair with Tracey Childs. He'd been married to Sheila Willet for over twenty years and she wasn't taking her husband's all too obvious public romance at all well and was, he said, throwing the furniture around at home. On top of that, Tony wasn't too happy about being darkened up for his part as *Abdul*, apparently anxious not to look too ethnic, although I tried to help by suggesting to him that this only heightened his appeal. I also had the impression that he thought the whole 'sitcom' thing was rather beneath an actor of his provenance. He considered himself a serious actor and wanted this acknowledged, which he encouraged by picking holes in John Sullivan's wonderfully crafted scripts, and sighing in a supercilious way at some of the more overtly comic moments, which unsubtle as they may have been, were viscerally funny. For all that, he was a perfect foil for *Boycie's* more extravagant persona, and I was sorry that he never featured in the series again.

In Sullivan's script, *Abdul* and *Boycie* plan to have some diamonds smuggled from Amsterdam to London. They don't want to do the dirty work themselves so they need someone to go over, with the money, to get them. They find *Del Boy* and drag him out of the Nag's Head to a secret meeting where they offer him £10,000 to act as courier from Holland to England. *Del Boy* winces and demurs, until the offer is upped to £15,000 – a 10 per cent cut of the £150K they expect to get for the stones in London.

Naturally, *Del* goes straight back to *Rodders* to persuade him to help, then hears that his old nemesis, *Chief Inspector Slater*, thinks *Boycie* and *Abdul* are dealing drugs, and is keeping a sharp eye on them. The next morning, as they arrive at the market, *Rodney* is very windy about the job and believes the trip will be very dangerous; *Del* managed to convince him that everything will be OK and they'll earn their £15,000 for very little effort.

When *Denzil* turns up, driving his lorry, he makes a point of asking *Del* to stay out of his life, as his wife, *Corrine* thinks he's an evil influence on him. Having got that off his chest, *Denzil* drives off.

The *Trotter* brothers get on with their day's activity, flogging dodgy watches with the Unique Selling Point of being able to play thirty-six different national anthems. When they find the police are on their heels, they scarper, but with their usual bad luck, they run straight into *DCI Roy Slater*. *Slater* was played, incidentally, by Jim Broadbent, a fine actor, who loved the series, and had been mooted, before Sullivan picked David Jason, as a possible *Del Boy*.

Slater is with his right-hand man, *Terry Hoskins*. At Sid's Café, *Slater* tells *Del* and *Rodney* that he's already onto *Boycie* and *Abdul's* latest drug deal, but admits that he doesn't know who's going to act as courier. He goes on to tell the *Trotters* that once he's dealt with this case, he'll be retiring from the police force. When the coppers have gone, *Del* phones *Boycie* and tells him *Slater's* on to him.

The chaos and disasters that follow are classic Sullivan and, with several sub plots unravelling at the same time, the episode easily fills the allotted 90 minutes.

Del having ended up in Hull by accident, and ever the opportunist, thinks it a great idea if he and *Rodney* sail to Holland in a hired boat instead of going through the airports being watched by *Slater*.

Albert, who's always claimed to be an experienced sea dog, is summoned up to Hull to skipper the boat. It's soon obvious that he doesn't have a clue how to navigate and he admits that he spent most of his time with the Royal Navy in the boiler room.

Their sea-voyage includes possibly the most expensive sitcom joke the BBC ever commissioned. As *Uncle Albert*, *Rodney* and *Del* are standing on deck, passing a North Sea oil rig, an incredulous oil worker spots *Albert* waving up from the small boat and shouts down to ask what their problem is.

'Which way's Holland?' *Del* calls back.

The disbelieving rigger points eastwards, and *Del* wishes him a cheery: '*Bonjour.*'

It was a great show to make. Part of it, in which *Boycie* wasn't involved, was shot on location in Amsterdam and the rest was shot in Hull. For convenience, the BBC had built sets of the Nag's Head in an old warehouse up there, and it felt strange not to be in our regular studio with an audience boosting us with their enthusiastic response.

The film unit had a great time in the hotel in Hull. With the whole team there, this was probably the first time we saw just how huge *Only Fools* was becoming.

On the second day, I found Nicholas Lyndhurst in the middle of a beastly concrete shopping mall being besieged by adoring women of a certain age. Later, when we went out to look for somewhere to play pool, every time we found a possible venue, the crowds would gather – and this was long before mobile phones and Twitter had entered our collective consciousness. Quite often from the hotel windows we'd see gatherings of scantily- dressed women waving up at us, and we noticed a slight genuflection in the attitude of the staff.

A film crew away from home is always inclined to behave badly and this adulation encouraged us to think we could get away with anything. One memorable night, with only David, Nick and Buster being called next day, several of us decided to stay up drinking all night. We'd been joined by a few local doxies, as well as our indomitable production manager, Sue Longstaff, a tall, rangy, strong-minded character, who had a penchant for cameramen and took no prisoners. Quite late on, when I made the mistake of questioning how much booze she could hold, she grabbed me by the wrist, gazed blearily into my eyes and spoke in a husky passionate voice. 'I bet I can drink more tequila slammers than you, Challis.'

I shrugged, as if engaging in any such contest would be a mere formality, and ordered up the first few salted glasses, feeling as if I was going out to bat against a team of ten year olds. At the back of my befuddled mind, I was aware that I hadn't engaged in a serious tequila slamming contest for a long time but I wasn't discouraged.

I got as far as ten salt-edged glasses of the fiery lighter fuel before my shoulders hunched, my eyes filled and my head sank in submission on to the table between us.

Sue looked at me with a mad glare of determination in her squiggly eyes, downed one more, raised her arms in triumph and promptly collapsed.

As we came to, we decide to help our recuperation with a hopelessly drunken soda-siphon fight until breakfast time, when we ordered champagne and felt very pleased with ourselves.

A sober member of the unit who had just come in, scrubbed, shaven and with eight good hours sleep behind him, sat on our euphoria and flattened it like an elephant on a whoopee cushion, when he told us the weather had changed so we had to report for duty for a full day's shooting at 9am.

It was a hard day. We staggered, stumbled, and mumbled, desperately stifling yawns and hopelessly trying to remember lines. I found myself cursing all Mexicans, especially those responsible for making the hideous brew that was burning my brains up from the inside, while I tried to assume the calm air of self-confidence which characterised *Boycie's* manoeuvres.

Ray Butt, our director, although an enthusiastic boozer himself, wasn't amused – especially with his production manager, the still almost legless Sue Longstaff. But he must eventually have forgiven her, because she became an essential member of the team and stayed for five or six years.

Seeing the degree of public recognition to which the stars of the show had risen, Ray was quick to remind us how tenuous was our hold on this celebrity. He was good at putting us down. 'You may not be the best actor we've got,' he would say, 'but you're certainly the cheapest!'

Another time, when Roger Lloyd Pack was trying to show me a card trick he'd just learned, and we'd missed our call to stand by, Ray had crept up behind us.

'If you two have got a moment,' he said, 'perhaps you'd like to join us? I can make *you* disappear, you know.'

We had seen evidence of this, over the years of the show, when favourite little scenes we'd made never appeared in the finished version – usually a result of John Sullivan's habit of writing about ten minutes more than we needed. This practice of his made sure that if a scene hadn't really worked or was little substandard, he wasn't forced to use it. But sometimes we couldn't help thinking that one of our scenes might be cut, simply as a punishment for bad behaviour.

After a few weeks of rattling up and down to Hull, I was glad to have a little more time to spend with Sabina. She was always surprising and stimulating; her normal attitude to life was rather like a naughty child's: there were always boundaries to be crossed – though never so far as to cause serious trouble.Everything had to be funny, and a challenge. Soon after we'd first met and were touring the National's production of *The Rivals*, we were in Plymouth with an eclectic and rousing company. There was Edward Petherbridge, a fey, hyper-theatrical virtuoso actor, who almost smelled of stage curtains; an Irish actor, Niall Buggy; Fiona Shaw; the beautiful Anne-Louise Lambert; Sabina, Barry Rutter, Patrick Ryecart and me.

One night after a wonderful, booze'n'mirth-filled evening in a Plymouth restaurant, Niall, Anne-Lousie and Fiona – egged on by a mischievous Sabina – decided they'd like to go skinny dipping. We left the restaurant and all trooped round to a spot on Plymouth harbour where the swimmers stripped off on the shingle and rushed into the sea; I could feel Sabina tense with high excitement at this unruly behaviour as they emerged naked and glistening in the moonlight.

I enjoyed a little unruliness myself and loved taking things to the limit, and I was aware that we were both of us fairly dangerous people to be with; we were pathological flirts, and recognized this in each other, which tended to add a frisson to any group encounters. In a perverse way, one thing that held us together was our mutual distrust, especially when one of us had been working away from London.

Chapter 2
From Prussia with Love

In the spring of 1986 Sabina was cast in a fresh production of Tom Stoppard's *The Real Thing*, for the New Theatre, or *Theatr Newydd* as they call it in Cardiff. The play had been produced in London for the first time in 1982, when it won the *Evening Standard* Best Play award.It is still recognised as one of Stoppard's major works.

It is his exploration of the meaning of love, in which the main protagonist is a writer – very likely Stoppard himself – who, by flaunting his superior intellect and a kind of charisma that only great success can bring, seduces a young actress, *Annie*, (played by Sabina) away from her husband, affable but dim actor *Max*.

The cuckolded man struggles against the tide, rails against the unfairness of what has happened but in the end submits and sinks into a puddle of self-denigration and inadequacy.

The actress has been tempted away in part, of course, by the perceived promise of future prestigious work, although, as is turns out, this is never realized.

Stoppard himself, as was well aired at the time, had done a bit to wreck the life of one of the National's top directors, Michael Rudman, when he spirited Felicity Kendal away from him (they have since been reunited) to create the role of *Annie* in the original production of *The Real Thing*.

In his incisive examination of love, Stoppard aims to find how it most truly manifests itself. Is it that lurch of the heart at first sight, the thrill of the chase, a tantalising glimpse of greener grass?

Or is it the long-term, shared trials and experiences – 'Been through it all together, and come out the other end as best mates and comforters'?

Does love exist at all? Or is it a mere construct that we must sustain to justify our own existence and procreative urges?

Stoppard's exploration of these themes against a backdrop of the vain uncertainties of writing and acting, plus his own personal history, make the play especially potent. I don't know when he and Felicity Kendal started their affair but she had been in the first production (with me) of Stoppard's uproarious *On the Razzle*, so he certainly saw a lot of her then. But it can have been no coincidence that when he and the director were casting *The Real Thing* for the first time, he announced that what he was looking for was a 'bossy blonde'.

While Felicity was with Michael Rudman, Stoppard was married to Miriam. I had met Miriam when I'd been up to Cambridge a few years before to help Stoppard illustrate a talk he was giving about his work. And I had warmed to her very much; I found her a clever and engaging woman, who made a genuine effort to connect with people she met.

Stoppard's own apparently supercilious remoteness, and what I can only – and reluctantly – describe as his intellectual arrogance, are evident in the character of *Henry* in *The Real Thing*, for instance in a speech about perfect writing, where he uses the effective metaphor of a batsman, possessing a fine bat, who perfectly judges the timing of a stroke from which the ball is hit away to the boundary without any sound or apparent effort, compared with the player wielding a mere bat-shaped plank of wood and the random unsatisfactory results that provides.

There is no escaping the autobiographical self-knowledge that informs the character. Although not a weakness in Stoppard as an artist, this sense of superiority can be, as I'm sure he knows, a disability in dealing with his fellow men.

I recalled how when I was working on *Razzle*, he appeared on the *South Bank Show* with Melvyn Bragg, whom he managed to tie in knots, by simply not answering the question and offering nothing instead. I asked him afterwards why he hadn't wanted to be interviewed by someone who could handle what he was trying to say.

He looked back at me quizzically. 'If he'd been clever, I wouldn't have done the show.'

I found this almost sociopathic attitude in him irreconcilable with the man who, just eight years before, had sat in my room in a run-down New York hotel to thank me with some humility for holding together his play, *Dogg's Hamlet and Cahoots Macbeth*, which he was sure he hadn't yet got right.

When I took the rattler down the Brunel Highway to South Wales to see *The Real Thing* for the first time, I wasn't surprised to find that

Sabina had formed a cosy, flirtatious relationship with her leading man. This situation, in a dash of *deja vu*, seemed eerily familiar. I managed to brush it aside at the time, which I think kept it in check, although I recognized its echo later on in our relationship.

With no stage production of my own to get on with and a break in shooting *Only Fools*, I had a few more TV parts – in Lenny Henry's show, as a manic Mexican, again (perhaps someone had spotted me in Jimmy Cricket's *And There's More*), and an episode of a series, *Chance in a Million*, with Simon Callow and Brenda Blethyn, where, in the familiar surroundings of a pub, I was cast as a seedy, lascivious drunk. These were not memorable experiences but I've always taken the view that work is work, and that it was preferable to take most of what was offered (within reason) than to wait around for better offers.

In any case I was firmly established in my career path now as *Aubrey Boyce*, whom I was booked to play in five more episodes in 1986, starting with a favourite of mine, *From Prussia with Love*, which we filmed in June.

I was delighted when I heard that Sue Holderness had been called back to play *Marlene* for a second time. I'd heard that John and Ray had been very happy with her first appearance a year before and were expecting to include her more in the sixth series.

John established that one source of conflict and bicker between *Boycie* and his spouse would be their difficulty in conceiving children. At one point, *Del* accuses *Boycie* of 'firing more blanks than the Territorials'. The irony of this hit me hard. I tried to think back to any time when I might inadvertently have referred to my own problems in procreation: if I hadn't, it was a bizarre and slightly painful coincidence.

In *From Prussia with Love*, John took on this very personal and tricky issue and, through laughter, managed to remove the pain a little and leave people shrugging philosophically and smiling over it.

Working his way with skill and sensitivity through a minefield of potential political incorrectness, Sullivan has *Del Boy* telling *Boycie* and *Marlene* that he thinks he can help them 'have a baby'.

'I know where there's one going,' he offers.

Boycie gives him a sharp sideways glance. 'What? Knocked off?'

'No, no; it's all pukka,' *Del* protests.

In fact, he's come across a German *au pair* girl who has 'fallen pregnant' but doesn't want to keep the child.

Rodney of course assumes that *Del* intends to sell the baby to *Boycie* and is outraged by his brother's callousness.

Del denies this and proceeds to make arrangements to produce the baby for *Boycie* and *Marlene's* approval when it arrives.

The *au pair* gives birth to a fine healthy child. As *Del* is well aware that *Boycie* is dead anxious to have a boy, presumably for some kind of dynastic reasons, he's very put out when the baby turns out to be a girl.

Nevertheless the presentation goes ahead. *Boycie's* reaction to the child's gender is classic. 'It's amazing! Everything you buy off him has got something missing!'

When the problem is apparently compounded by the baby girl being brown, *Marlene* coos over her with delight and Sullivan takes more risks with political correctness in *Boycie's* reaction. 'Good God, Marlene! I might be able to convince people into buying my cars; I might be able to convince them that you conceived and gave birth in ten minutes flat, but how the hell am I going to convince them that my grandad was Louis Armstrong?'

By having *Marlene* fall in love with the little brown baby and wanting her to become part of the family, Sullivan removes any racial undertones from the scene.

The episode ends with the *au pair* changing her mind and deciding that she wants to keep her baby after all, while *Boycie* and *Marlene* are left to carry on trying.

Marlene was in my next episode, too, *Video Nasty*, in which *Rodney* innocently becomes involved in the making of a soft-porn flick by his one-time chum, *Mickey Pearce*. I was delighted that the *Boyces* who, as a couple, had greater scope for providing plot lines, were now becoming well and truly ensconced in the series. By the following year they were appearing in almost every episode that was made.

Against this background of growing confidence and security in both our careers, Sabina and I were managing to find a level between our two potentially self-destructive natures, which suited us both. Sabina, to her credit, still spent a lot of time on her mother, Margo, who had somehow been tossed rather helplessly on to the shore of a sea of tribulations.

Her former husband, Bill Franklyn, a man who liked to be in control of as much as possible of his life and of those around him, to some extent took responsibility for her – at least to the extent of coming round to remind her to send a birthday card to his new wife and interfering with her financial arrangements.

Margo was partially to be blamed for allowing him to get away with it. Although since his departure from her, she had, as a beautiful and potentially engaging woman, been pursued by plenty of suitors, she'd always declared that Bill was a hard act to follow and none of them were up to it. Although Bill's undeniable qualities weren't especially profound, this may have been true; in any event, she had never formed any kind of long-term liaison with anyone, and as prospects became more distant, had got into the habit of spending a lot of the time on her own, feeling sorry for herself.

Once when we rushed round to Westfields Avenue to answer a piteous panic call, we found her sitting helplessly in her shambolic front room, surrounded by a clutter of unsold *objets* and chunks of nineteenth-century lath and plaster, soaking wet from a deluge that had caused the collapse of the ceiling above her as a result of a leaky bath tap.

Within minutes Bill, also summoned, had arrived and immediately got on the phone to berate her insurance company and anyone else he felt he could effectively harangue on her behalf, pulling celebrity rank wherever possible.

By that stage in my life I was getting better at accepting that other people did things differently and there was little to be gained by getting annoyed with them or trying to change their outlook, however irrational it may have appeared. And this applied to my own parents, too. One could only stand by and watch, I concluded, as they allowed themselves to descend into a downward spiral of uncompromising mutual reproach and unhappiness.

My mother's health was going downhill, in direct response, I suspected, to her own dissatisfaction with life. On the whole she liked Sabina, or, at least, appreciated that there was a bit of 'class' about her and, still unaware of my infertility, hinted about it being time I settled down and had a family. But Mum didn't entirely trust Sabina. She resented her tendency to be a little supercilious around her, and wasn't slow to remind me of the mess I'd made of my first two attempts at marriage. Besides, I was aware by then that there'd always been something of a power struggle between my mother and whatever woman I was involved with.

My father always liked seeing Sabina when I took her down to see him for birthdays and high days. He seemed to welcome the presence of another female within the family circle and he would take her hand, looking meaningfully into her eyes.

'And how is John?' he would ask, although he never asked me. For the most part, however, he was becoming increasingly intolerant of anyone who didn't agree with his own bitter views on life, the government, God, and the human race in general... and was suspicious of those who *did* agree with him! He was clearly drinking a lot – more than he openly admitted to – and I had to resort to spying on him to discover just how much he was consuming.

On one occasion when he suggested we went out, ostensibly to walk my mother's dogs, when we'd driven up to park by a parade of shops off Ashtead Common, just around the corner from where I'd been incarcerated as an estate agent twenty-five years before, Dad declared that he was going to pop in and buy a bottle of R. White's Lemonade – 'A lovely drink, that!' – while he attempted to slip a half bottle of Booth's gin into his coat pocket without my seeing it.

He made some lame excuse for staying in the car while I took the dogs off onto the common and when I returned there was a heavy aroma of gin on his breath.

My mother had told me that she kept finding bottles, empty or partially depleted, all over the house and garden – even in the cistern of the downstairs lavatory. She was clearly suffering from the effects of this, and cast herself as a collateral victim of alcoholism by joining a support outfit called Al Anon, where she was encouraged to write about her experiences, and met other people with whom she could air the problems of living alongside an alcoholic.

I later learned that my father's half-hearted, almost deliberately botched attempts to conceal his alcohol purchase from me were classic symptoms of a distinct stage in the inevitable, slippery descent into Alzheimer's.

I was very sad when my mother told me it had all become too much for her and she was going to move out. She had sold her old family home in Bath after her father's death and bought another, more modern house up towards Lansdown on the edge of the small city.

Now, after torturing herself with doubts and guilt about abandoning my father, she announced that she was going to move permanently down to the West Country and leave him to his own devices.

She justified this, too, by its closeness to a hospital that had the facilities to deal with a virulent skin condition from which she was suffering.

I offered to take her and a carload of her possessions down there, and as we set off in my trusty Honda Accord from the house in Sunnybank, Epsom, I caught sight of Dad in my rear-view mirror. He was rubbing his hands with glee at the prospect of spending an uninterrupted spell with his mistress – a bottle of Gordon's Dry Gin.

As Mum and I set off to take the old A4 through Reading, Newbury and Chippenham, past the prehistoric tump of Silbury Hill, she didn't look back once. This has always seemed to me a desperately sad way to end a marriage that had already lasted over four decades, when just a little compromise might have averted it and given them a few happy last years.

I know I've referred more than once in these memoirs to some aspects of my demeanour and, I suppose, my height, which have caused me very regularly to be cast as a policeman on television.

One of the strangest and, I guess, the apex of my career playing plod occurred in mid 1986, when I was summoned to play a copper opposite a small piece of grey felt rag known as *Roland Rat* – the same celebrity rodent who'd been invited in by Greg Dyke in 1983 to put TV-am more soundly on the map, which he did with great success.

Now he'd been elevated to a more prestigious time slot and was as popular as ever. I enjoyed him a lot; he was brilliantly operated and very funny. Before the show had started we'd sit either side of a table, in character, and discuss how we should do the show. It was quite bizarre to work with a character with whom one carried on quite erudite conversations without ever seeing the man who spent these encounters invisibly, beneath the table with his hand up the witty rat's jacksie.

I enjoyed it, but after just the one appearance, when I was asked if I would come back, I felt that one could spend only so much time in the company of a rat before one developed a bit of *ratitude*. Besides I was sick of being a policeman, and I declined the offer.

Soon after that, on a characteristic whim and the spur of the moment, Sabina and I set off in the Honda to drive down to Italy. Bill Franklyn was a great fan of all things Italian and the glamorous Amalfi coast. Sabina had often travelled there with him and she was anxious to share her affection for the place with me.

Before we went, Bill took it on himself, in his usual didactic way, to give me a crash course on Italy and Italian driving habits.

Nothing, he said, could be worse than dealing with Latin drivers, their lack of skill and excess of histrionics, as well as the dangers of driving on the wrong side of the road.

It didn't do any good to tell Bill that I'd been through all this before, knew it and experienced it probably as much as he had. After all, anyone who had tackled the *rond-point* around the Arc de Triomphe as I had during the Paris rush hour should be prepared for pretty much any kind of traffic madness. In that particular death trap I've actually found myself facing cars head on!

We ferried across the Manche, put the car on the train to Evian, from where we drove past the lake up into the Alps. On the way up through the dramatic mountainous approach to the Brenner Pass, after a longish pit stop in a bar, I found I'd left the car headlights on; the battery was flat and the car had to be bump-started. Sabina was highly unamused and chilly about it. Actresses don't on the whole like to be seen pushing cars – especially Hondas – in public.

Naturally, when we got there, I could see and feel at once why Sabina loved Amalfi and Positano so much. This beautiful coast appealed strongly to a dangerous, romantic side of my nature but as usual, in my effort to blend in with the locals, I couldn't control my urge to imitate the voice and extravagant gestures of the native Italians and had to stop myself from breaking out into lusty renditions of *O Sole Mio* (the Elvis version).

Walking through the pine and lemon-scented lanes that straggle and zigzag up some of the most picturesque cliffs in Europe, Sabina and I talked of marriage. We boldly addressed the issue of no possible issue and the irreversible damage done to my procreative equipment when I was a child. She accepted it and we started making plans for a wedding. I wasn't drifting into it with my eyes shut, like I had with Carol Robertson twenty years before and I hadn't been bounced into the idea, as I had been by Debbie Arnold, my second wife, but I can't deny that there were questions nagging at me. I was still doubtful that both our own, quite distinctive and – it had to be admitted – self-centred personae could settle down and make the required compromises with our vanity. Nevertheless, by the time we'd driven back to England, the idea had firmly taken root and started to grow.

That autumn, October 1986, we were happy to sign up to a joint gig, in a new production of the play in which we'd first met, Sheridan's *The Rivals*. This time it wasn't a National Theatre production and we both had bigger roles when the show opened at the Theatre Royal, Windsor.

I enjoyed being back in Windsor, well-stocked as it was with memories, occupying a goodish chunk of my own personal history. I recalled with pleasure my time working in that theatre as a dresser with Mark Piper, when he was still a teenager. Every time I saw the mighty Copper Horse, a statue of a mounted George III, at the end of the Long Walk in the Great Park, I remembered my walks up there with Carol, or, on the way to Ascot, the field where we'd pulled in to canoodle in the car and I had, with youthful romanticism and regrettable naivety, proposed to her – memories which led to the occasional stab of guilt for having left her there in the thoughtless, scatty way I had.

It was great to be back on stage again after a run of TV work. Although this was a straightforward, provincial production of Sheridan's classic, it was very well directed by Stephen Barry and cleverly designed by Lee Dean, who was to feature in my career quite a few times in the future. Sabina and I had a great time renewing our relationship with Sheridan's brilliant writing in the different roles in which we'd been cast. This time I played a diffident, irresolute *Falkland*, while Sabina was a lovely, saucy *Lydia Languish*, paramour to *Jack Absolute*. The show was made special by the presence of June Whitfield, whom I'd always loved, as *Mrs Malaprop*. With her bright little blue eyes, hers was a more glamorous and blousy version of Sheridan's famous creation than Geraldine McEwan's had been for the National.

Twenty years after this, when she had become famous all over again as *Eddy's* mother in *Ab Fab,* it was lovely to see June when she turned up in *Boycie's* life as *Marlene's* mother. Also in the cast of *The Rivals* were her daughter, Suzy Aitchison, and Christopher Strauli, who'd been in *Keep it in the Family* with Sabina, all adding a nice homely feel to the show.

Intriguingly (in hindsight), a very young Clive Owen played the *Coachman.* What we all noticed about him at the time was his rather brooding, listless and unforthcoming nature. I would never then have picked him as a future movie star – which shows how much I know.

Friends who came to see the show, who'd also been to the National production, said they preferred the simplicity of the Windsor version, faintly damning the National for feeling rather self-consciously that, if they must play a classic, they always have to dig out some new, undiscovered facet to it.

After two and a half weeks, we moved on to Bromley, which used to have a tie-in with the Windsor theatre in those days. But I was to be back there under the shadow of the royal castle several times in the future, and in subsequent years I had a few classic panto outings for producer, Lee Dean.

Once the New Year was past, I didn't need much pushing to join Sabina in a search for a house we could buy together. I was far more sanguine about the idea than I had been when Debbie had demanded the same, and was very happy when we found a charming little house in Trehern Road, Mortlake, just upriver from Barnes.

It was a tiny brick terrace house, built presumably for some kind of artisan about 150 years before. A two-up two-down with very steep stairs and the bathroom brought indoors, it had a garden to re-arouse my gardening juices (which had been sorely deprived in Sabina's flat). There was room to swing only a smallish cat, but I immediately got stuck in and was reminded, with the pleasure that the passing of time can lend, of my happy days as a landscape gardener in Twickenham during the drought year of 1976. There were already some good roses in the garden, a ceanothus and some viburnum. I started by adding some climbers – jasmine and morning glory – to wind their way up through the existing trellis.

Beside these, I planted some of my favourite vegetables, like courgettes and squashes. From one of these, which seemed to grow like the man-eating plant that did for me when I was *Scorby* in *Doctor Who*, I produced the largest courgette I've ever seen, in fact a sizable marrow by the time I found it, the only fruit, buried beneath deep layers of its own foliage, which had produced only the weediest visible specimens.

The house itself was as tiny as a doll's house, really far too small for us but we loved decorating it. Sabina was able to bring into play her taste and knowledge of diverse decorative *objets*, a battered eighteenth-century watercolour beside a Victorian child's sampler, a pair of chipped Staffordshire lovers and Shelley tea sets. The small windows were curtained with much ruching and frilly ties. Our road was one in a little network of narrow streets close to the railway. Of the two closest pubs, one attracted a clientele of shiny-suited men and dark glasses, with women to match and expensive-looking cars outside. The other had an altogether rougher edge, used by unsophisticated 'lovable rogues' like my former business partner from the St Margaret's Hotel, Leslie Churchill. The regulars were duckers and divers of the 'gotta make a living some'ow, mate' type. I was made to feel welcome in both establishments, although by now I'd more or less licked my serious pub habit. Moreover being *Boycie* was making pub visits a little fraught and sometimes uncomfortable, as aspirational con men frequently wanted to tell me how their schemes matched up to those of my fictional alter ego.

Soon after we'd moved in, my mother arrived from Bath for the first of several visits to Trehern Road. It was clear that her health wasn't getting any better. The subcutaneous cancer from which she now suffered seemed to be spreading and opening into painful blisters. However that didn't stop her wanting to join in and be part of everything that was going on. She relished the regular contact with the theatre world, which she'd aspired to so much as a younger woman. And there was no doubt that she enjoyed the connection with Bill Franklyn, of whom she'd always been a fan. She was certainly pleased that I was with someone who – in her terms – had 'a little quality'.

Nevertheless, with her continuing, vague reservations about Sabina, she didn't hold back in expressing her opinions about the way we'd done up the house.

'I wouldn't have used those curtains down here,' she would say through pursed lips, 'they look a bit bedroomy.'

Sabina's jaw tightened as Mum went on. 'It's strange, but the colour you've used in the kitchen reminds me of my mother's house in Bath. Isn't it extraordinary how these things come round again.' It wasn't meant as a compliment.

After some bristling and a few sharp intakes of breath, Sabina gritted her teeth, trying to control her indignation. I explained later that my mother must have been suffering from a combination of losing her influence over her only child and heart problems from her debilitating disease.

I went down to Bath to see her as often as I could and occasionally ferried her back to Epsom for a fraught reunion with my father. They would at first clasp each other in a ritual display of affection but would soon revert to their old sniping and bickering. Sad to say, I don't believe either of them realized how ill the other was and their manoeuvres had the look of a sort of macabre last waltz as the lights in the ballroom died.

Chapter 3
Third Time Lucky?

Neither of my parents came when, in May 1987, Sabina and I were married at Richmond Register Office, with a blessing at the church in West Temple, Sheen. We celebrated afterwards in a large room overlooking the river in the Boileau, a sprawling '20s pub at the top of Castlenau, by Hammersmith Bridge.

This was my third wedding reception and a pretty riotous event. No doubt some of the speeches were received in a spirit of irony, if not undisguised cynicism. A few days afterwards, taking advantage of a brief window in our work schedules, we presented ourselves with our smartest luggage at Victoria Station alongside the Pullman coaches of the English end of the Orient Express. In those pre-tunnel days one took the English train to Folkestone, to be ferried in a special lounge to Boulogne, and boarded the wonderful old blue-liveried *wagons-lits* there. The exquisite marquetry and brass fittings of the sleeper cabins, the tinkling of the jazz pianist at a concert grand, cocktails in the bar, and the elegant formality of black-tied men and dressed-up ladies in the dining-car seemed to evoke great waves of nostalgia and yearning for a time that was long before our own. For both of us it was a very romantic trip and my first visit to the ever-magical city of Venice.

Like a lot of people who are visiting Venice for the first time, I was struck most immediately by how much the canals pong. They are, after all, for the most part, rat-infested open drains – not to say sewers – which is why you never see anyone swimming in them... unless they've fallen in blotto, when the risk of catching Weil's disease is quite high.

However one's olfactory organ seems to become accustomed to the odour of drain quite swiftly and enjoyment of the extraordinary and unique qualities of the jewel of the Adriatic is not seriously impaired.

I'd seen innumerable documentaries about Venice, magazine articles and, most potently, Nic Roeg's eerie film *Don't Look Now*, filmed at a time of year when the narrow canals and alleyways are filled with mist, not tourists. Seeing these places, so well known from

Third Time Lucky?

afar, for the first time in the flesh is a truly uplifting experience, because for once the reality out-trumps expectation. The Rialto Bridge is magical, as it has been for 500 years. St Mark's Square, the Doge's hangout, San Giorgio Maggiore (Big George's), floating on the lagoon opposite St Mark's and the network of alleys and tiny bridges, the gondolas full of Japanese being pushed through the grimy water by bored, handsome gondoliers are unforgettable sights, which is, perhaps, the reason so many people go back again and again (apart from inhabitants of Las Vegas, who have large tracts of the city recreated on their doorstep – lucky things!).

Sabina and I were staying in a moderately-priced hotel which was in fact a charming and tatty old palazzo on the Grand Canal. With their gift for these things, it seems that the Venetians have known about shabby chic for at least two hundred years.

Sadly, though, despite all this stimulation and beauty, Sabina was unwell. Something had got at her stomach – maybe the water, possibly the excitement of it all – but she insisted on staying in the hotel, where she could lie down all day. Thus for most of our stay, I ventured out on my own, self-indulgently stopping at everything that interested me and swiftly passing by that which didn't. I loved all the treasure houses, the churches stuffed with wonderful paintings, sculpture and decoration – murals by Tintoretto, a ceiling by Rubens or Michelangelo; while in the church of San Pantalon, (Holy Trousers) I found a magnificent ceiling painting of the martyrdom of San Pantaleon, painted by Gian Antonio Fumiani. I wondered how on earth Fumiani had painted something at such a height and unpromising angle, particularly after learning that he had fallen to his death before finishing the thing.

Of course, when I saw signs to the Arsenale, I had to investigate. While there's no football pitch there, it turned out to be a fascinating complex of buildings where for centuries the great Venetian navies used to store their firepower. After several days spent wandering on my own through the narrow, crowded streets I was beginning to feel a little hemmed in and claustrophobic on what is after all a small island but luckily Sabina recovered enough for a boat trip across the lagoon to some of the other islands. First stop was Murano.

This little island, just north of Venice itself, produces some of the world's most beautiful glassware and, curiously, some of the world's most revolting and tasteless glass objects. But the glass-blowers are all happy enough to churn out this ghastly stuff by the bucketload, for it seems there are always punters for rank crapolata – like someone once said (Rupert Murdoch, probably) no one ever got poor by underestimating public taste.

But for all the downside of Venice – the crowds, the over-priced restaurants, the awful tourist tat the vendors sell, the pong – its beauty and sheer uniqueness will always come out on top and I've enjoyed several return trips since my honeymoon with Sabina.

In the summer of 1987 Sabina and I were enjoying Trehern Road, which had become a busy meeting place for our friends, although that wasn't always a good thing. While we were there, we had what we thought was the brilliant idea of having a party for the casts and crews of our two respective shows, *Full House* and *Only Fools & Horses*, both very popular at the time. It seemed perfectly sensible to combine two groups of actors and TV production people, with all that two TV sitcoms should have had in common. Most of my cast came (though David Jason couldn't at the last minute) and all of Sabina's. But instead of bonding through the similarities of their work, the gathering developed into what resembled the after-match tea between two rival prep-school football teams, where members on each side would look shiftily at one another and conversation was restricted to mild insult and snide innuendo. Evidently the common experience of making TV sitcom was eclipsed by the differences in social standing of the characters in the two shows and the party was a disastrous failure.

As it happened, with no new episodes of *Only Fools* being made that year (apart from a later Christmas special), I wasn't all that busy, although there had been a few other outings on TV, including some sketches with Griff Rhys-Jones and Mel Smith for their show. So, when Sabina and I were offered another job working together, I was more than ready for it. This time we were to be in Bernard Slade's hit American stage comedy, *Same Time Next Year* at the new Thorndike Theatre in Leatherhead. The Thorndike, a state-of-the-art modern building, had replaced the old theatre I'd first known nearly thirty years before. Back then, as a teenager, I'd been a trainee estate agent in the town and had watched Donald Wolfit cruising the streets like an emperor, while appearing there in a great production of *Cromwell at Drogheda*, an experience which had done a lot to trigger an urge to go into acting myself.

Same Time Next Year is a highly-structured piece of comic theatre based on a relationship which is unlikely but nevertheless bears examination. It features a man and a woman who meet up at the same place every year to commit adultery. In these circumstances the unpleasantness of infidelity is somehow diminished as the two parties discuss their spouses with genuine fondness, while the action, so to speak, continues over forty years.

Essential to this, of course, is that the two protagonists have to age as the play unfolds; starting in their twenties, they end up in their sixties. The inherent difficulty in this was exacerbated for me by becoming partially deaf just after we'd opened; I felt as if I were carrying on a dialogue with a blanket wrapped around my head, so that I could hardly hear myself, or anyone speaking to me. The problem suddenly disappeared during the second of our two weeks but when I could hear myself again, I was so appalled by what I sounded like I had to make some dramatic adjustments to my performance. However, if anyone noticed, they said nothing to me, while I was made a little more uncomfortable by the fact that the next production at the theatre was announced during the interval of every show, with a reverence that made our production look very modest by comparison, as if to suggest that next week the audience would be able to see some *proper* theatre, rather than an irrelevant, populist comedy starring a TV face with impaired hearing, who was probably twenty years too old for the part!

Shaw's *An Ideal Husband*, with the distinguished director, Patrick Garland, they announced, would star Simon Williams, Lucy Fleming (there's a surprise, we thought, as Lucy is married to Simon Williams), and Alexandra Bastedo (another surprise, for she is married to distinguished director, Patrick Garland). Most of us, and perhaps especially actors, suffer from a little paranoia, not helped now for me when I reminded myself that perhaps I'd only got the part in this bizarre American comedy because it was directed by another distinguished director, Bill Franklyn, to whose daughter I happened to be married.

But I received a pleasing little blast from my distant past when, the day before our run ended, a nice-looking woman approached me in the bar after the show and gazed up at me with twinkling blue eyes.

'You don't remember me, do you?' she asked.

A dozen possibilities swam before my eyes, until, in the nick of time, I got it. 'Yes, of course I do,' I said. 'You're Christine Shaw, and we were at Tadworth County Primary together.'

Her face showed that she was delighted I'd remembered and so was I. It's always good to have evidence that your memory hasn't packed up altogether. What was more, I bet no one ever came up to Donald Wolfit and said anything like that to him in the bar after, when he was appearing at Leatherhead in *Cromwell at Drogheda*.

When my mother next came to stay with us her health was not improving and I was a little uneasy about asking her if she wanted to come to a party we were holding at Sabina's mother's cottage in Little Chelsea, not far from Sabina's old flat. But she insisted on coming.She loved the idea of being part of the real acting world to which she'd always wished she'd belonged, instead of the am-dram world she knew. She was aware that she'd be dealing with a more sophisticated gathering of people than she'd been used to among groups like the Tadworth Players, but was, I think unprepared and out of place with the newer, more cynical attitude of modern theatricals. Her fantasies of gentlemen actors and *grandes dames* of the theatre spouting arch witticisms at each other were quite out of date – if they'd ever had any reality. To my distress, I could see that she was really struggling with the language and mores of the profession as it was now. In the end she crept off to the kitchen and started doing the washing-up – not an activity for which she was best known. Back at our house the next day, obviously depressed and not well, she found a bowl of walnuts, which had come from a tree in Bill Franklyn's garden, and scoffed half a pound of them at a sitting, before being violently sick.

I took her back to her house outside Bath. She had given a room in the house to a lodger (who probably never paid any rent). Colin was one of what my father used to call her 'lame ducks'. From now on she spent much of her time in bed while Colin ventured from his litter-strewn room to look after her. In fact he was quite canny with her and adept at judging her volatile moods. I recognized this and was grateful for it. If a crisis developed, he would ring me and I would try to get down within a couple of hours.

Although Sabina often came too, she'd grown no closer to my mother and she didn't get on with Colin. I would find myself trying to keep the peace between them, while my mother was waning upstairs.

But Mum had retained her surprising sense of practicality. 'Darling,' she wheezed, 'now that I'm dying, I'm going to give you the car, as I'm obviously never going to drive it again. But I'm not going to sign the house over to you, because I don't want you to be in a situation where Sabina thinks she can have a half share in it. I mean – you know I like her, of course, but I don't trust her.'

To be fair to Sabina, although my mother showed some prescience in this, I didn't believe my wife was particularly acquisitive about my material possessions.

The last time I saw my mother in her own house, I was getting into my car outside, and she was sitting up by her bedroom window, smiling weakly and waving. I was sure that next time I came to Bath she would be in hospital, which I didn't think she would like much.

Fortunately when she was moved into hospital she accepted the reality with dignity, and although she now had to be helped to do almost everything, she fought off the humiliation of it with a great effort to retain her independence. She still followed the horses on TV, while ogling John Francome, and loved to dwell on the old times when theatre, dancing and romance had filled her life.

'If I were twenty years younger,' she boldly told one young doctor, 'I'd be out of this bed in a jiffy, and you'd have to run for your life.'

And while religion had never been important for her before, she started asking to be helped to the chapel where she would pray.

A few months before, Sabina and I had booked an autumn trip to Sicily, where the sun was still hot and the lemons were ripe. The thought of meandering though the empty, sleepy, cicada-buzzing mountains where Al Pacino had once roamed in his breeches and butcher's boy hat was very appealing. I was worried about going now, with Mum looking as pale as a sheet and speaking in a whisper but she wouldn't hear of us cancelling our holiday and hated the thought of being a dampener on anyone's life. She even seemed to rally a little and the staff at the hospital tried to assure me she would be all right at least until we got back in a fortnight.

I was relieved. I needed this break, drained as I was by driving up and down to Bath, worrying about Mum and also my father, who wasn't in much better shape by then.

On the day before we left, I spent a few hours at the hospital with her, holding her hand while we watched *Korky the Cat* flickering on the TV, before giving her a hug, telling her that I loved her and that she wasn't to spend too much on the horses.

As I left, she smiled at me. 'God,' she whispered. 'I could murder a glass of champagne.'

I blew her a kiss and on the way out arranged for the nurse to get her a bottle of Veuve Clicquot.

With a reasonably clear conscience, I set of with Sabina for Sicily. From Palermo we flew south to Catania from where we took a ferry, which offered the most picturesque introduction to Syracuse. This crumbly, ancient and beautiful port, right on the south-eastern corner of the island was absolutely soaked in history; over the past three millennia it has been conquered and occupied by Greeks, Phoenicians, Romans, Venetians, Vandals, Ostrogoths, Byzantines and Arabs as well French and English crusaders, who had all stamped their influence on the place in the temples, churches and palaces they built (except for the Vandals, of course, who'd just done a bit of vandalizing).

The town nestled like a chip of white chalk in the rusty, rugged coast; the sea below us, where we sat for our first drink, lay still and deep turquoise, broken by sparkles of silver as fishing boats, great flashy gin palaces and little cargo ships slid silently across the surface. I thought of the two *Antipholuses*, the *Boys from Syracuse*, as the Hollywood film makers had called their version of the Bard's dotty *Comedy of Errors*, where the twins are so absurdly confused in a way which only a playwright of Shakespeare's eminence could get away with.

Looking for a place to eat, we couldn't resist the allure of a small *trattoria*, where we sat at battered iron tables on a stone-flagged terrace beneath a vine-clad trellis, from which dangled large clusters of plump, dark purple grapes.

It was, I thought, your dream Italian family restaurant where you're treated like an honoured guest and you feel they can't do enough for you. Sicilian charm seemed warmer and more authentic to us than the suave gushing of the chicest Italian restaurants in London, where the head waiters think they can kiss your wife as soon as you've eaten there a couple of times.

Amid the wonderful aroma of good food cooked in olive oil and the competing musty scent of the oleander, we looked over the dazzling town, down on the sea and felt very content. Sabina was in her element, her eyes glowing and her skin somehow already tanned. The sense of authenticity we felt about the place was confirmed by the presence of a number of other diners, who were clearly locals, and one family gathering in particular at a table close to us.

A dark-eyed old matriarch with silver hair gathered in an elegant bun presided over two or three offspring and their younger families. Two handsome young men, with dark brown skin and jet black hair couldn't take their eyes of Sabina, who was, it has to be admitted, very eye-catching in a white shift dress. They made no attempt to disguise their ogling while they chattered away in torrents of Sicilian dialect, laughing and constantly throwing glances at us before they decided to summon a waiter. With a lot of gesticulation in our direction, they evidently instructed him to bring us a couple of plates, each containing a small baked pink fish.

I was suddenly alarmed at what this might have meant. Was it some kind of challenge? What, in the southernmost town of this island of Mafiosi did the despatching of fish to strangers signify? We were, after all, less than a hundred miles from the *Godfather's* home town of Corleone. As I became more uneasy, involuntarily communicating this to Sabina, a garbage truck growled by slowly and drew to a halt a few yards down the hill. The motor was turned off.

In the silence that followed, the family beside us had gone quiet, the sound of a dozen busy cicadas rubbing their back legs together grew louder and an onshore breeze rustled the vines above us.

I stared at the fish in front of me. Its dead grey eye stared blankly back at me and just the thought of eating it made me sick. The waiter stood by with what seemed to me like a deeply menacing smile.

35

'*Mangiate! E buono!*' he urged with what sounded like an ugly hint of a threat.

Was that it? I thought in panic. They would kill us with the fish for daring to enter their milieu and dispose of us in a garbage truck.

Sabina, who liked fish and seemed oblivious to the danger we were in, was already carefully slicing it away from its bony skeleton. She looked at me, puzzled, as if to say: 'What's wrong with you? It's just a fish!'

I'd hardly dared to look at our donors but snuck a quick glance. The two young men were looking at us, raising their glasses in salutation.

'Lucca Brazzi sleeps with the fishes,' I remembered. I couldn't defy them by declining their gift.

I look a deep breath and gingerly started lifting the flesh of my fish off the bone.

I forced myself to take a mouthful, controlling my urge to gag.

It was delicious – the most succulent Mediterranean *pesce* I'd ever eaten. I looked at Sabina who was now munching happily and at the family, who looked ecstatic that we'd finally got round to eating their offering. Some of them even started clapping and laughing.

We gathered through a conversation of mime and pidgin English that this was a fish peculiar to the region, and, as an *hors d'oeuvre*, one of the great delicacies of Syracuse.

To my shame, I went limp with relief when I realized I was panicking over nothing more than attack of my own blasted paranoia; that I was no kind of threat to the local Mafia. The garbage truck started up again and rolled off down the hill to go about its lawful business.

After that powerful introduction, we fell in love with Sicily and spent a happy week visiting the still bubbling volcano at Etna, the beautiful town of Taormina perched on towering cliffs, boasting an ancient, almost undamaged amphitheatre, where naturally I couldn't resist slipping down to the flag-stoned stage and spouting some Shakespeare, to the alarm of a few English tourists.

Being with Sabina away from the tensions and competitiveness of our usual lives, we were as relaxed together as we'd ever been and the lingering, niggling doubts that I'd had about us being married seemed to dissipate like the morning mist in the Sicilian autumnal sun.

Our sojourn there was a little marred one morning when I lost my wedding ring while floundering in the turquoise sea. The following day, 13 September, as Sabina and I frolicked in the swimming pool, the pool attendant called across to me, beckoning me to the poolside phone. It was Colin, my mother's friend and self-appointed carer.

My mother had died during the night.

By stomach dropped like an express elevator. My first instinct was to blame myself. If I hadn't gone, I convinced myself, she wouldn't have died. And what the hell was I to do now? I couldn't possibly stay on holiday, although it wouldn't make any difference to my mother now – but then mourning is always more about the feelings of the bereaved than those of the deceased.

Sabina agreed that we'd have to go straight back and I set about finding a flight.

There was nothing for three days, which we managed to cut to two by entrusting our lives to a clapped-out Rimini Airways spanner bag.

We drove straight from Gatwick to the Royal United Hospital in Bath, where I gazed on my mother's unmoving face for the last time. She was sixty-seven and died through heart failure brought on by a leaky valve, as her mother had. I was desperately sad to see the poor old thing so frail and thin and looking slightly cross, as if somehow betrayed by life, while my father, eighty miles away in Epsom, was failing completely to deal with his own self-inflicted problems. I couldn't help crying over the bitterness that had developed between the two of them and, with a measure of guilt, I felt sure I could have done more to reconcile them.

At this distance in time, I doubt that was the case; the truth was that there'd always been an underlying tension in what was fundamentally a marriage between two incompatible people. I learned about the reality of this more directly, I suppose, after I'd allowed myself to fall into the same condition for a period of my own life. It must be something that happens to people far more often than it should but then again, I guess this kind of risk-taking, punting against the odds in choosing a partner, is essential to the evolution of the human species, in order to provide greater genetic diversity.

While I looked at her, I started thinking of rather strange aspects of her behaviour since she'd been admitted to hospital. She'd called me, for instance, just before we'd left for Sicily to tell me that she didn't want flowers at her funeral. Instead, she wanted everyone to plant a tree in her memory. 'No flowers, but plant a tree for Joan,' she insisted.

When she'd rung off, I'd called the hospital to ask what drugs she was on.

'Oh, yes, she was a bit high, wasn't she? Sorry!' They didn't sound it.

When Sabina came into the room with me to see my mother, she rather unexpectedly crossed herself, as if she were entering the house of Dracula but, despite her ambivalent feelings about my mother, she was very supportive. She understood completely when I burst into tears while ordering the forbidden flowers; she could see that losing my mother had hit me harder than I could have imagined. And this wasn't helped by my father's reaction when I went to see him to break the news.

Telling him was awful. He looked at me, puzzled. 'Oh dear,' he said, apparently not very moved, 'what a pity. When will she be home?'

'Dad, she won't be coming home, ever.'

He looked annoyed. 'That's all very well; she can't just go away on holiday and not come back.'

'No, Dad; *I've* been on holiday and *I've* come back, but Mum has died – and she won't be coming back.

He shook his head. 'Well, I don't know, I really don't. Nobody tells me anything!'

When I went back to Bath to organize Mum's funeral, I found that all the burial places in the city were full and I had to look elsewhere. I found a spot on the hills to the south, overlooking Bath, near the Radstock road. I knew she would have liked the place; she and I had often been up there to walk the dogs.

My father came – or rather, I went and picked him up from Epsom myself the day before the funeral. I'd asked him to be in his best suit, and somewhat to my surprise, he was, sort of – his jacket and trousers didn't match, he hadn't shaved and he had odd shoes on.

I remembered my Uncle Albert wearing similar footwear to a funeral in Sheffield, when Aunt Milly had to point it out to him.

'Aye,' he'd said. 'Ah've another pair like this at 'ome.'

I gave up trying to persuade Dad to change and only got him into the car with a struggle. He'd hardly been in a car for ten years or so and couldn't handle the journey at all. He kept flinching and moaning about the speed, although I couldn't have been driving more sedately.

Once we got to my mother's house, Sabina and I sorted out sleeping arrangements for him and us for the night before the funeral. He took a while to settle down in strange surroundings, although in the middle of the night, he evidently thought he was back home and blundered into our room, convinced it was the lavatory. I was embarrassed on his behalf and it took some time to get him to change his mind and show him where he should go.

I'd let everyone I could think of – family, friends, former colleagues – know about the funeral and most came to the service, presided over by the vicar of the church where Mum and Dad had been married forty-six years before. I felt there was at least a nice symmetry to the arrangement but Dad seemed completely unaware of the connection.

As we entered the church and walked up the aisle behind the coffin to its place in front of the altar, I took Dad's arm, which he immediately wrenched away with a sharp snort. Once we'd made it to our places on the front pew, he spent the whole service tutting and sighing, as if he'd rather be anywhere else.

I could see the concerned faces of the people around us, whom he'd known most of his life but he ignored them and grew even more irritated. He treated his wife's other mourners as if they were all total strangers, undoubtedly causing quite a lot of hurt with his eccentricity.

Afterwards at my mother's grave, which I'd been to so much trouble to find up on the hill, he refused to get out of the car. After a lot of persuasion from the driver, Sabina and me, he grudgingly climbed out and shambled up to the graveside, where he carried on muttering and sighing grumpily.

I felt bad about even bringing him now, although I had been determined to, perhaps to shake him out of the misery that seemed to have been consuming him, making him increasingly bloody-minded and antisocial as he aged.

Now, though, he was behaving worse than ever, and apparently doing it deliberately, as if some evil spirit had taken him over. I had been hoping desperately that at least seeing his wife going for the last time, he might have relented and shown some vestige of the love he'd obviously had for her as a young man. But there was not a flicker of regret or affection for her in him.

I felt devastated that I had failed so completely to bring about any kind of final reconciliation between my parents. It was a very unhappy day.

I spent the next couple of months dealing with my mother's estate, such as it was, and filming the next great feature-length *Only Fools* Christmas special.

My mother had left me about £20,000 in shares and the house, which sold for £60,000. I sold the shares and passed some of the money I got for them to my father's only other living relative, my Aunt Enid, who lived frugally in Sheffield. Enid was my father's youngest sister, who had been married to an eccentric, possibly certifiable hoarder, whose house was so jammed with junk he'd accumulated that there was no room left in the place and she'd had no option but to try to find a place of her own.

I'm happy to say that, twenty-seven years on, Aunt Enid is still going strong, and writing regular letters of complaint to the BBC about their failure to run a fifth series of *Green, Green, Grass* (she is family, after all).

The Frog's Legacy was one of John Sullivan's typically convoluted plots of expectations raised, brought to a frenzy by *Del Boy's* relentless optimism, only to be dashed by impossible obstacles.

Del Boy, *Rodney* and *Albert* have been asked to the wedding of *Trigger's* niece, *Lisa*. *Trigger's Auntie Renee* makes an appearance, played by Joan Sims. Joan, of course, was something of comic legend for playing highly strung, often sexually-charged women of a certain age. It was said that the always hilarious Dick Emery had based a lot of his female characters on those created by Joan. I was naturally excited to be working with someone I'd grown up watching in comedies like the *Carry On* films which had been huge hits from the '50s on, and she couldn't have been better in her role with us; but sadly, for some reason I never gathered, she seemed uncertain of herself and didn't appear to enjoy her time on our set.

Auntie Renee, who had been *Joan Trotter's* best friend, talks to *Del* about the legendary local 'gentleman' thief, *Freddie 'The Frog' Robdal*. She tells him that his mother met *Robdal* and they became friends (in fact had a brief affair) before *Rodney* was born and while she and her husband *Reg* weren't getting on. *Renee* claims that *Freddie Robdal* was a cultured man, interested in French wine and paintings. He and his gang had broken into a London bank to steal £250,000 in gold bars; the rest of the gang were caught but *Robdal* got away with the gold and hid it. After he'd died (by accidentally sitting on a detonator while working on another bank raid), it was found in his will that he'd left the hidden bullion to *Del* and *Rodney's* mother.

On the basis of this story, *Del* embarks on a quest for the lost gold, having theoretically inherited it from his mother on her death.

It turns out that *Uncle Albert* knew *Robdal* a little during the war but he's incredulous when *Del* suggests that *Robdal* had had an affair with a married woman who lived on the estate. However, *Del* is wondering why he left everything to his mother. He also mentions a rumour that *Robdal* and the woman had an illegitimate child, who would be about *Rodney's* age now. This begins to worry *Rodney*, although *Uncle Albert* dismisses it as a mere rumour.

In the meantime, *Del* gets *Rodney* a new job, as chief mourner for the local funeral directors. *Rodney's* not happy about it but as a result, finds out that *Robdal* had bought a coffin from the firm when they first started business, for a 'friend' called *'Alfred Broderick'*. Rodney quickly sees that *'Alfred Broderick'* is an anagram of *'Frederick Robdal'*, and concludes that *Broderick* didn't exist and the coffin had been used to hide the gold and was buried in a fake funeral.

But *Albert* now tells them *Freddie Robdal* had been a frogman in the Royal Navy, so he had buried the gold at sea, planning to recover it later but was killed before he could do it. While *Del* vows to find the gold, Rodney can't help asking *Albert* about his resemblance to *Robdal*. Although *Albert* still dismisses it as a rumour, he does acknowledge that they do look a bit alike. But *Rodney* is unimpressed. 'Freddie the Frog? Killed himself by sitting on someone else's detonator. What a plonker!'

Of course, the gold was never found but this episode laid the foundations for a theme that John Sullivan was to explore twenty-five years later, when he conceived the idea of *Rock and Chips*, a prequel to *Only Fools*, which features Nick Lyndhurst playing *Freddie Robdal, Rodney's* dad.

Chapter 4
Assorted Villains

Sabina and I had loved living in the little house in Trehern Road but there was no doubt that is was just too bloody small and by 1988 we were both working fairly consistently (for actors). As my mother had left me a bit of money, it felt like time to trade up. After a little searching, we found a house we both liked in the snootier environs of Sheen Lane. It was a distinct step up the housing ladder – certainly up the hill, towards the park, for despite its nearness to Trehern Road, the south side of the Upper Richmond Road was altogether more salubrious.

Number 8 was near the top of Observatory Road, a good-sized terraced house, on which someone had spent a few quid in the recent past. The floors were Swedish timber – in a good way. We had three bedrooms, a study on the first floor and a garden in which you could have swung several cats. The front was well planted with a few alpines, aubretia, arabis, campanula and bluebells. The rear garden wasn't so tidy. It supported a sizeable magnolia, a few gloomy shrubs and a neglected, weed-strewn patio area. I set to work on sorting out the paved section, anxiously trying to recall all the cock-ups we'd perpetrated on behalf of clients with our attempts at paving ten years earlier in the days of Churchill, Challis and Slater – by now fondly remembered through the distorting mist of time.

Settling in to Number 8, we both felt we were going in the right direction. Sabina certainly aspired to a bigger dose of glitz in our lives and she loved being in a distinctly smarter house – it was certainly the poshest house I'd ever lived in. We could just about afford it; we were both working a lot, with the added interest of the antiques trade with Margo. I particularly enjoyed being in a house in a leafy suburb with the park on our doorstep. It felt to me like living half in town and half in the country.

We hadn't been in the house long when our neighbour paid us a call. I opened the door to a potty-looking female who seemed determined to tell me her life story and several additional tales of woe. 'You see,' she said, 'my children have robbed me – every penny, dear, and now I've barely enough to feed myself.'

She looked quite fit and well and her clothes had certainly been expensive.

'I can't even afford my cigarettes,' she said, 'and, d'you know, they're the only pleasure I get *these* days. I should love a packet of Players Navy Cut,' she went on wistfully. 'I can't bear those horrid little cigarettes with tips, can you?' she challenged.

'Oh no. Absolutely,' I agreed, hastily stubbing out my pathetic Silk Cut.

She was warming to her theme. 'Tips, spats, whatever you call them, they're just for perverts. I don't mind Balkan Sobranie – those gold tips aren't tips at all, they're just for decoration – to show you which end to put in your mouth – though of course it doesn't matter, because it's only tobacco either end. Anyway, they're too expensive. I think it's disgusting! Just because they're coloured pink or blue, I mean that doesn't make any difference to the taste, does it?'

I tried discreetly to rummage through my pockets and wallet, without producing any evidence of great wealth. I found a small fistful of change and gave it to her. She looked down at the coins in her hand with a peremptory sniff and scuttled off down the road, I presumed to the tobacconist.

After a few enquiries among our other neighbours I discovered that the little woman did a regular begging run, up and down the road, although, curiously, only on our side. I wondered vaguely if that was reflected in the relative value of the houses. It seemed she was making quite a living by begging, although she was in any case a very rich woman, with a large family, who simply viewed her eccentric habits as a source of amusement.

On Christmas Day, 1987, *The Frog's Legacy* had been watched by 14.5 million and there was little doubt that, after five seasons, there was still a lot of life in *Only Fools*. However, there were no plans to make any more until the next Christmas special, so I was glad to have been offered a good run in five episodes of a new television drama, *Wish Me Luck*. I'd got the job through one of those benign accidents of fate that (although we are loth to admit it) are so crucial to an actor's career.

Among the assorted thespians, TV and film folk who played for Bill Franklyn's cricket team was a TV producer called Colin Shindler.

Despite being a famously ardent Manchester City supporter, he wasn't a bad bat, though he once fell foul of a rather strange aspect of our matches.

When we played against village teams in the bucolic backwaters of Hampshire or Wiltshire, we would sometimes encounter a tendency in the more rustic elements of the village side to show a bunch of fairies from Lunn'on how real men played. More than once, massive, blacksmith-style characters with sideboards like legs of mutton and biceps as thick as a ship's hawser would hurl the ball down the wicket at us in a way the Australians facing Harold Larwood would have recognized, with the missile pitching short and bouncing straight up at our unprotected heads.

One of these evil balls caught Colin Shindler on his forehead with a loud, wince-inducing smack. He collapsed, shrieking like a girl on a roller coaster, and fell to the ground clutching his head, convinced (he excused himself afterwards) that he would suffer serious brain damage and would have to spend the rest of his life as garden veg. As it happened, he was barely hurt at all because the ball had only glanced off his skull.

He survived and it was soon afterwards that he introduced me to Gordon Flemyng. Gordon was directing *Wish Me Luck*, a series for ITV about undercover agents in contact with the French Resistance during World War II. As *Victor Travussini*, I was a Frenchman whose cover had been blown in France, and had come to England to help direct operations across the channel. Warren Clarke – one of Dennis Waterman's hard-man chums – was typecast as a horrid, podgy German person and the lovely, demure Jane Asher was a female agent handler. It was good to be playing a more romantic role for once and I enjoyed my wartime canoodling with Jane Asher. I liked her and got to meet her husband, the extraordinary cartoonist Gerald Scarfe, whom I'd always admired for his political stuff and his work with Pink Floyd.

Through Jane Asher and Gerald, I met Terry Jones – a former Python – and subsequently worked with him on a series of spoofy satirical vignettes for a pilot he was making. I loved doing this and was grateful for the opportunities I'd had over that year of playing a great variety of characters on TV, just as I had in my early days in repertory theatre.

I also did some work in the very popular *Ever Decreasing Circles*, a cosy, enjoyable production starring Richard Briers and Peter Egan, who had directed the Aldertons and me in *Rattle of a Simple Man* a few years before. Also in it was Penelope Wilton, who was married to a colleague from my far away RSC days, Ian Holm. I'd worked with our 'esteemed director' Harold Snoad, too, on a few occasions, although on this show, Peter Egan seemed to be doing most of the directing, while Harold just pointed the cameras, sometimes through specially-made flaps in the scenery – a technique for which he was justly famous.

It was a very jolly show to be on. Richard Briers, egged on by Peter Egan, enjoyed a giggle, which led to some hilarious sessions on the set. After the show, it was great to meet up with connections who had come to watch the filming, like Ian Holm, who'd come to see Penelope, and Peter's wife, Myra, whom I knew from *Rattle* days. On one occasion Myra brought along a tall, striking female friend called Carol Davies, to whom I managed to say a fleeting 'hello' before being whisked smartly through the stage door by Sabina, who'd also come to watch.

It's extraordinary, with hindsight, what that fleeting 'hello' led to and how it was to change my life – albeit a few years later.

However, I was back on the familiar trail with my next role, in *Relative Strangers*, playing an unappetising character, the natural father to a truculent youth (played by Mark Farmer) whose stepfather was Mathew Kelly.

The show was written by an interesting up-and-coming duo, Laurence Marks and Maurice Gran, both intensely interested in comedy writing and committed Arsenal supporters. They sat me down to grill me about John Sullivan's methods, while they clinically dissected the plots of all the *Only Fools* shows they'd ever seen.

I felt a tad disloyal, sensing that they considered themselves in direct competition with John. They went on to become very successful, with several popular series – *Goodnight Sweetheart*, with Nicholas Lyndhurst, *Shine on Harvey Moon*, with Kenneth Cranham and two that I was involved in – *The New Statesman*, with Rik Mayall and *Get Back*, with Ray Winstone.

I enjoyed their company, as well as sharing the highs and lows of supporting the Gunners. We watched a few games at Highbury and had a few meals together and played a bit of Trivial Pursuit, before they went off to America, where they became very big for a while. When I met them, there was no doubt that they were vying with John Sullivan to be the most successful comedy writers of the '80s but I always felt that John had the edge – the magic touch when it came to everyday relationships and characters that the public saw in themselves. For a while he had *Only Fools, Just Good Friends,* and *Dear John* all running at the same time. It wasn't surprising then that he, like Marks and Gran, was being courted by the Americans, who have rated British writing talent very highly for a long time.

The Sullivan format they liked best was *Dear John,* a sitcom about a Lonely Hearts Club for divorced folk, featuring the amiable Ralph Bates as *John Lacey,* but John wanted them to consider *Only Fools.* 'It's the most watched of all the shows I've done,' he said.

The American producers shook their heads. 'We can't put a character like *Del Boy* on network TV over here – people might get ideas!'

It seems that they saw *Del* as a totally dishonest character and a negative role model. They completely missed the subtle point that he was a loser with a big heart and recognizable moral values – a man who did all he could to keep his family together, took a beating for his brother, stopped a riot and interrupted a mugging while wearing his *Batman* outfit. Indeed, whatever scams he got up to, he always failed to pull them off. And to think, the Americans rejecting these sound values belonged to a nation that chose Richard Nixon for president!

Life in our new house in Observatory Road was working well. We had much more room to entertain than we'd had in Trehern Road and it was just a few minutes walk from the big open spaces of Richmond Park. It was handy for the shops, too and even handier for a good, smart pub, the Plough in Christchurch Road. I still enjoyed pub life (although Sabina didn't), for the wonderful levelling effect it produces and the sense of brotherhood among the regulars, although I've found this is less marked in the smarter pubs; for something less hoity-toity I would sometimes wander down to the scruffier establishments I'd frequented in the more banausic quarter down by the river in Mortlake.

Inevitably, life had also become, by degrees, more expensive and it was as well that Sabina and I were both keeping steadily employed. Although there's always a danger of being typecast when you've been in a big show like *Only Fools* for a long time, the exposure certainly helps and, luckily for me, there were producers around who were prepared to let me loose in other roles. Given that there were no outings for *Boycie* until the next Christmas special, I was very grateful for the work.

But most of the parts coming my way continued to be of a certain, sinister type. The next was in another Harold Snoad production, *Don't Wait Up*, starring Nigel Havers, where I was a shady con man, flogging dodgy watches. I did ask myself why I was offered so many of these parts on TV. After all, on stage I'd been in anything from Noel Coward, Restoration comedy and even the Bard himself but as soon as the cameras came up close and personal on my face, it seemed I was scuppered.

In *The Bill*, for instance, I played a bus driver who'd gone tonto because his wife had left him. He'd smashed up his bus with a sledgehammer, then driven it at high speed (for a bus) around the neighbourhood, before landing up in someone's neat little front garden. Rather sensibly, in the circumstances, he'd done a runner and led the police a merry dance until he was caught, banged up and questioned before being severely reprimanded with a mallet and told not to do it again.

My next director was Keith Washington, with whom I'd worked at the Mermaid and in rep at Harrogate in the early '70s. I'd acted under his direction in *Lovers* there and subsequently at the Orange Tree. After that he'd gone on to direct at the Royal Court with some success.

In the episode of *Casualty* he directed, I was cast as a man who had gone to a party dressed as a rabbit, got very inebriated and, together with another yuppy dressed as a chicken, had exited the party through a plate-glass window a few storeys up. The injuries this caused triggered a trip to A&E and earned a serious ticking off for getting slaughtered and wasting valuable hospital time and space. This was a subplot to the main story about the reluctance of a father to allow his dying son's organs be used for transplants. He wouldn't let his son's body be used for what he described as 'vivisection'.

However, his mother believed the boy would have wanted to help. A patient in desperate need of a donor was wheeled in, a meeting was arranged, the father's wishes almost prevailed but in the end a life was saved.

This strongly emotional, finely balanced argument was treated with such sensitivity by Keith that the programme won an award for Outstanding Social Drama.

I'd also been in a play by Howard Brenton, which he'd directed, *Christie in Love*, focussing on the reviled multiple-murderer, John Reginald Christie. It was not a pretty play, so much so that when I invited a casting director to come and see me in it, he declined. 'Please don't ask me to come and see that revolting play at *lunchtime!* I'm sure you'll be lovely.'

It may not have been a pretty play, but it was very powerful, depicting both the depth of Christie's depravity and society's ambivalence towards it, seen through the eyes of two very different policemen – one an old-school, authoritarian type, the other, a younger, more questioning junior, eager to understand what had happened and why. Keith had worked with Mike Leigh and had adopted some of the idiosyncratic director's free-form techniques, which made it an exciting and demanding style of direction. From there Keith went on to direct a lot of drama for the BBC.

During this busy year I tried to find time to run an allotment down by North Sheen Railway Station, which I loved, although I soon discovered the true cost of growing your own vegetables – if you factored in your time. I worked out that it would have been cheaper to have them delivered in one of Mohammed Al Fayed's Harrods vans, though, naturally, one would have missed out on the therapeutic value of delving your hands into clods of earth, and would have had to fork out, as it were, the cost of a few sessions with a shrink instead. In any case, it seemed that every time I got stuck into some serious work with the spade and hoe, I would get a call from my agent and the whole thing would go backwards again.

At weekends we still enjoyed helping Margo with her stalls at Covent Garden and Beaconsfield Antiques Fair when we could. This meant early starts and fending off gangs of voracious dealers who appeared as soon as you got the gear onto the trestle table. They would be on it like a flock of vultures dropping on a carcass in the Serengeti, and you needed a skin like a Serengeti rhino to deal with the snarls of ridicule and derision at the descriptions on the labels, and the prices, of course.

When the early birds had dispersed, clutching their cut-price worms, the stall would be overrun by what Margo called the PPPs – Pick up, Put down and Piss off.

One of our friends, the silver dealer Richard Francis, would sit and grin benignly while punters would come up to his stall, pick up pieces of obvious silver plate, priced at a fiver, and ask if they were solid silver (as if!) then try to haggle down to 50p, having already been told by Richard what his best price was.

Richard allowed them to faff around for a bit until he'd had enough and spoke to them in level, honeyed tones. 'Now, you've had a good look, why don't you just fuck off?'

I couldn't do that, but I realized it would have been a great way of releasing the frustration these people caused.

It was a good summer, light years away from where I'd been (just over the river in Twickenham) in the hot, dry summer of 1976, when I'd seriously considered leaving the acting profession for good to become a professional gardener. Luckily, I was saved from that fate when my business went bust. Now I was making a few quid to spend on our leisure time. Sabina and I had a lot of friends to party with, I played tennis and cricket as much as I could, and we had a regular dose of short breaks, often to Cornwall, sometimes to more exotic destinations in France and Italy.

My mother's legacy, from the sale of the house in Bath that had such mournful memories for me, had helped fill our house in Observatory Road with the frilly curtains and white-painted furniture that was the prevailing look Sabina most admired. She seemed happy. I thought I was happy.

We were both chuffed to be booked for a run in John Vanburgh's Restoration comedy, *The Relapse*. It was being put on by Peter Woodward (son of Edward) and Kate O'Mara, with the company they had formed, the British Actors' Theatre Company, known, quite appropriately as BATCO.

This unusual company had no director – everybody was free to direct everybody else – and it was intended to be an egalitarian set up where everyone was on equal footing, regardless of the part they were playing. I didn't know if Kate had formed this company because she wanted to cast herself in all the juiciest female roles or because she knew she was undirectable – either reason was plausible!

The result of this official lack of direction, as one might have predicted, was chaos. There was great deal of disagreement among the actors in the company over direction and the urgent need to have one's views heard encouraged a lot of shouting – sometimes quite loud.

It fairly soon emerged that the more experienced among us had a better idea of what worked and what wouldn't, although Kate's tendency to switch hats between producer and leading actress didn't help. It became clear quite soon that the company had split roughly into three groups: the 'Big Four' – those of us who had been on the telly, the 'Tracksuit Rehearsers' – young things yet to make their mark and the 'Lower Tier', which mainly consisted of musicians.The Tracksuiters spent their time exercising, warming up, warming down and doing a lot a moody running about.

One of our 'Big Four' decided to relegate himself to the Tracksuiters group and be 'just another member of the ensemble' but the whole device smelled bogus since he was the best known of us all. To show willing, he did throw a lot of ideas into the pot, although most sank to the bottom.

Richard Heffer, on the other hand, besides being a charmer and a good actor, was also an academic from Cambridge and an avid 'text' man, which meant he was constantly correcting other people's misreadings and misinterpretations. With the unconscious condescension of the over-educated, he provoked much resentment from the younger actors, though admiration, too from the more aspiring ones.

Sabina and I were inevitably tarred with sitcom *schtick*, so we weren't taken seriously at all and provoked even more resentment when we suggested improvements.

In practice, what this demonstrated was the clear need for someone to sit outside the action, looking on, and see it as a whole – in other words, a director. The result of BATCO's free-for-all was a mishmash of very good scenes and some that didn't work at all. Even Ed Berman, my boss from a few years before in the British American Repertory Company (or BARC), who was a notorious liberal and democratic operator, would not have allowed this artistic anarchy to reign.

One member of the company who seemed aloof from the action – indeed, it seemed, outside the whole production – was Peter Adamson. I remembered him, of course, as *Len Fairclough*, from the short stint I'd done on *Corrie*, when I'd found him always entertaining, if mostly drunk, with a dash of bitterness about life. Now, eighteen years on, he was still mostly drunk, still bitter and a lot less entertaining.

He couldn't seem to decide if the whole BATCO concept was beneath him or above him and he managed to contribute nothing to the tortuous joint directing process. He'd opted to play *Sir Tunbelly Clumsy* as entertaining, mostly drunk and rather bitter.

I had the role of *Worthy*, a sinister, Machiavellian ladies' man, forever plotting to prise the women away from their proposed husbands under the guise of matchmaking.

Worthy's collaborator in this was the equally conniving *Berinthia* (a 'young' widow), played by Kate O'Mara in heroically vampish style. Our self-appointed Tracksuiter, Roy Marsden (formerly *Chief Inspector Dalgleish*) played *Lord Foppington*, a rich, dandified, silly arse.

Somehow the show lurched into some kind of recognizable form, and we set out on the road a little nervously.

The company's shambolic tendency was reflected in our first performance in our first venue. We arrived in Oxford to find that we were, apparently, completely unexpected. There were no posters to be seen anywhere around the town, which was hardly surprising as they were all still in a bundle in the manager's office.

We dashed out with them and spent the next few hours persuading any shops or households who would listen to put them in their windows, in their cars, on their front doors, trees in their garden or, in one case, wrapped around their dog when they walked them through the Parks.

Once we sorted out the publicity, without much help from Peter Adamson, our egalitarian non-hierarchic company had to help with the 'get-in' – heaving the set, the costume hampers and props out of the transporter, explaining the lighting set-up to the local sparks, getting the right costumes to the right place and making sure the scenery was where it ought to be. It reminded me of my days in rep with the Penguin Players in Bexhill, a quarter of a century before.

On our first night in Oxford, our efforts were rewarded with an audience of three men and (possibly) a dog – perhaps the dog that had worn the poster. As the week went on things improved but I realized it was always going to be hard to sell a show whose egalitarian principles didn't permit promoting the 'stars' of the show.

I know I won't be universally popular for saying so but I've always felt that political attitudes and thespians don't mix, however enthusiastically they are embraced. Look at dear old Glenda, from the grandiloquence of *Queen Elizabeth I* in Court, to the back benches of the Commons, once she'd become responsible for writing her own speeches!

From Oxford we headed west towards the mighty dinosaur's back of the Malvern Hills and the theatre in Great Malvern, which clings to the lower slopes on the eastern side. It's a distinctive town, founded on profits from the gentle industries of education and spa water. It seems to have a particular architecture all of its own, early Victorian multicoloured stone, held together by extravagant snail pointing. This rather genteel atmosphere has made it, like Harrogate, a gathering place for theatre enthusiasts of a certain age and income. They were always going to love a Restoration comedy.

Sabina and I shared a house with Richard Heffer. Early in our short run there, the 'Big Four' of us – Roy Marsden, Richard, Sabina and I – had arranged to pull on our walking togs and bound up to the top of the nearest Malvern peak when, just as we were about to set off, I was called away to do a voice-over in London.

Before I left, I watched them set off up the hill, Sabina between them, all linked arm in arm – two naughty boys whisking my wife away with a jovial cry – 'Don't you worry... we'll look after her!' – offered and taken in good spirit.

Roy, the self-downgraded 'Tracksuiter' had several times expressed his admiration for Sabina and with his well-oiled charisma had taken to referring to her as 'Wonder Woman', which soon morphed into 'Wanda'.

He would catch me and take my arm, with a thoughtful lowering of one eye-lid. 'What about your wife, eh?' He would shake his head. 'Give, give, give, all the time.'

Cynically, I replied to myself. 'So you can take, take, take, eh?', while the bogus Tracksuiter plunged on, piling on the charm.

I was complimented on my 'skills' in comedy and character invention. 'I wonder if I could borrow a bit of advice from you,' he went on smoothly. 'I need some help with my comedic problems. The trouble is, you see, I've only ever done drama.'

I was flattered. I didn't see then that this was a device for gaining my trust, allaying – when it came to it – my suspicions, while he referred to his own wife with gentle irony, as 'The Gauleiter'.

I watched the three of them for another moment or two as they walked away, laughing and ragging one another. I wondered why I felt a little uneasy as I walked down the hill to catch the London train. The town possessed a wonderful Victorian station with colourful, wrought-iron decorations and an old-fashioned tea-room into which at any minute one expected Trevor Howard to burst, breathing heavily in anticipation of his tryst with a dewy-eyed Celia Johnson. I thought of her cuckolded husband, sitting at home in a moquette armchair, puffing on his big-bowled pipe, while he listened to the wireless and I half expected a steam train to thunder through the station, whistling vigorously as it thrust into the tunnel at the end of the platform.

When I got back from London, Sabina and the other two seemed to have bonded even closer. Roy and Richard had worked together in the 1982 series *Airline* and knew each other well. They indulged in a certain amount of unspoken communication, in which Sabina was keen to join. Richard was a natural, incorrigible flirt; Sabina, like me, was an habitual flirt, while Roy could trowel on the charm, like a profligate Irish bricky with a pallet of mortar.

To some extent, of course, the flirting reflected the action of the play and we were all, on the face of it, getting on well in a joshy, theatrical sort of way. Sabina was *Amanda* – a little as she'd played *Lydia Languish* in *The Rivals*, an ingénue among the crafty schemers trying to seduce her away from her husband, *Loveless*, played by handsome Richard Heffer.

With the two chaps and Sabina getting so close, I felt a little left out. I looked more closely at Kate. But no, I didn't really mean it – she and I were far too experienced to slip into a relationship of convenience and besides, I reminded myself, I was married to Sabina.

By the time we reached Billingham, a '60s horror of a town dedicated to the production of chemicals and adjacent to some of the most beautiful parts of North Yorkshire, the show had settled into an acceptable, if fitful rhythm. I'd taken on an additional small cameo character part of a mad old shoemaker and I relished the return to what I did best – prancing about a stage, wearing colourful clothes and being a chameleon.

It was during this third leg of the tour that I was first aware of an identifiable change in atmosphere among us 'Big Four'. Sabina was distracted, evidently pre-occupied with something that didn't concern me. So, as it happened, was Kate, who was sharing a house with us this time. I deduced that the young man in the company she'd been seeing wasn't performing satisfactorily (at least, off stage) and she'd been prompted to turn her sights on Richard Heffer, who, to her angry frustration, was showing no reciprocal interest. Kate was very upfront about this kind of thing in a way I found endearing. She saw no point in disguising her evergreen urges. 'I'm just not getting old,' she declared frankly. 'I mean, I'm sure I'm going to still be having my periods when I'm ninety.'

Sabina, on the other hand, held her cards much closer. She was impervious to my gentle inquiries. 'I'm fine,' she fluted airily. 'I'm fine, absolutely fine. Why do you keep asking?'

By the time we reached Newcastle and the wonderful Theatre Royal, relations between us were clearly strained. The 'Big Four' of us carried on doing everything together. Roy took us down to show us an extraordinary arts co-operative that he had financed and helped his brother set up. It was in an old warehouse in a dilapidated part of the city where countless artists, artisans and craftsmen all beavered away merrily like the elves in Santa's toy factory. Even with my own cynical suspicion of socialist utopias, I couldn't help being impressed that Roy had used the money his success as an actor had brought to give others a chance to realize their own creative potential. It was, in any event, consistent with his efforts to show he was on equal terms with the other members of the company, regardless of his greater role.

At the end of our week in Newcastle, relations between Sabina and me had deteriorated badly. Our habitual double-act repartee had been replaced by irritable bickering, sighs and moody shrugs.

If I strayed into contentious areas, comments that would normally have raised a laugh and a wicked comeback were met with expressions of angry derision. When she started putting me down in front of the others, I had to get to the bottom of it. She was adamant that nothing was wrong with *her*, and went on the attack.

'You're so crass and bloody naive,' she hissed at me.

I didn't deny it, but she'd known that long before we were married.

The company's visit to Hadrian's Wall and Housteads Roman Fort would normally have been a great treat for me, fascinated as I am by historic piles of stone (I'm even living in one now), but the enjoyment of it was marred by my growing feeling that someone else must be behind the changes in Sabina's attitude.

At one point, when I'd been poring over some piece of Roman history, I saw what looked to me like a secret conversation going on between her and Richard Heffer.

Could it be, I thought as an absurd dread gripped my innards, that she had finally succumbed to his relentless flirting?

But there was no other sign of it that afternoon, and I decided that I must be imagining things and that the cause of Sabina's discontent lay elsewhere.

From Newcastle we travelled across England to the Grand Theatre in Blackpool. During the week in which we stayed in the blowsy old seaside resort, I had to commute almost every day to Bristol, where we were shooting scenes for the *Only Fools* Christmas special, *Dates*, when *Del Boy* meets *Raquel* for the first time, through a dating agency.

As usual, the BBC expected everyone to be available at a moment's notice as soon as they wanted to shoot. As there always seemed to be delays in fixing dates, most of us had gone on and taken other jobs. As a result of the inevitable conflicts of work, the BBC had to ferry Roger Lloyd Pack, Ken MacDonald and me back and forth from all corners of the kingdom so that we could fulfil our obligations.

Although I was delighted to be working with the chaps again in what was one of the best of the *Only Fools* 'specials', I couldn't stop

Chapter 5
Restoration Drama

Christmas 1988 came and went – a brief interlude in the run of our show at the Mermaid. Sabina and I did our duties in the round of present giving to Margo, Bill and Susie and my father, as grumpy as ever in Epsom. There was no overt rift between Sabina and me, but the sense of apartness I'd first felt while we'd been touring *The Relapse* did not diminish and the inexplicable chill between us lasted over Christmas into the New Year.

This wasn't improved when, arriving a little early for an entrance in the play one evening, I saw a swift withdrawal of hands between Sabina and Roy.

I was *almost* sure that this was the conclusive piece of evidence of what I had been suspecting for some time but, being English and not wanting to cause a scene, I pretended to treat it as a joke.

'Unhand my wife, sir,' I hissed, quoting from the play.

But I suddenly felt marooned, marginalized, external to secret things that were going on. 'What the fuck do you think you're doing?' I went on, a little less jokily.

'Oh come on,' Roy chuckled. 'We're all good friends, aren't we?'

'Darling,' Sabina cooed, taking my wrist. 'You're being a little paranoid, don't you think?'

I really hoped that was all it was. I *wanted* to be mollified and allowed myself to be. We were, it was true, all very close after our hectic tour and living in and out of each other's lives in shared digs. Besides, at one point I'd suspected Richard, and Sabina couldn't be having an affair with both of them... so perhaps it was neither, and we really were just a close, happy band of strolling players.

The following weekend, on Saturday morning, Sabina had gone off to keep an appointment for remedial work on some part of her anatomy, while I wandered down to the local hardware store to buy a bit of kit to do a chore she had requested. It was the kind of crisp, bright January day on which I love to get out into the open, and after I'd got what I wanted, I had an overpowering urge to get in the car and drive the short distance up through Sheen Gate into to the wonderful open spaces of Richmond Park. I knew there was a car park on the right just inside and planned to leave the car there and get out for a good long stride across the rolling sunlit grassland.

Almost as soon as I drove into the car park, I saw a small Honda whose registration number, without even reading it properly, was familiar and I felt suddenly nervous. Focussing, I saw that it was Sabina's car, when she should have been at a body-repair shop in Putney. Before even registering it, I was aware that there were two people in the car and they weren't doing the crossword together. They were busily engaged in what looked like more than a friendly embrace.

Almost numb with dread at what I was about to discover, I drove slowly in front of the car and as I did, the man looked up from what he was doing and saw me. It was Roy Marsden.

Looking pretty horrified himself, he gave an automatic response by putting on a rictus smile and giving me a cheery little wave. Beside him, Sabina's face appeared.

I drove on, almost frozen with shock at the enormity of what I'd just seen.

Oh, Christ! I thought. *What the hell do I do? We've got a show tonight!*

Another wave of nausea hit me as I drove out the other end of the car-park and headed for home.

After some deep breathing, I tried to adopt an attitude of steely determination that would let me handle this vicious blow to my emotions – and my pride, of course – with some dignity. Then my guts kicked in again and I felt violently sick.

As if in a trance, not hearing any outside sounds, I drove back down Sheen Lane. I parked the car and let myself into the house I'd enjoyed buying and doing up, like birds with a nest, with the woman I'd just seen wrapped in the arms of another man – and not just any other man but the leading man in the show in which I'd been immersed with Sabina for the past twelve weeks.

In an attempt to find some kind of replacement therapy, I blundered about, making coffee, tidying up, fiddling with plants in the garden, while I tried to face up to the sheer indignity that this affair must have been going on under my nose, with everyone else, my friends and colleagues all seeing it and the fact that my wife must have had such little regard for our marriage that she couldn't be bothered to resist the idea – couldn't even wait until the run of our show was over before rushing off to cheat on me.

I was jerked from the storm of resentment and angry thoughts whirling round my head by the sound of a key in the door.

Sabina walked through into the kitchen where I was waiting. She looked calm, but apprehensive. 'We should talk,' she said.

'Too bloody right!' I snapped, immediately letting go of my dignity, and cursing my lack of resolve.

Sabina stayed calm. 'I think it's best if I leave home for a bit, to get some space to sort myself out.' Familiar words, I recognized – clichés from a hundred marital dramas.

'I... you...*what?*' I burbled unhelpfully.

'Look, I'm going to stay with Natalie for a while and see how things go.'

Natalie Forbes was her friend from the TV series *Full House*, in whichshe and Sabina had worked together. I had nothing against Natalie; she was attractive, frothy, not one of the great thinkers, but good fun. She'd been through a few dramas herself, and there was a tale that Ralph Bates' wife, Virginia had once turned up on her doorstep and landed a good right hander on her pretty blonde head – though I never heard why.

I guessed that Sabina wanted to be somewhere where it would be easier to keep up contact with Roy.

'Will you be seeing more of... him?'

'I expect so, now and again. We hardly know each other yet.'

'I shouldn't think there's much more to know,' I snapped back, foolishly. 'I mean, what the hell are you doing?'

'Please don't get angry,' she said, with a note of alarm in her voice. 'After all, we've all got a show to do.'

'Show? A *show*? Who cares about the fucking show! Our bloody marriage is more bloody important than any show.' I was gobsmacked, wounded, and very indignant that she didn't seem to appreciate the scale of her disloyalty.

Bizarrely, my mind suddenly reverted to a similar scenario, when I'd first met Sabina, and she'd delivered the news to her previous boyfriend, Michael Cameron (who had referred to me as 'John Callous'). She had told me with a distinct frisson how he got so angry he'd smashed one of her favourite ceramic figures. Perhaps what was happening now was simply part of a cycle of need in her life.

That evening, we made our separate ways to the Mermaid and, still quite overwrought, I had to deal with changing in the same dressing room as the man I'd found wrapped around my wife in Richmond Park that morning.

He was patently nervous too and if Richard Heffer hadn't known before what had been going on, he certainly did now. He did his best to keep the peace between two men he knew as good friends and colleagues. It wasn't easy. Snarled words and observations kept escaping from me.

'Nice sort of a shit you've turned out to be,' I muttered in low, vicious tones as I got to my feet. Roy took a quick step back, thinking I was going to thump him. I didn't, though. I've never thumped anyone; I'd be too concerned about hurting my own knuckles. But I did pick up his make-up box, with a view to hurling it across the room, though some innate professional instinct stopped me in time. I didn't really know what I wanted to do; I was massively confused by what had happened, and frustrated that I didn't know how to react. Besides, with my own self-esteem so wounded, I wanted simultaneously to lash out and steal off to lick those wounds.

Roy, drawing on his great reserves of ersatz dignity, tried to look understanding and fair. 'Now, look, we can talk about this in a civilized way, like reasonable men,' he suggested tentatively.

'*Civilized?*' I bellowed. 'What's civilized about sneaking off with the wife of a so-called friend and colleague?'

When I was changed and made up, I went along to Sabina's dressing room and asked her again what the hell she thought she was doing with an arty-farty, bogus poseur like Marsden. Sabina reacted like a starchy hospital matron dealing with a recalcitrant patient. She gave me a couple of pills to calm me down, whether they were Valium or the pills she took to settle her own unreliable innards I didn't know but the tension backstage was electric by now.

The whole company seemed to know about the showdown that morning and someone from the management came down with a message from Peter Woodward, who ran the company with Kate O'Mara. If I wanted to take a couple of shows off, they said, that would be fine.

But for years I'd lived with the maxim that the show was the thing, the show must always go on, and so, feeling a little saner after the pills had kicked in, I went on.

When it came to it, my performance was somewhat marred in my scenes with Sabina, when I kept bursting into tears, whether of rage, humiliation or frustration, I couldn't say; perhaps all three.

Even though all the other players were sympathetic, with much back-patting, I hated the fact that everyone knew about Sabina and Roy and had clearly known for some time. Perhaps I'd known too but had been in denial over it. It seemed to me whatever it was that had made me drive up to the car park in Richmond Park, it had been for a purpose – for me to be confronted by the truth and deal with it.

After the show, driving with Sabina on the way back to Observatory Road, I had a strange turn in my inner ear which seemed to destroy my sense of balance, so that I couldn't drive. I had to get out on the Embankment and walk up and down, with my head on one side. A wet wind drove up the Thames, while Sabina sat in the car looking sour and sceptical.

We spent a painful night, in the same house but without contact. In the morning Sabina was still adamant that she was going and packed her clothes into a clutch of suitcases, while I stood by, foolishly haranguing her – knowing as I did it that it was the worst thing to do.

'I suppose you'll soon be shacked up with Roy, then.'

'I told you,' she snapped. 'We hardly know each other!'

That made it worse. I was livid now, though I managed to avoid doing anything stupid or shameful as I watched her drive away with a carload of clothes to Natalie Forbes' house in Shepherd's Bush.

As her car turned into the main thoroughfare at the bottom of our road, my battered self-esteem encouraged me to wonder in a paranoid way if I was witnessing an example of Life imitating Art, of a woman seduced, like the character Sabina had played in Stoppard's *The Real Thing*, by the attraction of perceived artistic superiority and a kind of intellectual superciliousness that supported it. But then, I reflected more rationally, I could hardly put Roy Marsden in the same camp as Tom Stoppard.

On my own, after the car had disappeared and I'd walked back into the empty silence of the house, I knew it was well and truly over. The bleakness in her cold, grey-green eyes had told me clearly that she'd come to a decision to close a chapter in her life; she wasn't going to be talked out of it; there'd be no coming back. We would never sleep together again.

I played an old Stones album, which did nothing to help my mood, but at least it calmed me as I tried to identify my own contribution to the collapse of my third marriage. I was old enough by then to see that whatever else one person does to cause a split, it's nearly always with some impetus from the other's behaviour.

I was flirtatious, I knew, but this was an inherent part of my character – a simple enjoyment of female company – which meant nothing serious, and I hadn't been unfaithful to her once during the time we were married. Sabina was flirtatious, too, although evidently it sometimes meant something to her.

I certainly drank too much but that is an endemic hazard for members of our profession, of both sexes. I was pretty cavalier about my finances but all the bills got paid in the end, even if it did sometimes take a large man coming round to discuss my "elff" to make me cough up. I suppose I'd always been aware that our bouncy, joshing relationship had been bolstered to some extent by our natural tendency to play the most convenient role. Without using it as an excuse, either for Sabina or me, this can often be a problem, especially for people with healthy egos and low self-esteem (which is not such a contradiction as you might think in the thespian world). In the end, marriages to people outside the profession tend to have a better survival rate. In our busy, almost glamorous lives, we hadn't stopped to encourage one another to look too hard at the fundamental incompatibilities that lurked beneath the surface of our relationship.

In the meantime, we had another two weeks of *The Relapse* to run. Luckily, during that time I was already working on the early episodes of *Only Fools*, Series 6, which helped to distract me from the horrors of appearing on stage every night with my estranged wife and her lover.

I had to grit my teeth sometimes to stop myself from lashing out at Roy when he tried to explain, without much apology, how it had happened. At the same time, he tried to bring me back on side by telling me how much he admired my comedic skills and how lucky I was to possess them. I hated working with him now but what was especially galling was that while Roy had been deploying his oily charm before I realized he was lusting after my responsive wife, I'd got him a nice one-off guest appearance in *Only Fools*, which was due to be shot on the first weekend of February, three weeks after *The Relapse* closed. I was not looking forward to it, and although I could probably and not unreasonably have had the booking scratched, I chose not to show that kind of weakness.

Soon after Sabina had moved out, various people turned up at Observatory Road, apparently to commiserate. Sabina's old friend, Louisa Rix, whom I'd always liked, came round for a chat. She told me she was very sorry such a lovely relationship had had to end.

'But you know, darling,' she said shaking her head earnestly. 'You'll have to prepare yourself – she may not be coming back.'

I felt I already knew that, but I didn't want to hear it from anyone else.

'And,' she went on, with a disapproving tilt of her chin, 'I hear you kicked her car.'

It was the first I'd heard of it, though I suppose I *might* have given it a token boot up the exhaust as it sped away down the road *en route* for Shepherd's Bush.

Louisa's husband, Jonny Coy, met me in the pub later. He was genuinely upset and flabbergasted over what had happened. He'd seen Sabina the evening before.

'I asked her what the hell she was doing,' he said. 'I told her that you and she had had such a wonderful relationship – so warm and witty, and real – it was absurd to walk out on it!'

I guess it had been all those things, as far as they went, but always at a superficial level, it seemed now. Or how could she have been so brazen as to pull off a stunt like she had, with one of my colleagues, right under my nose?

To Jonny, she'd tried to justify her actions as being a lot more than mere infatuation with the biggest stag in what was, after all, a temporary and not very large herd.

'Besides,' she'd said. 'John never paid the bills on time.'

That was true enough, I told Jonny.

'But it's not grounds for separation!' he asserted strongly. 'And she also said she wanted babies.'

'That hurts,' I protested. 'I accept that she may be finding the biological clock ticking a lot louder now but before we got together seriously, I was completely up-front about my infertility. She said that was OK, she could live with it.'

Privately, despite my own sense of loss and battered pride, I'd come to recognize that, in the end, the urge to procreate was just as strong in a modern, sophisticated western woman as it was in any tribal virgin in the Amazon jungle, and I had to respect that.

By the last week of *The Relapse* at the Mermaid, after I'd somehow managed to sleep-walk through the previous three weeks, I was near the end of my tether. But I was given some let-up from my gloom one evening by finding a character from the past in my dressing room. In fact, I was astonished and, in an unexpected way, rather relieved when, out of the blue, my idle, unreliable and not entirely honest former partner in the St Margaret's Garden Centre poked his head around the door.

Michael Slater looked fit, well, tanned and chirpy. I told him so as I shook his hand and greeted his wife Alison who was with him. Always a bad keeper-in-touch, I'd seen very little of either of them since I'd stayed with them in their Earl's Court flat after I'd split up with Debbie, my second wife, six years before.

'Where the hell have you been?' I asked, genuinely pleased to see him, although I didn't really know why. I told him about what had happened between me and Sabina (whom they knew a little) and invited them to come round to Observatory Road soon.

At last *The Relapse* finished at the Mermaid. It had been enough of a success there to have yielded a worthwhile profit, which we all shared equally (after Roy Marsden's extra salary had been deducted). I said goodbye to Sabina, not expecting or even wanting to see her again. I knew I would see Roy in a couple of weeks when we'd be working on the *Only Fools* episode in which I'd got him his part.

Sabina came round to the house a few more times, mainly to discuss what we were going to do with it. The last time she came, she announced that she and Roy were both having counselling and suggested I should too.

I pointed out that counselling didn't appear to be helping her much, which may have been unfair; she might have been in an even more unsatisfactory state without it. Bizarrely, shortly after that, Louisa Rix left Jonny Coy and it turned out that she was having counselling too.

A few days after Sabina's visit, I came down to answer an early morning knock on the front door. Outside, shifting from foot to foot, was a grave-faced man in grey shoes and a beige anorak, who announced that he was from one of the nastier tabloids.

'Would you care to make a comment on what's been going on?' he asked in a weasely, nasal voice. 'Sorry to hear the news, by the way. We know who's involved.'

'No,' I said, already closing the door.

How the hell had they found out? I wondered.

I watched the paper for the next couple of days, but nothing appeared about me, or Roy or Sabina, so I guessed they didn't, in fact, have a clue who was involved.

Sabina got in touch to congratulate me on my great 'show of strength' in dealing with the tabloid, and went on to say that Roy had left his wife and two children and was now tormented by self-recrimination. Sabina sounded unimpressed by this show of vacillation and weakness and seemed to be hinting at the possibility of a reconciliation between us.

I asked her bluntly if she had slept with Roy.

'Since you ask a direct question, the answer is yes,' she told me.

Frankly this was no surprise but the clear articulation of it drew a line in the sand for me.

Within this obviously strained relationship, Sabina and I had to decide between us what to do with, 8 Observatory Road. The house was something for which we'd worked hard and it meant a lot to both of us. We'd planned it as a stepping-stone towards our future together. Now it had to be disposed of, like an obsolete cassette recorder, irrelevant and surplus to requirements.

We agreed that for the time being the most sensible thing to do was to rent out the house while we decided how to proceed from there. In a rather bizarre coincidence, one of the first people who arrived to look at it came with a hefty blast from my complicated past.

She was my former agent, Caroline Dawson, who'd found me all my earliest television work back in the '60s. She had also become my lover and I'd bought my first dog, the Prune, with her. In another ironic twist of fate, she was now Roy Marsden's agent and must have been responsible for negotiating the secret deal on his salary that had been made with management at the Mermaid and which had upset the rest of the company so much. But it was fun to see her again and she agreed to have lunch with me in a few days' time, on the strict condition that I did not ask her to become my agent again.

She brought her old friend and our former flatmate, Doreen Jones with her to lunch and we chattered away as if we were back in 1968. I'd had a great time when I lived in their flat – the first time I'd lived in London – when I used to occupy my 'resting' time between acting jobs with working around the antique dealers of Portobello Road, where I got my first taste for the trade.

The two women were sympathetic about the recent hurt and humiliation I'd been though with Roy and Sabina. 'What a bastard!' Caroline exclaimed, even though he was her client.

I left lunch feeling fairly drunk and a lot better about myself. Caroline didn't take the house but she did buy one almost opposite and moved in a few months later.

After that, Sabina's influence began slowly to ebb from my life. It had been a pretty horrible time, but, although we never think we'll mend after these things happen, most of us have enough survival instinct and personal resilience in the end to be able to look back and say – what the heck, these things happen and life goes on.

Afterwards, Sabina herself didn't fare perhaps as well as she might have hoped. She and Roy split up, she never remarried and, sadly, never had the children she was hoping for. Her career, too, seemed on the downhill side of its parabola, although she continued to put in appearances in *East Enders* and *Coronation Street*.

Mike Slater came round to see me at Number 8 while I was packing up and getting ready to let the house. It seemed quite strange that I hadn't seen him for so long, considering Mike had been quite a big part of my life for some years. I guess our paths had diverged and I'd had less spare time to keep in touch.

He and Alison could see that I was still sore over Sabina; they were supportive and sympathetic, and I found I was glad to see something of them. In a way, Mike, who really knew very little about my world and the personalities involved, was the right person for me to be talking to. I was glad, too, to let go of my own problems for a bit and hear about everything he'd been doing.

Mike said that he'd done fantastically well (as usual) in the appropriately vague field of Public Relations. PR has always been a catch-all term for a variety of nebulous functions related to sales, presentation, schmoozing and so on. I couldn't elicit from him any precision about his function, although Alison volunteered loyally that he had been 'headhunted' by some impressive outfit I'd never heard of. However, perhaps things were going less well now, or Mike was becoming more idle, because they told me with great excitement that they were planning to move to Portugal.

Mike had a wheeze he was very anxious to tell me about. They were going to sell up in London and buy a bodega, near Lagoa, apparently a charming old Portuguese town in the foothills of the Monchique in the Algarve.

'But what are you going to do there, or don't you need the money?'

He glanced at me as if I were mad, for thinking he would do nothing and perhaps for thinking that he might need the money, while I knew that he was by nature idle, and, by habit, skint.

He touched the side of his nose in a continental gesture. 'I've hit on a fantastic way of making money out there, from the soil.'

'What – *gardening?*' I asked with disbelief.

'No, no...' he said testily. 'Aloe vera.'

At this stage, the plant with a name like a bad British sitcom was becoming more recognised for its curative properties and often cropped up in articles about health and wellbeing, so I was vaguely familiar with it. Although the Romans had known and made use if its qualities, it was only recently that it had excited the interest of the mainstream western world.

Mike banged on. 'The market for it is enormous – for potions, lotions, sun cream, shampoo, cuts, grazes, as a soothing ointment – probably as a sex aid of some sort, too, I wouldn't be surprised.'

Despite my instinct to distrust any claims made by Slater for anything and although normally cynical about wonder cures and their true efficacy, I could see that growing the stuff might well have commercial possibilities.

Michael, maybe taking advantage of my vulnerability, was full of it and when we went out for an extended drink afterwards, I was so relieved to get away from the Roy/Sabina saga that I sat and let him bang on about his new project, embellished by a large helping of his usual old bullshit. It soon became clear that it wasn't only my jovial company and a renewal of our friendship he was after but also some money to put into the aloe-vera plantation he was buying.

I suppose he thought my regular appearance in *Only Fools* meant I had accumulated large piles of wonga. He was wrong about that but, as it happened, I was still sitting on several tens of thousands of pounds, the residue of what my mother had left me. I had retained my interest in growing things and it occurred to me that investing in a plantation on the sunny southern slopes of Portugal might provide a handy income at times of future scarcity, as well as a warm bolt-hole when not much else was going on. Besides, my trust in the workings of 'fate' – as close as I got to any 'religious' beliefs – urged me to feel that Slater turning up with this proposition when my life was crying out for a new direction, when my mother had left me an entirely unexpected sum of money, was obviously pre-ordained and couldn't be ignored. I was quite drunk by then and I told him that, absurd as it might seem, I could be interested in going into business with him again. By the time we parted, he was quite high and very optimistic, while I went home wondering what on earth I had committed myself to.

Chapter 6
Little Problems

By the time I came to work with Roy on the episode of *Only Fools* that I'd engineered for him, my anger with the man had relented a little and he and I seemed to have reached a kind of truce, if not a very cosy one. He was obviously still feeling guilty as hell and made a point of telling me again how much he admired my comedy skills and how lucky he felt to be involved in our little sitcom.

In *Little Problems*, Roy played a Peckham villain called *Danny Driscoll*. Although, in the circumstances, I could probably have persuaded John Sullivan and Ray Butt to write the part out – they always had too much good stuff in the can anyway – I wasn't going to give anyone the satisfaction of seeing me cave in to my emotions like that. Besides, it did the show good to have a few better-known actors coming in from time to time; and if it did the show good, it did me good, I told myself pragmatically.

In fact, the first choice for the role of *Danny Driscoll* had been Anthony Hopkins – not only a great actor, but also a big fan of *Only Fools*. He rated John's writing very highly, along with the strength of the ensemble performances it produced. Sadly, he couldn't do it: he was otherwise occupied in some little horror film about lambs.

In what turned out to be a brilliant fifty-minute episode, *Danny* turns up to collect a debt from *Del Boy* with his little brother, *Tony*, played by Chris Ryan (best known for his stint in *The Young Ones*). John Sullivan gave them some memorable lines:

Tony: I hear Marlene's up the spout.
Boycie: Yeah...
Danny: When you find out who done it, let us know and we'll sort him out.

And later, to *Mike* landlord of the Nag's Head:
Danny: OK, Guv'nor. I wanna buy everyone in this pub a drink. Here's a pound... and I want change.'
Boycie: Large Cognac, please, Michael.

There was an additional element of authenticity to this episode, supplied by Patrick Murray. Patrick played a nice dodgy character called *Mickey Pearce*, who appeared from time to time. Between filming the location shots and finishing off the studio stuff in front of a live audience, Patrick had arrived home with several bags of shopping. He'd opened his front door, tripped over the doorstep and fallen headlong into the hall, breaking his arm on the way and getting a great gash in it too. We'd been told before he came into the studio that his arm was heavily plastered. After a quick raid in the BBC props department, we all put plaster casts on various limbs and sat around waiting for Patrick to arrive for rehearsal. We hadn't done it to hurt him but to take the sting out of the situation for him with laughter and a show of sympathy. But this presented John Sullivan with a problem. *Mickey* couldn't suddenly appear in the Nag's Head with an arm in plaster without an explanation. John, as usual, turned it to his advantage. The *Driscolls* were already the main protagonists in the plot, so it was no stretch that he and his friend *Jevon* (played by Stephen Woodcock) had somehow crossed *Danny* and *Tony Driscoll* and had been punished for it – hence *Mickey's* arm in plaster, and *Jevon* appearing in a rather fetching neck brace.

Shortly after working together on *Little Problems*, Roy rang me and suggested we meet up for a drink on neutral ground, an anonymous little café in Covent Garden, to have a chat, man to man. I agreed but I didn't feel forgiving. When we met, I told him bluntly that I felt cheated and humiliated by his behaviour with Sabina and that he'd shown no sensitivity or civilized restraint. Like the father of an errant daughter, I asked him what his intentions were.

'John, I promise you, it's serious,' he said, gravely nodding his head. 'I really love her. I'm sorry you're hurt, of course, but it has been a joy to work with you.'

I got up and left him to pay for our drinks.

The next time I saw Jonny Coy, I told him about my chat with Roy.

'But weren't you bloody angry with him?' he asked.

I realized then that I'd reached a turning point when I answered, quite truthfully, that I wasn't angry anymore. Although the humiliation of it still stung, that was just about male pride, which was more than compensated for by a sense of relief that I had discovered relatively early in our marriage the true nature of a woman in whom I had placed my complete trust. She had been quite prepared to carry on with Roy, bigger stag as she saw him, without any consideration for me.

Little Problems had been the last of four *Only Fools* episodes I was in, where production partially overlapped the last couple of weeks of *The Relapse*. Before it we'd done *Danger UXD*, *Chain Gang* and *Sickness and Wealth*.

Danger UXD demonstrated wonderfully John Sullivan's ability to handle the grubbiest material and make it work without resorting to outright crudity. The stars of that episode were a group of blow-up dolls, which *Del* had bought from *Denzil* – very cheap, of course – to help him out of a hole, under the impression that they were *toy* dolls, not adult sex objects.

It turns out that they are factory rejects because they had been sent out ready-inflated with propane, and were potentially lethal fire-hazards. It was a great script but, off camera, most of the laughs came from the trouble the props people had moving the dolls around. After filming one scene, the dolls couldn't be deflated and had to be transported by two of the lads back to the unit hotel, still in all their grotesque, fully-inflated glory. They managed to get them into the lift without being spotted and headed up to store them in their rooms for the night.

Halfway up, the lift stopped and a respectable-looking couple got in. Their jaws dropped in horror at the sight of two young men taking these open-mouthed, shell-shocked looking plastic women to their rooms.

'It's OK. We're doing a film,' one of the lads tried to explain, digging himself deeper.

The horrified couple said nothing and got out at the next floor.

Chain Gang emerged as one of the favourite episodes. It's a beautifully plotted story of *Del* and *Boycie* being out-conned by a superior practitioner of the art, although, in the end, they get their own back – and their money. *Boycie* has a wonderful and much loved scene in a restaurant, when the con man pretends to choke and keel over with a heart attack.

Boycie, with magisterial self-regard, declares. *'I am a doctor. Stand aside; let the dog see the rabbit!'* – a line which I am frequently asked to reproduce, even now, twenty years later.

By this stage, now into its sixth season, *Only Fools* was achieving unbelievable viewing figures – nearly 19 million for *Little Problems* – and we were all feeling pretty pleased with ourselves. Inevitably with a show like ours which heavily featured two principal characters, there had developed a bit of a 'them and us' atmosphere on set. David and Nicholas had most of the plot to deliver and most of the lines, so they'd got into the habit of rehearsing on their own at one end of the rehearsal room, in their set, depicting the flat in Nelson Mandela House. Buster, as *Uncle Albert*, was part of those rehearsals but not part of the very close empathy that existed between the other two, which left him slightly out on a limb. We satellite characters, *Boycie*, *Trigger*, *Denzil*, *Marlene*, *Mike the barman* and, to a lesser extent, *Mickey Pearce*, usually revolving around *Del* and *Rodney* in the Nag's Head, made up the next tier in the show's hierarchy, followed by the guest stars, like Roy Marsden or Jim Broadbent, followed by the one-off, bit part players. Reigning supreme at the top of the stack, of course, was John Sullivan, the show's creator, who fiercely guarded his fiefdom.

As the importance of our own characters within the ensemble had grown, we'd begun to feel a little neglected and taken for granted by our producers, who seemed to spend most of their time with the top two. As David used to say: 'If in doubt, follow the money.'

Tony Dow, our director, was aware of this divide and did his best to bridge it by involving the satellite characters as much as possible. In one episode, I was wearing a sweater that I thought was dead right for *Boycie* – smoky grey with a linked, crenellated motif across the torso.

David was full of ridicule. 'He looks like the Mayor of Casterbridge, for Gawd's sake!' he exclaimed sourly.

His own sweater, featuring a large fluffy black and white cat, was even sillier.

'I don't think you can talk about sweaters,' I responded.

'At least mine says something!' David retorted.

'Yeah, *Pussy!*' Tony Dow chipped in, just like that.

It was like a piece of Sullivan's script – a perfect set-up with a great tag.

Tony needed this kind of tact to keep things on an even keel, especially as most of us (though not Buster) had already been on the show for eight years. He had been AFM (assistant floor manager) for much of that time too, and, it seemed, groomed by the 'management' for the director's job. He had got his chance when our original producer/director, Ray Butt had to leave in the middle of a show to look after his sick father. Tony had held the reins ever since, with the help of Gareth Gwenlan, one time Head of Comedy at the BBC, and now a freelance producer. He and Tony Dow remained with the show in tandem until 2001.

The success we were having with *Only Fools* to some extent made up for the shock and potential misery caused by the sudden and unexpected meltdown of my marriage. I was pleased, too, that despite the collateral damage it had caused, my last effort on stage in *The Relapse* had done so well. I felt like a grown-up actor as well as a successful comedy turn.

My stock among the *Only Fools* cast went up considerably when Kate O'Mara turned up at the North Acton rehearsal rooms (known to us telly actors as the Acton Hilton). Kate was rehearsing something quite different but we met up for lunch and I was able to introduce her to David Jason, who was a great fan and had always wanted to meet her. She was a true star, and responded to him at her slightly wicked, vampy best, which delighted David.

Later, when we were alone, she was very solicitous about what had happened at the Mermaid. 'You must keep yourself nice and busy and make lots of plans to take your mind off what's happened and put it all behind you.'

I had plans, all right. I'd let Observatory Road very easily to a Japanese family, who treated the place with great deference. When I want back to check a detail on the lease, I was asked to remove my shoes before entering my own house.

I had gone to live with my old friend, Keith Washington and his partner, Madeleine Howard in a two-up two-down terrace house in

Thornton Road, Mortlake, a part of South West London now very much on the ascendant. Luckily they had a spare room.

Keith was still wrangling with his ex-wife over access to their son, Tom, who was living with his mother, but at least Keith and Madeleine were settled and he was a lot happier than when I'd seen a lot of him, ten years before.

At the blessing of my marriage to Sabina, Keith had read a John Donne poem about the wonders of love, which he had done movingly and with great panache. This seemed now to make him an appropriate person to help pick up the pieces after the failure of the marriage.

I was living in what felt like a state of suspended animation. Despite the success I was having, I really had no clear idea of where my own career was going: in fact, very few actors, in the unlikely event that they were being honest, would say otherwise. It is true to say that in popular television you are as desirable as your last set of ratings, while in the other more esoteric areas of acting, luck, serendipity and hard graft in the networking department all play a part.

I was entirely aware by then that *Boycie* had become an immutable presence in my life (although I would never have predicted that twenty-five years on, in restaurants and other public places, I would still encounter nasal cries of '*Where's Marlene?*')

While *The Relapse* had been running at the Mermaid, I'd had a taste of this. A steady stream of *Only Fools* fans were waiting for me outside the stage door each night for an autograph, including one man, who, when I asked him if he'd enjoyed the show, seemed unhappy.

He spoke with a strong Birmingham accent. 'It was all roight, I s'pose,' he said unconvincingly, 'but we were a bit disappointed, reelly.'

I was mortified. 'I'm sorry to hear it; why was that?' I asked, well aware that some parts of the show even now weren't quite hanging together.

'Well, you wasn't like him at all! The only reason we came down from Solihull was because we saw you were in it. They should have told us!'

'Oh dear, I am sorry,' I said, relieved in some respects. 'But the trouble is there weren't many second-hand car salesmen around in seventeenth-century London,' I said, probably more flippantly than I should have.

'I know you think we're all stupid,' my fan went on, 'but it's this sort of lack of information that's driving people away from the theatres.'

I simply couldn't think of a suitable answer and busied myself scribbling on his programme. I almost felt guilty that people were coming here to see me as *Boycie*, and were finding something so far removed from the character and his metier, that they were positively resentful.

Peter Adamson, known as he was for years for his *Corrie* persona of *Len Fairclough*, must also have disappointed a few fans. He was giving a great, rumbustious performance as *Sir Tunbelly Clumsy* when his agent told him one night that an important casting director was coming along to see him. He warmed up beforehand with so much falling-down water that by the end of the show he'd completely forgotten that he was supposed to meet the Big Cheese in the bar after the curtain and he never showed up, leaving us to explain his absence.

'He's very ill, I'm afraid. It's a miracle he got through the show tonight,' the casting director was told. 'Oh, thank you, yes, I'd love a drink.'

We guessed, good actor though he was, that Peter was still terrified of being put under the microscope and having his talent examined too closely. We knew it wasn't lack of talent that was the problem but excess of booze and it didn't look as if that was going to change.

Once I'd put Observatory Road and its memories of life with Sabina behind me and I'd moved into Keith and Madeleine's house, I became obsessed with the idea that Mike Slater's proposition had turned up in response to the demands of fate, specifically to show me a new direction to take after Sabina had put an end to the last phase of my life. Slater had a Dutch partner in his proposed aloe-vera growing enterprise and they were looking for investors.

'We've already raised all we can ourselves,' he explained, 'but we need a little more to clinch it. It's a bloody nuisance we have to bring in partners at all. Once it's up and running, it can't fail. It'll be a licence to print money.'

I managed in my excitement to forget entirely that every time I'd heard that phrase used to describe a proposition, it had always turned out to be a licence either to flush money down the lavatory, or to make a big bonfire out of it. Fate, I was convinced, had decreed that I should take this gamble – if indeed it were a gamble – and besides, Mike was a very old chum who'd seen me through some of the leaner periods of my life. He wouldn't let me down...

I'd coughed up the money I'd promised Slater, and he had shot off with Alison to set up home and consolidate the purchase of the plantation with his mystery partner. With no immediate job in hand, I was anxious to get out to the Algarve as soon as possible to see what was happening to my investment.

I flew to Faro, hired a car and found my way through the small hills to Lagoa, which, as Mike had described it, was a charming town of well-worn stone with a fine patina and ancient vines clambering up the walls. I found Mike's house on the edge of the town. The entrance was a small postern, set in a much larger pair of carriage doors. The door creaked open and there were Mike and Alison in the beautiful, flower-filled courtyard of an old stone bodega, with breakfast still on the table, and a lunchtime bottle already open. A run of stables and an old winery occupied three sides of the flagstoned yard, while on the fourth, beside a high retaining wall was a dark swimming pool, shaded by eucalyptus trees and a large bougainvillea.

After all the hassles and gloom of dealing with my former life with Sabina, this looked more or less like paradise.

Mike and Alison welcomed me fulsomely and clearly saw my arrival as an excuse for an extended bout of carousing. We seemed to spend the next few days on a continuous binge around the bars and cafés in the 'talking squares' of Lagoa, Portimao and Lagos.

I'd seen Sabina just a few days before I'd left to sort out our proposal for the eventual sale of the house at Observatory Road. Now, over endless cups of coffee with the Slaters in the mornings, wine and brandy into the afternoons and evenings, I took the opportunity to get a lot of bad stuff out of my system by talking about it and they were happy to let me ramble on.

'She had the gall to ask me if I thought maybe we should get back together,' I expostulated, 'after all the shit she'd put me through! She said we could get some *focus* on our lives. I thought we'd had plenty of bloody focus before, until she took her eye off the ball and kicked it into touch. I suppose Roy's been backtracking – not delivering on his original promises. Maybe she's discovered that the biggest stag in the herd is made of straw, with feet of clay,' I droned on, happily mashing my metaphors. 'Mind you, the last thing I heard she was still with him. I bumped into Bill Franklyn, her father, at a voice-over studio, and he was quite apologetic – blamed her entirely for always trying to create new crises in her life, to give her a foothold up to the next level. He said he'd love me to come and play cricket with the Sargentmen again this summer but there's no way I will, not with her swanning about and Roy bloody Marsden lurking there.'

I suppose Mike was listening, although, in truth, the ability to listen wasn't one of his strong points. One never knew quite what he was thinking about – if anything. He was one of those people who turn out to exist only on the surface and appeared to want an easy, uncomplicated sybaritic life, without having to give too much thought to how it was going to be paid for, while Alison tried to plug the gaps by running a fairly chaotic B&B at the bodega.

Around the bars, Slater introduced me to dozens of other expats, most of whom were running restaurants and bars, all of whom appeared to be great *Only Fools* fans, wanting signed photos of me. We were offered in return any number of free drinks, free meals, even a free hour each on a jet ski, which was a very uncomfortable experience for me, with my marked lack of aquatic skills. While I could manage driving off in a straight line at great speed, the minute I tried to turn, I seemed to be leaning the wrong way and I'd go off in one direction while the wretched little thing shot off across the water in the other. I found it very difficult to remount without immediately tumbling over the other side.

We ate out all the time, sampling seafood in Portimao (great), paella in Lagoa (so-so) and 'All you can eat' Argentinean beefsteak somewhere in between. It was hectic, non-stop and easy to forget the gloom of the last few months. But when there were down moments, I would go up on to the flat roof of the bodega and reflect on the shambles I'd made of my personal life so far, and what, at the age of forty-six, I should do next.

I persuaded myself that it would be therapeutic to walk, and set off on the five-mile path across the hills to Silves. I loved it. The journey gave me a lot to think about and the satisfaction of arriving at the unspoiled medieval town, founded by the Romans when they'd built their beautiful (and strategic) bridge across the River Arade. After the Romans, the Moors had occupied it, to be turfed out again by Christians in the El Cid era.

Although Michael was very unconcerned – or just uninterested – in the technical and financial side of the aloe-vera venture, he did show me all around the plantation, which, to my untutored eye, looked very pretty and full of potential. The plantations lay on the lower slopes of the Monchique in crescent rows of young aloe plants and above them, a newly-dug reservoir, which would irrigate them through a pumping system that was being installed. There were a few employees in evidence and it all looked surprisingly organized for an enterprise run by Michael Slater.

The key to it all would lie in their first harvest that autumn, when the fat, juicy leaves of the aloe would be gathered and stored down in the docks at Portimao until a buyer could be found at the best price. After that, Mike said, with a worrying gleam in his eye, dividends would be paid to shareholders. It all sounded much more predictable than my usual precarious livelihood and in my current unstable condition I felt very optimistic about earning a nice little income from my investment over the years to come.

We went off on a few excursions up the mountains, for which I volunteered to drive, as Michael was more or less permanently drunk. He had always claimed to have been some kind of racing driver in his younger days and he backed up this claim by being the most appalling back-seat driver, sporadically clutching his head, pumping his heels into the footwell, gasping loudly every time we went near a cliff edge and constantly trying to tell me how I should be driving. In the end I got so sick of his relentless barking of absurd instructions that I stopped, got out and told him he could take over. This was a mistake, because he was so pissed that he often bumped into things and would spend a lot of time explaining how a stationary truck was to blame for a collision, while we came quite close to death on several occasions.

On my second weekend at the Slaters' Alison had to fly back to

England and Mike announced that he had committed us to looking after two female Danish friends of an acquaintance of his. They were, he explained, on holiday from Spain, where they worked as physiotherapists in one of the Costa resorts.

Margaretta and Inge turned out to be a great double act and it was clear from the minute we shook their warm brown hands that they were going to provide a lot of entertainment. Inge Christensen, the younger of the two, was a sassy, blue-eyed, rangy blonde, who looked a man straight in the eye and gave him as good as she got in a lovely, sexy Scandinavian accent. I had the impression that neither of them was in the habit of taking prisoners. We spent the first day on the lash, with the occasional break for food or sleep and arranged to meet them the following morning on the beach.

As we approached, Inge unfolded her long slender legs and rose from the sand to greet us. Apart from not having a dagger strapped to the waistband of her bikini, it could have been Ursula Andress heading up the beach to grapple with Sean Connery.

I felt myself shiver with arousal and gulped involuntarily, already sensing that this was going to be a very exciting day. And so it was, cruising the bars, dancing on the beach, lying semi-naked on the roof of Mike's bodega... it was like a teenage boy's dream sequence. Inge smoked incessantly and with vigorous intensity, while she hurled back the local Portuguese plonk at least as fast as me. The more she drank, the more she developed a fascinating, wild, angry air, which the masochist male in me found very appealing. The banter, the flirting, the sexual tension didn't flag all day until we had to put them on a train at Lagoa for their journey back to Benalmadena, near Fuengirola, on the Costa del Sol.

Astonishingly enough, Inge and I hadn't been to bed together but from the rudimentary animal communication that had gone on between us, I knew that Inge was interested in seeing me again. And I was sure I felt the same.

She gave me her address – apparently a remedial centre for sports injuries, as well as geriatric limb conditions, (of which, I guessed, there were plenty on that coast).

Shortly after that, with my mind refreshed, my body exhausted and half-poisoned with alcohol, I had to get back to England for the summer filming of the next *Only Fools* Christmas special, *The Jolly*

Boys' Outing.

It certainly was a jolly outing, on and off screen. The whole gang was in top form and it became more of a holiday, with most of the shooting in Margate. Around the town, at the fairground, by the seaside, we threw ourselves into the challenges.

Winston Churchill would have been impressed. 'We will film them on the beaches, in the fields, on the streets and in the fairground. We will *never* go back to the hotel,' he would probably have observed.

Most of the time, we didn't get to bed when we were supposed to (in anticipation of the next day's filming), and once I stayed up all night with Nick Lyndhurst and Ken MacDonald in the jacuzzi, taking it in turns to be drinks waiter. We were joined for a time by two ladies, although my recollection of what happened and when they left is inevitably hazy.

This episode, *The Jolly Boys' Outing,* was incredibly good fun to make and, perhaps as a result of this, the favourite of a large number of *Only Fools* fans.

John Sullivan had based the idea on similar trips undertaken by an ex-servicemen's outfit from his part of London. They got together every year for their coach trip to the seaside and always came back as if it had been the highlight of their year. That was how it felt for us – dancing around to the music – and there's a great shot of Roger Lloyd Pack, Ken MacDonald and me, all hammering away on our air guitars to Clapton's *Lay Down Sally* as it blasted from a fairground speaker. Between shoots we were daring one another to go on the hairiest rides in the fair. Some, whom out of kindness I shan't name, were as windy as bean curry and wouldn't go on anything. Ken as usual overdid it, full of booze, with the inevitable consequence. We behaved like children on the beach, all rushing down to the sea together, squealing like schoolgirls as the six-inch surf rolled in.

As always on location work, we had to endure an awful lot of hanging around and surrounding our locations was a permanent ring of onlookers, camped there all day with their primus stoves and teapots, ogling everything we did – eating at the chuck wagon, taking a trip to the Honey Wagon (upmarket Portaloo), traipsing in and out of make-up or wardrobe. I was regularly being hailed with cries from the multitude –'*Come on Boycie, give us a wave!*' or worse, '*Give us a laugh!*'

At Margate, we were in the proverbial goldfish bowl but, for myself, I never resented it, nor ever have since. It was these enthusiastic fans who had given us the joy of being a part of what was already one of the most popular sitcoms in the history of television.

Sometimes, though, the onlookers almost overwhelmed the location and would get mingled with the crew. As a result, the producers hired a security firm to guard the perimeters of the locations.

During one long boring gap between filming, I turned to the bulky geezer standing beside me. 'I've got to have a stretch and get some fags,' I said.

He nodded co-operatively. 'I'll come with you.'

I was grateful for the security. I cleared it with the director's assistant and we pushed our way through the crowds to the promenade where the shops were.

I bought my cigarettes (it wasn't a crime to smoke in public then) and offered one to my burly minder.

'Do you do a lot of this kind of work,' I asked, by way of polite conversation.

'What sort work?' he asked,

'You know – security and that.'

'No, never, really, mate. I'm a supermarket manager. I'm on me lunch break. Could I have your autograph?'

Looking back over twenty-five years of *Only Fools*, I guess that *The Jolly Boys' Outing* was as good as it got. I still have a wonderful photograph of us all in front of the Halfway House pub on the road to Margate, in beautiful sunshine, all looking happy and proud – and, of course, twenty years younger. The whole gang is there, with Ken MacDonald and Buster Merryfield – now, sadly, no longer with us. I think it must have been a happy time for all of us.

Filming that episode certainly helped me to forget the pain of everything that had been going on a few months before. I was still very conscious that my third marriage was over, through no fault (or not much) of my own. I still felt vulnerable and inadequate but the defences I'd raised had worked to some extent and most people mistook this protection for an inner strength I didn't really possess. Still, as long as it was working, I was content to live that lie.

After filming in Margate, I was booked for another voice-over at Angell Sound. I arrived to find Roy Marsden was doing the other voice part with me. I wanted to turn around and walk out but I deliberately drained any expression from my face and carried on. Roy's demeanour was surprising. He was obviously nervous at seeing me and, it seemed, still quite guilty about how he'd behaved. He was deferential, almost unctuous, calling me 'Guv'nor', for some reason.

I seldom saw him after that, although when he took over as artistic director of the Mermaid Theatre in 2003, just before it closed, he offered me a couple of jobs there. Despite the fact that he and his wife, Polly, had divorced as a result of his liaison with Sabina, that affair hadn't outlasted the year. I think he must have had a taste of how Sabina could be, for he'd made no move to marry her. In the summer, she'd taken him to one of her father's Sargentmen cricket matches, where she'd flirted extravagantly with a number of the other men she knew there. She'd always been one of those women who got a charge out of seeing two men wanting her at the same time. I guess Roy must have recognized then, if he hadn't already, what he was dealing with.

While I was busy and *Only Fools* was getting more and more viewers with each episode, I was able to put on a fairly convincing face. Inside, though, I was wobbling and making erratic, knee-jerk decisions – like my aloe-vera investment – to take my mind off the failure I was feeling.

Another knee-jerk, random decision was to ring Inge and fly out to see her in Spain. I guess I thought it would help me to escape – to 'move on', as everyone kept telling me to do.

Once I'd got to Benalmadena, I found Inge at first quite wary and putting on an unmistakable show of Nordic feminine independence. 'You can't just come down here and think you can have whoever you want,' she told me.

I'd already sensed that there was strong defensive streak in her, as if she were determined to resist being 'exploited'. So we circled one another for a few days, testing the air, sensing the vibrations between us. I knew I had to get back to London again in a few days for a voice-over and the sexual tension mounted until, the day before I left, when

Inge and I went to a flamenco bar which, with lamentable lack of judgement, encouraged the punters to have a go at flamenco dancing. I'd already been spotted for my *Boycie* persona and was vigorously urged to get up and participate.

It must have been a pretty horrible sight, my attempts at heel-tapping, hand-clapping, foot-stamping, arm-waving, pit-sweating flamenco movements but at least on the way back, Inge slipped her muscular little arm through mine. 'I suppose I can let you sleep in my bed tonight,' she whispered huskily.

Inge lived in a small flat a little into the foothills just north of the town, where I was to spend a lot of time, on and off, over the next few months. The extraordinary thing about her was that the difficult, spiky aspects of her character would in anyone else have really put me off but in her case, and perhaps because of my own insecurities and low self-esteem, I found it gave her a grisly fascination, as a constantly renewing challenge, and I was somehow ensnared by her unrelenting trickiness.However, I still had to make a living and the voice-over work was consistently providing that between bigger jobs. Inge was disgusted that I should be employed in such a fatuous way.

'Nobody ever paid me for anything I said,' she complained and her resentment suggested that she thought my frequent trips back to England were a mere self-indulgence on my part.

Despite the regular bursts of hostility between Inge and me, there was also a great physical chemistry, which I've often found rather dangerously overcomes any rational considerations in a relationship. We also shared a slightly perverse taste for exploration and adventure. We loved getting around, clambering up inaccessible gullies and tracks, as well as seeking out bars, ice-cream parlours, obscure *al fresco* eating places and, most importantly, identifying and mapping *servicios* of an acceptable standard in our neck of Andalusia.

A decent hygienic 'facility' was hard to find, especially inland. Although fastidious British tourists had been invading that part of Spain for thirty years, what was deemed adequate by the natives was usually out of the question for more prissy Northern Europeans. Very often all that was on offer was a hole in the ground, surrounded, if you were lucky, by cracked, discoloured porcelain, although more usually by a slab of local stone. While most of the time a chap could cope, for the ladies squatting over these things, with a handbag held swinging between gritted teeth was a gruesome form of hell. Add to that the usual absence of paper and the nightmare was total. Inevitably, as Inge and I sought out superior suitable facilities, she vigorously expressed an independent Danish woman's resentment at a male's ability to deal with emergencies simply by stepping behind a rock, a cactus or a growth of broom and unzipping his flies.

More positively, we had a wonderful trip to the great Alhambra Palace on the hills above Granada. We revelled in the tranquillity and beauty of the Moorish architecture and soothing atmosphere of the water gardens, which seemed to bring us closer together.

I loved the history of Southern Spain which had for centuries been an outpost of Islamic civilization and, curiously in the light of more recent events emanating from the Moslem world, far more advanced in urban sophistication than the rest of Europe at that time. The cities of what is now Andalusia were places of learning, with street lighting and proper sanitation, when London was still a warren of dark, stinking alleys and open sewers.

Despite the closeness brought on by occasional bursts of emotion shared with Inge, at the back of my mind I knew – although I wouldn't admit it to myself – that I was rebounding from the Sabina debacle like a squash ball hit in fury, with a bit of top spin so you never knew where it would land. However, I couldn't stop myself coming back to Spain again and again. I guess I needed the uncertainty of Inge's feisty company to keep me on edge and for the adrenalin rush it gave me. But my frequent absences led to even greater tension between us and when Inge had had just a couple of glasses of Pinot Grigio, she could become a wild beast at any perceived infringement of her right to Scandinavian-style gender equality and would fight viciously to make her point.

A regular mantra of hers was that people should have the guts to stand up and tell others what they really were. This didn't work for me, of course. I told her I was an actor precisely because I had no idea what the real me was!

She didn't like that and tried to explain what she meant by using as an example a female Swedish rock star – married with two beautiful kids – who had suddenly recognized a fundamental truth about herself, and announced to a stadium full of fifty thousand people that from then on, she was going to dance at the other end of the ballroom, so to speak.

I wondered how this had affected her husband and lovely children. 'Surely,' I suggested, 'some things are best left hidden, to protect the people you love?'

This provoked a tirade, a full-frontal attack on me, my profession, my personal integrity, and, indeed, my manhood.

'You are just in love,' she hissed through her teeth, 'with the glitter, the false posturing, egocentric world of the preening exhibitionist. Look at you – colourful showy clothes, always projecting your voice, winking at men.'

'*Winking at men?*' I protested. 'All the other stuff maybe, but not that!'

'You do it. I've seen you. You don't even know that you're doing it, do you?'

I certainly didn't know that I was winking indiscriminately at other men but I vowed to her that I wouldn't do it again. She refused to take this seriously, mainly because at this stage in her rant she seemed to have lost all contact with reason and I started laughing. Her perspective was so preposterous and so unfair. In any case, even if she really thought these things, it was totally unreasonable to dish them up all at once. As I had just told her, some things are sometimes – indeed often – better left unsaid.

These extraordinary tirades could erupt frequently and without warning. But between them it was exciting and edgy and this made me want to go on working on our relationship, such as it was. In a sense I believe I was suffering an addiction to the drama and the adrenalin it kept pumping into my system.

Coming back from London one time, I drove all the way across France, to reach the border at Perpignan and took the road south along theMediterranean, taking three days to reach Benalmadena from London.

By the time I arrived, Inge was spitting with fury. 'Didn't you think of the danger? Didn't you think how worried I would be?'

It didn't do any good telling her that I was a forty-six year old man, in tolerably good health, who could read a map. I suggested, not entirely convincingly, that what I had done was a kind of gesture, like the Swedish rock chick coming out as a lesbian in front of fifty thousand of her fans.

She retorted that at nearly fifty, I was displaying the immature reactions of a child of seven. But if I walked out after one of these knackering broadsides, she would beg me to return and when I did, she would greet me with an angry scowl. 'I never wanted this, you know – it's just stupid!'

I left again, and this time drove halfway across Spain to Toledo. That evening as the sun went down I sat in the Plaza Mayor. The day had been bone dry and dusty; the *cerveza* was cool and golden. It was time for reflection.

I rang Inge. After a brief conversation, I was on my way back to Benalmadena.

Once I was there, for a brief interlude, all the absurd accusations were forgotten again in an intense, seemingly profound coming together, until the after-love drinks came into play and the first bottles were empty.

I was treading on eggshells again: worse than that – eggshells on a mined Normandy beach!

I saw the danger signs as her top lip began to curl. 'You cannot be a serious person,' she growled. 'In any case, a person of your age should not be pretending to be other people. Who are you, for God's sake? I don't even know who you are! Maybe you don't!'

I didn't answer. This was well-ploughed land. I sighed, gathered up my stuff and left again.

This time I drove all the way to Santander in the north west of Spain and got myself onto the Plymouth ferry before I could change my mind or make any ill-judged phone calls.

Back in England at two in the morning, I got turned over by the customs so thoroughly I thought they must have had some tip-off. They took the car apart – and it was a modest Ford, not a drug-runner's Range Rover. They went through my luggage in minute detail, took away all my videotapes – presumably to look for porn – and put the sniffer dogs into the car, where they found nothing but an old congealed chocolate bar and an entrance ticket to the Alhambra in Granada, which I thought I'd lost.

I guess I must have looked pretty odd by then and a prime suspect for trafficking anything dodgy – a long-haired face off the telly, driving his mother's old car off a ferry at two in the morning. After finding nothing, they had the good manners to apologise and make their excuses.

'We can't be too careful, you see. Just last week we had a couple, in their seventies driving a battered old Triumph Herald. We found 500 vinyl LPs in their luggage in the back. Each one had been split, filled with cocaine and stuck back together again. We only stopped them because they seemed to be smiling and waving a bit too much.'

'I wasn't smiling and waving,' I protested.

'No sure, you weren't.'

I certainly didn't feel like smiling and waving now. I was utterly drained physically and mentally, almost quivering with the tension I'd been under since leaving Inge's apartment and I fell into the Holiday Inn (where I'd stayed when I was touring with Sabina in *The Rivals*), collapsed and slept for the next fifteen hours.

That evening I arrived back at Keith Washington's little oasis of tranquillity and comparative sanity in the quiet streets of Mortlake. It wasn't long before Inge's phone calls started. I was badly torn.

A lot of me, especially the irrational, corporeal aspects of my persona, missed her massively. On occasion the physical solace she had given me had been intense and overwhelming. But I was sure that her negative, destructive side was so intolerable now as to cancel out all the good she could do. I went to bed that night and for the next few nights determined not to give in.

On the fourth day back, on a routine call to Tim Combe, my agent, I was told I'd been offered the lead in a new production of Willy Russell's play, *One for the Road*.

The role was that of a youngish man, apparently happily married but at his wits' end about his safe steady, suburban existence. He was a man on the edge, trying to foment a mini-revolution, protesting angrily against the straitjacket in which society and 'the system' were constraining him – a character very well matched to my own circumstances. I also liked that it was a long way from the increasingly popular and potentially stifling figure of *Boycie*, with the added attraction that it was to play in Gothenburg, Sweden, alongside a Swedish version of the same play. I was told that most Swedes learn English thoroughly at school and liked to see the two versions of a play side by side. I said I'd take the job, suddenly very relieved that it precluded me from opting to go back to the Dangerous Dane in Spain.

In the interlude before going off to Sweden, I occupied myself with my father, who was still living on his own in Epsom. I made frequent trips down there, to try and sort him out. He was getting worse at coping and seemed to lack the will to help himself. I bought him an electric kettle so that he could make himself a hot drink or soup or at least boil an egg between his regular visits from social services. I showed him how to use it but even this seemed beyond him. He put it on the gas stove and it finished up as a blob of melted plastic, like a fake blancmange in an art deco kitchen.

'I tell you what, Dad,' I said, trying to think positively. 'Why don't I arrange for you to have meals on wheels?'

'How am I going to catch 'em, if they're on wheels?' he asked mischievously.

'No, no, Dad. It just means that someone brings them around in a van.'

'I'm not going to sit here and have my meals with someone I've never met,' he protested. 'And where's your mother, by the way?'

'Dad, she died a couple of years ago.'

'Oh yes, so she did,' he admitted. 'How insensitive of me.'

It was sad of course, but funny too, because he was so determined to be as independent as possible. I spoke to social services, telling them that I wanted to keep him out of care but I also needed to go away and earn a living.

They thought they could manage him, with the help of his next-door neighbour. I wanted to believe them.

We had already started rehearsals for *One for the Road* in London and had a couple of days in Gothenburg before we opened at the Lorensberg Theatre. Swedes have a wider appreciation of theatre than the British, and they made good, intelligent audiences. I loved doing the play. It was a great role but I was still shot to bits inside.

I was worried about my father, I was concerned that I didn't have

We few, we happy few
Image courtesy of BBC photo library

The Supergroup That Never Was
Lloyd Pack, MacDonald and Challis getting on down to
Clapton's 'Lay Down Sally' during the *Jolly Boys Outing*

One Between Three
Another award for *Only Fools* at the TRIC Awards,
Buster's finest hour

One of the great moments. "Not the Penguin Del Boy, More like the Joker!" Image Courtesy of BBC Photo Library

With Carol, Zimbabwe 1991 for Tusk Trust. Me wearing
a T-shirt with a Ronnie Wood elephant print

Zimbabwe - The *'Indiana Jones'* shot

Mavuradonna Wilderness, Zimbabwe, 1991. With Nick O'Connor, bush fighter turned tobacco farmer

With Carol, white-water rafting on the mighty Zambesi River. I'm the wimp in the yellow hat

Above: 1990, Carol and
Myra Egan at Airedale
Avenue, Chiswick

Right: 1992, Brown as
berries with Duncan
Heath after a holiday in
Hawaii with Carol

My very own show for BBC Radio 2
The 'graveyard shift' 4-6am

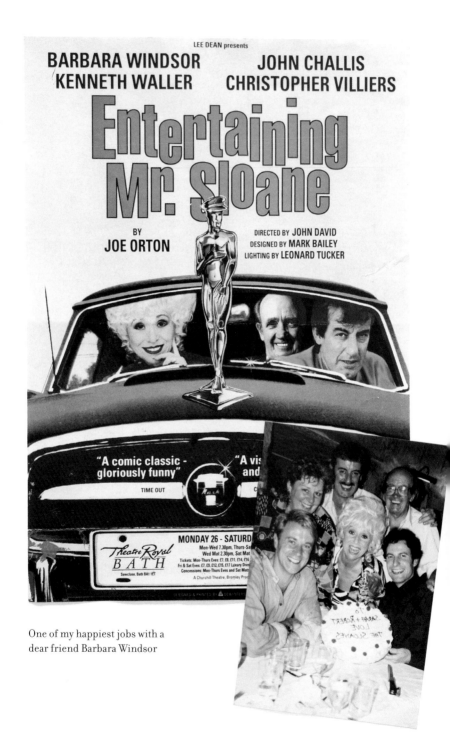

One of my happiest jobs with a
dear friend Barbara Windsor

2 June 1995. Fourth Time Lucky
We were only the third couple to marry at the Royal Pavilion, Brighton

Love 40: New Balls Please (Series 2)
Starring...
Back Row: Gary Martin, Philip Sherlock, Andrew Sachs & John Challis
Front Row: Mervyn Stutter & Moira Downie

With Roger Saul, founder of Mulberry and Sharpham Park Organic Foods.

The greatest pairing never to win… anything with Paul McNamee at the Mulberry Classic, Hurlingham vs Peter Macnamara & Anabel Croft

Artist Johnathan Heale at Lakshmi Lodge,
Birethanti, Nepal

Only Fools and Horses' greatest fan, memorabilia master
and fount of all knowledge, Perry Aghajanoff

Hooky Street

Issue 43

John Sullivan O.B.E.
1946 - 2011

One of the Great Nights.
As Nathan Detroit in *Guys & Dolls* with Anita Dobson,
Mandy Patinkin and Claire Moore

Wherever I go I can never escape from the Trotters

Above: With Sue and David
at my birthday party, 2002

Left: With Paul Barber –
my favourite rastafarian

Below: The cake,
a Jane Asher special

a place of my own in London – I couldn't go on squatting at Keith's indefinitely, but Observatory Road had not been sold. On top of that, I'd had a long conciliatory letter from Inge, regretting all she'd said, apologizing for her crazy behaviour. She explained that she hadn't realized how much I meant to her and could she come and see me in Sweden?

I didn't know how to react. I hadn't expected anything like this from her. I had carelessly told her which theatre I was working in because she said she'd like to send a good-luck card.

She went on to say that she was coming back from Spain to see her sister and parents in Copenhagen and she would finish that with a trip to Gothenburg.

This presented me with a conundrum I wasn't equipped to handle. The idea of a few days with the Dane was tempting – on one level at least. But would it solve anything in the longterm? Was it likely that she could alter her position to that extent for any length of time?

Frankly, I guessed not. I told her I'd see her in Gothenburg.

I was enjoying my first visit to Sweden, sharing a house with David Delves, the other male cast member but the house was quite a long way from the theatre and I was getting sick of sitting on trams. I decided to move into a serviceable apartment nearer the centre. I was intrigued by the slightly repressed coolness of Swedish life. Alcohol was strictly controlled and never advertised. If you wanted to drink outside your own home or place of work, you had to do it in a specially-licensed premises, of which there appeared to be very few. Actors, of course, are notoriously good at finding such places and our Swedish counterparts (and especially our Danish director) were not slow in introducing them to us. The rest of my English colleagues were less keen on this recreation and I was left to fly the flag for Britain in the lager-and-schnapps-chaser stakes.

When Inge was due, I hired a Saab and drove to Helsingborg to meet the ferry from Denmark.

For the three days she was in Sweden with me, we took a few drives out of town and we went to galleries but most of the time, when I wasn't at the theatre, we spent in bed together.

She was seeing me at work for the first time and watched with horrified fascination as I put on my make-up and scampered around the stage with a John Denver LP sleeve on my head. (My character expressed a strong hatred for John Denver, whose songs and persona, he thought, embodied the trite mundanity of human existence.)

When Inge left, we were on incomparably better terms than our last parting, although I was doubtful that would last. But we wrote to each other a few times during the remainder of the play's eight-week run in Gothenburg, until it closed and I had to return to England to check on Dad.

Dad's mind was wandering still but he didn't seem any worse. The social services were coping with help from George next door, who had kindly agreed to keep an eye on him. I thought it would be a good idea if I taught him how to leave messages on my answerphone, in case of emergency. This wasn't a success. I would come home to find among the crisp messages from agents and producers, my father speaking testily: 'Hello? Hello? (pause...) Hello?' followed by a heavy sigh of resignation and, 'Oh, bloody hell!' and the slamming down of the phone.

When I phoned back, he protested. 'What happened? I heard you, then you weren't there. Where the bloody hell did you go? How can you be there and not there at the same time?'

He was truly baffled, so I gave up. A friendly, businesslike woman from social services confirmed what I'd thought for some time, that he was in the early stages of Alzheimer's disease and said that I should be prepared for it to get progressively worse.

It's a frightening process, watching a formerly articulate and clever person sinking into confusion and speaking gibberish.

After a few exhausting months of failing to reverse Dad's inevitable decline, I needed a break, and decided it was time to go back to Portugal to see how the aloe-vera was performing. I rang Slater and told him I was coming. I also rang Inge in Benalmadena and she agreed to get over there too and meet me. I would then drive her back to Spain. Slater arranged for me to buy a small but roomy left-hand drive Citroen AX in Portugal for the purpose.

I flew out with Alison after a long dreary delay at Gatwick. When we arrived at Faro, Mike wasn't there to meet his wife, or me. He'd overslept, he later claimed. We had to take a taxi to the bodega and Inge was waiting there for me. I immediately got a bollocking for not phoning to check that she'd arrived safely.

Here we go again, I thought, but after that brief tiff, we were soon back on song and doing what came naturally.

News of progress on the aloe-vera crop was less forthcoming. On our last trip, Mike hadn't stopped talking about it. Now he was apparently not particularly interested and seemed uncomfortably vague.

'It's coming along OK,' he said. 'But, you know... the weather hasn't been great. We should be past that soon and then we can get on with the harvest – hopefully,' he added – ominously, I thought, and my first forebodings set in.

With some persuasion he took me out to look at the plantation and it all looked very promising in the sunshine. The leaves from which the essential oils are extracted were fattening up nicely, like plump green little fingers. I couldn't see what could go wrong.

The first thing to go wrong was that, once I'd driven her back to Benalmadena, Inge and I split up again. She'd got it into her head once more that I was just a feckless male and all males were the same – wanting it all, while the females had to have the strength, the guts to stand up and be counted.

After a week or two of this sort of stuff, I'd had enough. It was, I thought turning into some kind of relentlessly repeating farce.

In a state of emotional exhaustion, after a final, frank, inebriated discussion, I found I had the guts to stand up, be counted and say: 'I'm going!'

I got in the Citroen and pointed it north towards the Pyrenees. I left a message at Keith and Mad's house to let them know I was coming back and to ask if I could carry on staying there for a bit – I hoped they would agree. Observatory Road was still let to the Japanese tenants for another six months.

I had thought about going back to Portugal and developing a woolly idea I'd had about growing herbs in containers for English expats in Spain to plant into bigger pots or their garden beds. I almost convinced myself that I'd spotted a gap in the market. I could then sit back and watch the dividends from the aloe-vera farm roll in, while I supplemented that with cash from lucrative voice-overs and *Only Fools*, which was getting 20 million plus viewers by then. On top of that, the BBC were repeating all the earlier episodes, with the result that, although I wasn't in all the earlier ones, I was getting double bubble for all those I was in. But Slater had been so downbeat about the aloe-vera that I thought I'd do better to wait until after the harvest, when the wonga was supposed to start rolling in.

I turned my back on the Costa del Sol and drove away feeling free at last – free from guilt, from angst, and from constant inexplicable bollockings. I loved the drive back, cruising along empty roads I'd never driven, past cities and places with romantic names I'd only known from history and geography I'd learned at school – Salamanca, Pamplona, Biarritz, Poitiers, Crécy...

I stayed in *pensions* I found on the way and the joy of escape from a disastrous future sustained me almost as far as the north coast of France. After several, increasingly desperate calls to Keith Washington, I hadn't heard back from him and I was uncomfortably conscious that I had nowhere else to go when I reached London.

I didn't know if they were away or had simply given up on me. That was a possibility because before I'd left, they'd expressed the view, very strongly, that they thought I was insane to be going back to see Inge in Spain.

I got through customs at Newhaven without any trouble this time and arrived at Thornton Road about midday. No one was there but Keith and Madeleine's neighbour was in and fortunately he knew me. He had a key and let me in, assuming that they were expecting me.

Hoping for the best, I plonked my cases at the bottom of the stairs, staggered up to the spare room where I'd stayed before and collapsed, completely knackered, on the bed.

I woke, very relieved to hear a friendly 'Halloo!' from downstairs. They'd come back from a few days away, seen the cases I'd left in the hall and guessed what had happened.

I went down and laughed with them as they played back their messages, to hear the mounting panic in my voice in the several I'd left on my way up from Spain, pleading for somewhere to lay my head when I got to London. They welcomed me back, which was more than I deserved. I felt guilty and bloody foolish about the circumstances of my return, especially after Keith and Madeline had been so against my going back to see Inge but I also realised that at this point in their lives, I could be quite useful to them. Inge had always said about me that I was the 'best *au pair*' she'd ever had.

Now I did a bit of cooking for them, kept the place tidy and pottered around peacefully on my own, which I deeply appreciated after all the hassles over the aloe-vera project and drama of life with Inge in Benalmadena. When Keith and Madeleine were busy working, I could often be around for Tom, Keith's son, if he pitched up from his mother's, where he wasn't always happy. I was very glad to be back, sorting myself out again.

My father's situation, on the other hand, was becoming more of a problem. As soon as I'd got myself sorted out at Keith and Madeleine's, I drove down to Epsom and let myself into his house with my own key. Dad was sitting in his battered old chair with a sea of newspapers surrounding him all over the floor. His grey, haggard features showed no signs of interest in life as he listlessly watched a programme on television, one that he'd sworn he would never watch – even if he were dead.

In the kitchen there was even more of a shambles.The table was covered with empty paper bags of all different shapes and sizes. He'd always had a tendency to hoard – pieces of string, candles, lengths of electric flex, plant labels, jam jars and so on. I asked him what the bags were for.

'I'm looking for the right one,' he answered grumpily.

'What for?'

'I don't know, do I? What's it got to do with you?'

I sighed. 'How are the meals going, Dad?'

He scented the change of topic like an ill-tempered bear. 'Bloody people – coming round here all hours of the day and night. I just wish everyone would bugger off and leave me alone!'

It occurred to me that his irritability might well be a symptom of withdrawal from alcohol. He wouldn't be able to get his gin anymore. I couldn't see social services bringing it round or slipping out to the off-licence for him. And I doubted that his neighbour, George would either. Dad didn't mention it to me, though.

I wasn't feeling at all happy, especially when it dawned on me that from now on he would only get worse. I went outside and tried to calm down in the garden, working off my frustration on the army of invading weeds that had grown up, cutting back and tying in. The garden had been a very important part of Dad's life but when I went back in to talk to him about it, he didn't seem to give a damn any more.

In an effort to bounce him out of the gloomy introspective world he seemed to inhabit, I dug out some old photograph albums. I found pictures of him I'd never seen before, surrounded by young men and women who had worked with him in the Admiralty, clustered outside some long-forgotten, dreary office building in 1940.

Far from cheering up at the sight of his old colleagues, he burst into tears.

'They all went to Simonstown, you know,' he snuffled.

'What, in South Africa?'

'Yes, yes – where else would it be? The Strategic Naval Base for the Admiralty. I should have gone with them.'

'Why didn't you?'

He lifted his shaking head and looked at me with rheumy eyes. 'You bloody well came along, that's why!'

For me, a light appeared at the end of a very long tunnel – maybe this was the cause of the persistent and otherwise inexplicable resentment with which he'd viewed me for most of my life. I seized the chance to clarify this.

'Are you saying that if I hadn't been born, you'd have moved out to Simonstown and had a whole different career?' I pressed.

But the chink of light he'd offered – just for a moment or two – had gone already.

'I might have. I don't know. When are you going?' He looked bleakly up at me again. It was as if the window to his soul, which he'd just opened a crack, had been banged shut.

I shrugged. I'd get no further now. I tidied up as much as I could around the house, rang social services to make sure they were on the case and popped next door to see George.

George, an affable old boy of around seventy, told me that he'd had a few hairy moments with Dad. A couple of days before, my father had turned up at his front door, convinced that George's house was his own. It had taken George ten minutes, he said, to persuade Dad to go back, when he'd seen him safely into Number 8. He thought Dad had been drinking, he said, so perhaps he did have a source, or could still find his way to the off-licence. Later, I rang the services, who promised to keep an eye open.

Driving back to Mortlake, I reflected on the sliver of light my father had shed on his incurable resentment of me. At least knowing there was a recognizable (if not justifiable) cause for his attitude was some help in dealing with it. When I spoke to his GP later, he confirmed that there was little likelihood of Dad improving but he urged me not to feel bad about it. There was no point in ruining my life, too, over his condition.

Chapter 7
Stage Fright

After an uneventful and frankly unfestive season, my big priority at the start of 1990 was to find a fixed abode of my own. Sabina and I had finally managed to sell 8 Observatory Road and had divvied up the spoils. By lucky chance, I found a flat very quickly, just around the corner in Sheen Lane. I knew the building well – a converted Victorian mill of some sort. Keith had moved into one of the apartments there after his marriage to Joan had foundered ten years before. Mine was a ground floor and basement flat, with two smallish bedrooms at ground level and a kitchen projecting over a large basement living room.

I liked its quirkiness and I thought it would suit me very well. In early 1990 I was ready to buy it and a few weeks later I settled in for what was to prove a short-lived bachelor existence.

Between voice-over jobs, I spent my time watching rugby on the telly in the pub, drinking too much and feeling disoriented and sorry for myself. I wished I had more to do. Absurdly, despite the success of *Only Fools* and my ongoing key part in it, I was beset by insecurities about my own future. In any case, there were no new recordings planned for the show until the end of the year. As far as relationships were concerned, I'd to come to terms with the fact that I was incapable of good judgement about women and life in general and relied on far too flimsy bases for making such judgement. But I was in full agreement with whichever stout black American soul artist it was who sang: 'Every ma..an needs a woman,' and I was still feeling very lonely, when Inge – the Dangerous Dane – rang, out of the blue and said she'd been chucked out of Spain over a 'visa mix-up' and was coming to see me in England and could we try again? However much my reason told me this was a bad idea, I did nothing to resist.

Over the couple of days before Inge arrived, I tried to justify my decision to let her come by remembering the good, healthy physical bits of our relationship, which, although outweighed by the mayhem she could cause, were still very tempting.

When Inge turned up to experience everyday life in south west

London, not much sense of our past adventures remained. She came with me sometimes when I was working in voice-over studios, when she was still heavily critical of my making money from such a fatuously easy job – as she saw it – saying a few words on a commercial for fish fingers, which might take only ten minutes.

But to her credit, Inge quickly used her own ingenuity and considerable grit to get herself a job as a kind of wandering physiotherapist for the local health authority, dealing with knackered athletes and arthritic old crocks.

Despite the world's jubilation at the final unravelling of the old Soviet Union and the apparent death of communism, it was an uncomfortable summer for me. I didn't want Inge to leave but I was becoming increasingly depressed that nothing seemed to make her easier to live with. I admired her for having sorted out some work, determined as she was not to be too dependent on me, but I couldn't understand her constant desire to undermine my own already precarious sense of self-worth.

To compound my dissatisfaction with these circumstances, it was a lean year for work too, and I spent a lot of time away from the flat – in the pub, drinking, playing tennis and drinking.

In the autumn, though, things looked up. The seventh series of *Only Fools* had been scheduled, starting with a Christmas special, *Rodney Come Home* (in which *Boycie* doesn't appear), followed by another nine episodes, of which all bar one included him/me.

After seeing the very first episode in which *Boycie* appears, *Go West Young Man*, repeated by the BBC for the first time in September, nine years after it had first aired, I was back on the *Only Fools* set to record *The Sky's the Limit* followed by another four in quick succession, including one of my favourites, *Stage Fright*, in which *Del* persuades his girlfriend, *Raquel* to sing at a club with an absurdly tanned, crinkly haired *Tony Angelino* (wonderfully played by Philip Pope), who can't pronounce his 'R's – not a help when singing Roy Orbison's *Crying*.

Class of '62 featured Jim Broadbent as Slater, the bent copper who had appeared in *To Hull & Back*. He had invited all his schoolmates – *Del, Trigger, Denzil, Boycie* and the gang to a reunion in the Nag's Head, but he'd done it anonymously, so no one knew why they were there.

'I've just had a thought,' says *Del*, trying to work it out.

Boycie looks down his nose. 'Then lend it to Trigger,' he says beadily.

As Christmas approached I made my usual seasonal pilgrimage to Epsom, where my father had, for once, mercifully little to say. He was so weak now, that he hadn't the energy to berate me like he used to. He was just about coping on his own. For a while after that Dad got no worse but my visits to Epsom became no more enjoyable.

After a low-key Christmas, I jumped at the chance of another African adventure.

One of my friends from the Coach & Horses – the 'Barnes Office' – was planning a trip to Zimbabwe. 'Would you like to come?' he asked.

'Yes I certainly would!' I replied in a flash. 'Can I bring a friend?'

Bob Hankinson raised his eyes to the ceiling, but he agreed.

I had one more episode of *Only Fools* to do in January 1991, *He Ain't Heavy; He's My Uncle*, in which *Boycie* doesn't have a lot to do, apart from diverting a Ford Capri Ghia on the way to the scrapyard in order to sell it to *Del Boy*.

This at least offered some respite from the gloom that was enveloping me before our trip to Africa, gloom which hadn't been improved by Dad's condition taking a downward turn. He'd started wandering out and turning up fairly confused in different places, sometimes in the middle of Epsom.

'Somebody said I looked like a tramp,' he told me triumphantly when I came to rescue him one time.

They were right.He was wearing a greasy old trilby with the brim pulled down, a tatty, stained raincoat and shoes worn through on the sides because, now his feet were so bad, he found walking very awkward.

I tried to get him to a chiropodist in Epsom and got him as far as the door when he dug his heels in. 'I'm not going in there,' he said. 'I know what you're up to.'

He was becoming more and more paranoid about my motives and intentions. Everything had become a threat to him and he started not allowing people into the house, not even the doctor or social services.

Stage Fright

George from next door was at his wits' end, trying to keep tabs on Dad. 'You have to face it, son,' he said to me, 'you're father is, well... mad.'

The transformation of my father from a hard-working, intelligent, conscientious man into an entirely altered being, who only vaguely resembled his former self was tragic to see.

I thought of the pictures of Mum and him walking carefree along the promenade in Torquay on their honeymoon and tried to understand how this metamorphosis had happened. I sorted out more comprehensive care for him from the social services, but it was soon clear that he would need the kind of 24-hour specialist psychiatric and physical care he would only get in a nursing home.

I had to arrange power of attorney and then found he hadn't been cashing his state or Civil Service pension for over six months. His condition rapidly got worse. Once incontinence had set in and other ailments emerged, his doctor told me he must go into hospital.

He kicked up badly. On one occasion I had to tussle with him – the first time I'd experienced any physical aggression with him since he'd slippered me as a kid at our house in Tadworth. I hated it now, like wrestling with a stranger but in the end, with the encouragement of his GP and a Mental Health Inspector and a heavy heart, I signed a sectioning order. I was reassured that it was for the best and the nursing home he was going to was the best in the area for dealing with his kind of problems. For a while, Dad seemed to agree that something needed to be done. But when it came to it, he refused to leave the house.

In the end, two big male nurses manhandled him onto a stretcher and strapped him down. As they carried Dad out he threw me a look so vindictive it went straight through me.

I burst into to tears and tried to go with him but was advised it would be better to visit him in the home later once he'd settled in.

I couldn't imagine him ever being settled and the future looked pretty bleak for him. I set about cleaning up all the mess he'd created in the house at Sunnybank. When I got round to seeing him at the nursing home, the contrast was remarkable. He was clean and shaved, his feet had been done and he looked strangely calm, if a little spaced out.

The sight of the other inmates wasn't encouraging. A few were sitting helplessly in front of the flickering inanity of daytime TV. Others padded about on unfathomable missions, one muttering incessantly to himself. Another marched up and down like a guardsman. A man in what looked like red pyjamas appeared to be standing guard over the men's lavatory. The scene reminded me depressingly of *One Flew Over the Cuckoo's Nest*.

The staff told me they'd had to sedate Dad and it soon became clear that he wasn't going to be able to go back and live in Sunnybank. They told me we'd have to find a home where he could have the long-term care he now needed.

He seemed to me more than just a bit sedated. After that, I would sit for hours with him, sometimes in complete silence, or he would suddenly become alert and turn to me. 'I don't know, do I?' he would say. 'All these people are bloody mad!'

I found it mentally draining to sit with him, trying to make some kind of contact through the fog that seemed to have settled around him.

With a sense of gloom and guilt, I searched for a suitable residential home. I found it impossible to get any sense out of Dad over the choice but luckily I found a space in a very well run place nearby. One if its major attractions for me – on Dad's behalf – was that it had an aviary in the garden. Dad had always been a birdwatcher and I thought this would give him some interest. I also bought him a Walkman, with cassettes of all his favourite classical music.

It all looked good when I got him there and he seemed to like the place but that didn't last long when he started misbehaving. He'd soon had an acrimonious row with another of the inmates over the ownership of an HP sauce bottle; he got into the kitchens where he found a stack of sandwiches, waiting to go out, started stuffing them into his mouth and refused to come out.

More alarmingly, he kept going into the rooms of some of the female inmates and getting into their beds, which frightened the hell out of them. It wasn't long before I had an official request to return him to the nursing home, where, if he spoke to me at all, he complained about the number of 'men in red coats all over t'place'.

At least, though, he was more or less permanently comatose and not really capable of bad behaviour and his carers said he was stable now.

Nevertheless, he remained a source of constant worry, whatever else I was doing and it was with a sense of disloyalty that on a wet English winter's day, I felt mightily relieved to be boarding a plane with Inge at Heathrow to fly to the heat of South Africa. We were going to stay in Johannesburg for a few days before driving up to Zimbabwe, as I had done thirteen years before to tour Tom Stoppard's play, *Dirty Linen*. I had directed and played the lead role in the play while we were there because Peter Bowles, who should have been doing both, refused to enter a territory that had illegally seceded from the United Kingdom when Ian Smith had declared UDI.

Inge and I stayed with Bob's brother, Hank in Johannesburg. He had escaped from the former Rhodesia at the start of Robert Mugabe's unbreakable grip on the country. But soon we were heading north and across the Limpopo River. We spent a spectacular few days in the Hwange National Park – one of the best places in Africa to see herds of elephants, lions and their cubs, buffalo, rhino, hippos and some extraordinary sunsets over the Zambezi River.

I was loving it but despite all the wonderful natural beauty surrounding us, Inge, ever the truculent Dane, was still dissatisfied and finding no end of things to criticize as well as beating her monotonous drum over the callousness and fatuousness of male animals in general and human ones in particular. There seemed nothing I could say to convince her how pointless all this whingeing was. She carried on insisting that it was always the women who had the guts to stand up and tell anyone who was listening (and still awake) that they were there to be counted.

Bob Hankinson left after this, shaking his head in disbelief at her attitude – and in pity for me.

Inge and I struggled on to Kenya so that I could track down an orphan elephant I'd been sponsoring in the Tsavo Wildlife Park between Nairobi and Mombasa. This juvenile jumbo, Edo, had lost his mother, not through poaching, for a change, but through poisoning – perhaps an accidental intake of leaking battery acid, since elephants are notorious for investigating rubbish tips. And we think urban foxes are a problem!

Little Edo had been found wandering forlornly around the perimeter of the lodge and the staff had brought him in. They knew that elephant herds don't take in or nurture another elephant's offspring because the young rely on their mother's milk for some time.

Inge and I arrived at Tsavo in the middle of the night in a battered old VW Combi taxi that only just made it to the beautiful Safari Lodge. As all the thrilling, vibrant sounds of the African bush lulled me to sleep, Inge was still banging on about the injustice of male domination throughout the animal kingdom.

In the morning we were taken to the Daphne Sheldrick animal orphanage, which looks after orphans of all sorts – rhino, zebra, even warthogs. It has been hugely successful in rearing its inmates and preparing them for a return to the wild, again, with impressive results. It was staffed entirely by Africans, who showed a wonderful patience and understanding of the animals.

I was introduced to my juvenile protégé, who displayed complete indifference to the event, except when I had control of the feed bottle. But he bumbled about happily in an elephantine way with his chums and I was very proud to be a tiny part of this dedicated organization.

After a spectacular train journey through the dry bush to Mombasa, we flew up the east coast to Lamu. This tiny, peaceful island is one of the hottest places I've ever been, with the whitest sand and the bluest sea.

In one of the lovely little beach bars we met a man with a dhow on which he took punters out to snorkel among the inshore rocks. I'd always wanted to do this and booked up at once. I turned out to be better suited to this than jet-skiing and happily spent a day floating on my stomach gazing down at the most exotic sea-life I have ever seen.

Unfortunately I completely overlooked the fact that my neck would be exposed all day to the blistering sun. On the way back to the hotel, I started feeling nauseous and faint, with a tendency to hallucinate.

I barely made it back to our room off a bougainvillea-draped courtyard in an old colonial mansion, where I passed out behind the mosquito nets.

When I came round the hotel staff were gloomily convinced I was showing the symptoms of malaria, until a more qualified medico turned up and shook his head.

'No worry. Not malaria. It just the sun.'

That was a relief of course – if it were true – but I still spent twenty-four hours sweating like a rugby scrum – boiling then freezing, mostly delirious and no use to anyone. After another twelve hours, I felt like a wrung-out dishcloth but better than I'd been, and strangely, my guts, which had been giving me gyp for the past week or so, were back to healthy normality.

When we caught our plane back to England, I realized I'd enjoyed the trip, despite the heat stroke, but Inge was less sure. She said she was missing Spain and all her friends there but couldn't go back to work there as a result of her visa cock-up.

She also missed her family in Denmark, which spurred her to offer me an ultimatum shortly after we got back to Sheen Lane. 'The only reason for me to stay in London would be if we were married.'

I didn't need time to mull this one over. I chose directness of response. 'I have no plans to get married,' I said baldly. This evoked a longish harangue about gutless men who couldn't make decisions. And that, at last, was that. She slept in the basement drawing room of my flat and I spent a few tortured hours waiting for her to catch a plane to Copenhagen.

I was quietly confident that I'd finally managed to bring this most frustrating (although, admittedly, at times very exciting) relationship to an end.

Our trip to Africa had shown me unequivocally that we were fundamentally living in two different worlds (and that was putting it charitably). I'd tried very hard to accommodate her but we had just been what seemed like a million miles to try and find the key to our relationship and had completely failed.

As soon as I'd got back to England, I'd been to see my father. He was no worse than when I'd left, still existing in a kind of unknowing torpor; I was distraught that there seemed to be nothing anyone could do to help him return to anything like his old self and I couldn't help feeling that for him to have reached this condition was, at least in part, my fault for agreeing to have him sectioned and treated as a mental patient.

Thinking of him and what had gone on with Inge over the past year or so, I recalled a Stoppard line: 'The trouble with life is, it's mostly wrong, all the time.'

On my way back from seeing Inge off, I contemplated this depressing truth, determined to learn something from this latest clear demonstration of my inability to handle relationships.

The thick cloud of self-pity that still hung over me, despite the relief at not having to defend myself from Inge's aggression, was alleviated by a phone call from an old friend, Ian Masters. Ian and I had worked together on *Show Boat* in the Adelphi Theatre at least twenty years before. He had gone on to do very well in comedies like *No Sex Please, We're British* and *The Mating Game*, with Terry Scott and had now forged a strong reputation as a stage director.

Ian wanted to know if I'd like to appear in his production of Terence Frisby's *There's a Girl in my Soup*, for four weeks in May and June at the Mill at Sonning, on a sleepy stretch of the River Thames downstream from Reading.

The all-absorbing business of doing live theatre was a very different experience from the fickle promiscuity involved in making TV or delivering voice-overs which, in artistic terms, were more *'wham bam, thank you ma'am'* than real love. I knew it would provide excellent displacement therapy for a man going through a crisis of self-doubt. It had to be better therapy than pouring booze down my throat, which was the only current alternative. For, in a state of bleak humility, I was convinced that all my failures to date in the relationship department were my fault. Otherwise why had there been so many? Three washed-out marriages and a string of fleeting relationships that had gone nowhere, leaving me on my own again, at the age of forty-seven.

A season at Sonning did indeed turn out to be the perfect remedy and in the end provided more cures than I could possibly have hoped for.

Marc Sinden, son of Sir Donald, was to play the Peter Sellers role in *Soup*. We all got along very well and it was a fun show to be in. I hadn't worked at the Mill before, and it was my first experience of playing in 'dinner theatre', in which the audience eat their dinner and then watch the show on, as it were, the one ticket. It's a style of entertainment that the Mill has run for a long time, and the houses are always full, with a special sense of intimacy to them.

Stage Fright

Early in the four-week run, Myra and Peter Egan turned up to see Marc, who was an old friend of theirs. I'd met Myra Frances, as she was known professionally, when Peter had directed me (with John and Pauline Alderton) on stage in *Rattle of a Simple Man*, some ten years before. Now she was booked to direct the next production at the Mill for four weeks in July and August. She told me that since seeing me in *Rattle* she'd always kept me in mind for a role. 'I've got a part for you, if you'd like it,' she said.

I wanted to jump up and down and clap my hands (although I restrained myself). 'What? Oh God! Can't you get someone else? All right then,' I added magnanimously.

The thought of another run at Sonning cheered me up enormously.

In any case, working in Sonning suited me very well. The parts were interesting, it was a civilized place, well run and commutable from south west London and the short runs wouldn't let the job become boring. There were also windows in my schedule, which allowed me to pop down to Epsom and minster to my father.

I loved being back on stage, immersing myself in new roles, living them for weeks at a time and I'm sure that the process did help me to untangle myself from both my broken marriage the year before and my frustrating, exciting but ultimately pointless relationship with Inge. She was still keeping in touch with a few phone calls but I had successfully avoided succumbing to any lingering physical urges they may have provoked.

Marc Sinden had also been asked into the first of Myra's shows, a play called *Dangerous Obsession* by N J Crisp. I had a good part in what is a tense and complex drama. My role was a departure for me. *John Barrett* is an apparently insignificant character, who turns up out of the blue at the house of a well-off, middle-class couple somewhere in the home counties. The husband is out but the wife invites him in. He tells her that they have met before, at a business seminar, which both men had attended with their wives.

Did she know, he asks, that his own wife had died in a car crash? She did not.

The husband returns and *Barrett*, unseen by the couple,

systematically locks all the doors and slips the keys in his pocket. With a harsh change of tone, he makes them sit and listen while he tells them how the driver of the car that had crashed, killing his wife, had fled the scene, because he was having an affair with her. This driver had never been found. Slowly, relentlessly, he builds a case against the husband, showing incontrovertibly that he had been driving the car that had crashed.

Producing a gun, he points it at the man's head, and forces him to admit his guilt, thereby destroying the couple's marriage.

He is clearly relishing his revenge. As he prepares to leave the devastated couple, he takes a tape cassette from his pocket, on which he has recorded the whole confession. He holds it up. 'If you don't report my presence here, I won't make this tape available to the police.'

The husband is too shattered to speak. His wife answers. 'We won't.'

Barrett leaves, satisfied with his afternoon's work.

Marc was playing the husband and the beautiful Alexandra Bastedo the wife. In one memorable performance I delivered my exit line and waited for Alexandra's response before I let myself out.

She said nothing.

I waited, the tension mounted. I thought the only thing to do was to deliver my ultimatum again. Still she said nothing.

I couldn't leave. *Barrett* had to have his answer.

As Alexandra looked at me with a puzzled frown, Marc stepped in to rescue the situation.

'We won't!' he gasped, as if it had taken him all that time to get the words out, then he burst into tears.

Although it was the worst moment in the play for Alexandra to have dried, it happens to every actor at one time or another and, anyway, we all agreed afterwards that it made a much better ending.

Alex was a treat to work with in many ways. Her husband Patrick Garland was running the Chichester Festival Theatre at the time, while she was well known from the vastly successful TV spy series in the late '60s, *The Champions*. She was also rated one of the screen's great beauties.

My performance was hailed as a masterpiece of understated menace, marred for me by the fact that I had broken my little finger in a tennis match and it was in a straightening splint. There was nothing I could do to disguise it, sticking out in front of me, parallel with the gun I was pointing at Marc in a gesture not unlike the *shaka* sign used by the Hawaiian people as an informal greeting.

One day in July, during the run of *Dangerous Obsession*, Myra brought her great friend Carol Davies down to Sonning to see the show. Myra asked me to come and have tea with them. Over the Lapsang and fairy cakes, she introduced me to Carol, who reminded me that we'd met on the set of *Ever Decreasing Circles* a couple of years before. On that occasion, though, Sabina had whisked me away so rapidly I'd barely had time to focus on Carol.

Now I did. And I liked what I saw. Not only was she tall and Junoesque in a way that I'd always admired and which meant that I could talk to her eyeball to eyeball, she was also refreshingly straightforward and frankly un-luvvie. I had the impression that if I had shown her a spade, she'd have known what to call it.

I gathered that she and Myra had met at the Hogarth Club, a kind of theatrical health spa on Airedale Road in Chiswick. It was thirty yards down the road from Myra's house (although she always drove there), and she and Carol spent a lot of time in the gym. While Carol cycled and worked out on all the machines, Myra would gossip, and they became good friends.

After *Dangerous Obsession* at Sonning, I saw more of Peter and Myra and found I enjoyed their company very much. It was trait of Myra's that she was able to offer a sense of solidity to people at times when they were casting around for a little certainty in their lives, as I was at the time.

I'd been somewhat off-colour for a time while we'd been rehearsing the play and although I was partially recovered by the time it was over, I still wasn't quite right. I don't know what it was, but it seemed to be something more than a mere physical ailment. There was a line in the play, when I was holding a gun trained on Alexandra Bastedo that rang true. She's desperately saying to my character: 'It's all in your head, John; it's all in your head!'

I had been letting my condition control me, and finding outlets where they were easiest to find. When I wasn't working, I was in the

Coach & Horses in Barnes every night with my mind in a mess. As *Mo Green* said of *Fredo Corleone* in *The Godfather*: 'He was banging cocktail waitresses two at a time.'

Not quite in my case: one at a time, and a pub barmaid – just the once.

I'd worked with Peter Egan a few times during my career, first playing a small part in a TV show in the '60s, *Big Breadwinner Hog*, in which he starred. Like his wife, he was also a good director, as I'd found doing *Rattle of a Simple Man* with his chums, the Aldertons. He'd also starred in *Ever Decreasing Circles* with Richard Briers in which I'd had a one-off role. Getting to know him better, I liked him more.

Myra, thoughtful soul that she is, of course made it her business to make sure Carol and I had a chance to see more of each other. Carol was taking a few deep breaths after unravelling and escaping from a tricky, tangled relationship. She'd recently bought a basement flat close to the Egans, in Brackley Road.

She had been involved in showbiz for a long time, now mainly in the field of wardrobe, currently working on *The Phantom of the Opera* and we knew a lot of the same people. Shortly after our first meeting, Myra had said, rather cryptically: 'My friend likes you.'

'She ought to see a shrink,' I said, but after a few weeks, I began to sense that she was right, when I started to spot subtle – and not so subtle – hints of Carol's interest. It was a case of the spider and the fly – although I was, at first, a reluctant, resisting fly.

It wasn't that I didn't like Carol. I could see that we had a lot in common and beyond the merely physical. But I was realistic enough know that I wasn't in a reliable state of mind. I didn't want to start anything, only to let her down and experience yet another self-destructing relationship. I felt I'd already made so many wrong choices that my confidence was in shreds and I didn't trust myself ever to get it right, while Myra gently nudged things along and Peter stood and watched in the wings, an amused spectator. Could I really play this part, I wondered?

It wasn't long, of course, before I succumbed. After a jolly evening at Airedale Road, I walked Carol back to her little nest in Brackley Road. It was late, I was tired and emotional (in the real sense) and too full of booze to drive home.

Carol offered accommodation. I was accommodated.

She had to leave early in the morning for her job in the wardrobe department in *Phantom* at Her Majesty's Theatre in the Haymarket, where, among others, she dressed and undressed the lovely John Barrowman. Barrowman was *so* lovely, she said, that he was not averse to shedding all his clothes and walking around back-stage stark naked. I had the impression, from her description, that she wasn't averse to him doing it. Just before I left her flat, a message was left on her answerphone. It was a female friend.

'*Hello, Carol. Hope you're OK. Looking forward to seeing you soon. Hear you've got yourself a new man, darling! Well done!*'

'Well!' I muttered to myself, a bit like Frankie Howerd, 'that's a bit previous!' And I sat down to write her a note thanking her for her hospitality.

Within a month of meeting Carol, I had recognized that this was something entirely different from any of the relationships, marriages or flirtations in which I'd been involved in the past.

This, I knew, was real. For a start, Carol was real. She said what she thought; there was no dressing things up, or avoiding the issue. I loved that she was so tall and striking and yet at the same time, had such a great sense humour.

It turned out that she had a goodish back story of her own. She'd been born in Libya, where her father was stationed as a British Army officer in the post-war mopping-up operations. Returning to England aged three, she lived with her mother's parents in Martinstown, near Dorchester in the West Country.

Coming from old Dorset land-owning stock, she and her brother, Johnny had had an idyllic childhood. Carol's mother probably harboured hopes that one day her daughter would marry into some fine old Dorset family. In this she was to be disappointed. Like many full-blooded young females in the 1960s, Carol escaped to London, ostensibly to work in Bourne & Hollingsworth's stationery department, in fact just to be anywhere closer to the action than Dorchester.

She lasted six months at B&H, before enrolling into the London College of Fashion, just off Oxford Street, where she could extend a natural talent for dressmaking and design. As a young fashion student in London in the last convulsions of the Swinging Sixties, Carol got to know a lot of musicians and performers and had been known to ride pillion behind Jimi Hendrix wearing nought but a rabbit-fur coat. She was spotted while holiday-jobbing in Harrods' lingerie department by Peter Baker, choreographer and talent spotter for the Bluebell Girls. He always had his eye out for very tall, glamorous dancers and mannequins. At six foot one, Carol ticked those boxes. As a Bluebell, she would be one of a troupe of twenty girls employed to stand around in statuesque pose with hardly any clothes on.

Luckily, Baker introduced her to Raphael Olsen, an American of tiny proportions who had started out in Las Vegas doing an acrobatic dance routine with James Cagney and had since built up a spectacular cabaret act known as *Raphael and his Model*. His 'model' was always much taller than him (not hard) and (using a step ladder) he would dress them with extraordinary and outrageous creations, conjured up from lengths of silk and satin taken from a prop box and enormous hats lit up with fairy lights, trailing cloaks and feather boas. Clusters of diamanté added a splendid touch of 'bling' and at the final moment a miniature poodle called *Johnnie*, dyed pink to match the costumes, made an entrance from a secret pouch in a feather boa!

Raphael's current model had just become pregnant and he'd sent Baker an SOS for a replacement. The job description required the successful candidate to stand around in statuesque pose with hardly any clothes on. Carol was the successful candidate and took the job like a shot.

As Carol described the act, I wished I'd seen it. It was remarkably refreshing for me to be talking to a woman who, on the one hand, knew how the business worked (unlike, for example, Inge) but, on the other, didn't suffer from an actor's inherent need to pose and pout all the time (unlike, for example, Sabina), for despite having been an actor all my life, there were some aspects of actors of the opposite sex with which I was never very comfortable.

Olsen's was quite a famous act that was seen in all London's major cabaret venues. As a result of the exposure this gave her, Carol became much in demand. David Nixon wanted her for his TV show, *Magic Box*; Mike and Bernie Winters for their show and Eric Morecambe and Ernie Wise offered her a regular appearance on their

Saturday night programme. Unfortunately, Carol couldn't take up any of these offers as she was tied to Raphael's act and stayed with it for the next five years. By the time she'd finished her stint in it, she had got her DipAD from the School of Design and had met Patrick Curtis at an audition for *Queen of the Amazons*, starring Patrick's wife, Raquel Welch and Christopher Lee. The film called for a tall woman who could stand around in a statuesque pose with hardly any clothes on, a role for which Carol was, by now, very well qualified. Unfortunately she had also met her first husband, who wasn't so keen on the idea and a more conventional career beckoned, although it would always have a showbiz connection.

While the two Sonning plays were going on, I'd been able to keep up regular visits to my father, unrewarding as they generally were. As he'd shown no signs of being let off his by now powerful course of sedatives, he'd been moved to an altogether more hermetically-sealed establishment, where everything was very clinical and controlled, as if he were living in a laboratory.

I was struck that he was more comatose than ever, and the staff admitted that he'd been very agitated when he'd arrived and they'd had to up his dose again. I was guiltily put in mind again of *Nurse Ratchett* and Jack Nicholson's character in the *Cuckoo's Nest*, although I had to accept that there was no alternative.

A month later, after some kind of seizure, he was rushed to Epsom General Hospital. By the time I got there, he'd been stabilized and was sitting up in bed, awake but very wan. He didn't recognize me. I took his hand but he snatched it back just as he'd done at my mother's funeral four years before.

I was still there when he had another truly alarming seizure. He vomited violently and his eyes rolled right back in his head. I gasped in panic. I thought I'd just seen my father die.

But, astonishingly, they brought him back. He coughed, his eyes flickered open; he looked somehow apologetic and again gazed at me as if I were a total stranger.

A young doctor took me aside. 'Look, John, we've brought him back twice now. If it happens again, do you still want him resuscitated? I mean, there's no quality of life there and it's not going to get any better.'

I understood that pragmatically he was probably right but this was my father.

'You know I can't possibly agree to that,' I said.

The doctor nodded ruefully. 'I know.'

They made Dad comfortable and he fell asleep, while I sat there wondering what the hell to do. After half an hour, a nurse suggested that I go home and come back the next day.

I drove home with my mind in turmoil. Not knowing what else to do, I went to the pub, got monumentally drunk and dragged the barmaid back to my cave in Sheen Lane.

I woke up the next morning feeling bad in every possible way. I didn't recognize the barmaid who was still there but as the mist cleared I remembered who she was. 'Christ! Is the bar open already?' I asked.

I looked around to see the familiar surroundings of my own bedroom.

Later, I tried to work out what I was doing. I knew I'd been drinking a lot too much. Although since I'd met Carol I was beginning to see that what I'd found with her was probably something important, I seemed to be fighting the urge to commit and a pointless, one-off night like I'd just had was part of that process.

I went as often as I could to see Dad in hospital, although for a while, he still showed no signs of knowing who I was. Eventually, he improved enough to go back to the Oakfield Nursing Home in Ashtead and I was very relieved I hadn't consented to withholding resuscitation.

I couldn't get to the nursing home every day and when I did get there, I usually came away with the impression that it had made no difference to him if I was there or not. Nevertheless I felt bad that I couldn't go daily and that sense of guilt was only slightly assuaged when someone on the staff told me that a lot of the patients were just dumped there by relatives and were never visited at all. One of them hadn't had a visitor in ten years.

I got a small reward for my troubles and a little encouragement on one visit when Dad opened his eyes and appeared to let me in.

A nurse came into his room and asked Dad if he wanted a cup of tea.

'No, no,' he grumbled, then added, out of the blue, 'What about you, boy?'

'Thanks, yes,' I replied, provoking an impatient sigh from my father.

He fell silent. I drank my tea. After a few minutes, he grabbed the sugar bowl, stuffed every single sugar lump into his mouth, lifted the milk jug to his lips and downed the lot. He looked at me. I saw the hint of a twinkle.

'This tea's bloody cold!' he muttered.

In my excitement, I nearly spluttered my PG Tips all over the floor.

'Dad? Dad?' I whispered, eager to keep any contact with the 'old' Dad, the funny Dad, who'd loved surreal humour and laughed at the Goons with me when I was a kid. I allowed myself the sudden hope that he was coming back and this long stretch of non-communication was over.

A moment later, he fixed me with a monitory eye, as if to say: '*I know what you're up to.*'

And the window was closed.

I drove home, depressed as hell and grabbed the whisky bottle as soon as I'd got through the front door. It really hurt me that I seemed never to have had any real communication with my father. Reflecting on this, as I had increasingly, I now saw that as an only child, I'd found myself for much of my adult life being a kind of pawn in the curious struggle that had developed between my parents, each of them wanting me firmly in their camp.

The lack of connection with my one remaining parent lay, I think, at the heart of most of the uncertainties I harboured about myself. Whatever the outside world and the proliferating band of *Only Fools* fans may have thought, I felt, as an individual, that I was a total washout, with three failed marriages behind me, and no kids (probably a good thing, in the circumstances). To compound those failures, I'd allowed myself to start and stay with a ridiculously volatile relationship with the Dangerous Dane, which at no stage looked as if it could last.

Now that I'd met someone with whom I felt real and at ease, I didn't trust myself not to let her down and I was finding that I was drinking even more, maybe to avoid stepping up to face the possibilities, thereby encouraging fate to put the boot in again.

I talked about it to Myra Egan who, having directed me in some of the Sonning plays, had got to know me as well as anyone in the previous dozen years. She suggested I might like to talk to someone about my condition. I knew that she was a great listener herself and that she meant it constructively. I took the idea seriously and she introduced me to a friend of hers, Wasyl Nimenko, a well-known doctor with a wide range of corporate and high-powered clients.

Wasyl was a charming, jovial man who thought I should have a session with Susie, the in-house analyst attached to his practice. I agreed to an exploratory meeting with Susie, who had a lot of experience with performers of various sorts. She was also an able, all round psychoanalyst and I believed her when she told me that, as an only child, I was likely to have had a more complex relationship with my parents than was normal, particularly when communications had completely broken down between them. She suggested that my father may well have had issues of his own, which, of course, had never been dealt with – at least, not as far as I knew.

She advised me to take my time over writing a letter to my father, in which I should express all the doubts and frustations I felt about our relationship, his lack of encouragement and absence of approval for anything I'd ever done and how he seemed always to keep barriers up between us, as if forbidding my entry. It was only then, when I started writing about these things, that I realized just how painful this had been for me.

The letter wasn't intended to be sent to my father – and I could never have sent it – but as a means of identifying and drawing out all the bitterness and self-doubt in my feelings for him and I found that was undoubtedly a help in putting these emotions into perspective.

On the morning of 29 September 1991, I woke with a hangover again, in my flat in Sheen Lane with the phone beside the bed ringing in my ear. This time I was alone. I'd been out drinking, wherever booze and company were on offer, long after the pub had closed. I rolled over, managed to pick up the phone and grunt into it. For a few seconds, I couldn't take in that a female voice was telling me my father had suffered a heart attack during the night and was dead.

I shook my head to clear it. 'How can that be? I only saw him the day before yesterday!'

But the caller only repeated what she'd said.

I slammed down the phone, pulled on some clothes and drove straight down to Ashtead.

'I've come to see my father,' I announced when I got there.

But he wasn't there. They hadn't had a chance to tell me before I'd banged the phone down that his body was required for a post-mortem.

As I drove away to the mortuary, looking at the semi-rural fringes of London that surrounded it, not far from where my father and mother and I had walked the dogs in the old days, by the woods and meadows my father had loved, I thought it was not such a bad place for him to have died.

Hardly anyone came to Dad's funeral at the Anglican church in Ashtead. His sister Enid came down from Sheffield; Keith Washington and Mad came to support me. Although I had started to see more of Carol, she had never met Dad and I didn't feel I could ask her to come.

Near the grave, beneath the foliage of a flowering cherry tree, I said goodbye to my idiosyncratic father, and cried like a child. It must have been the realization that I had witnessed the final departure of the man who had brought me into the world and whom I had never really known. It was only after I'd passed forty myself that I'd started trying to find out what he truly was about and by then it was too late.

Enid cried too. He had never really talked to her, either, she said.

Back in Epsom, I stood in 8 Sunnybank, depressed and painfully gloomy about the deterioration of the place. Some pipes had burst and water had run down the stairs into the hall and living room; paint was peeling, gutters falling off and the garden looked like a bomb site. This was where I'd passed my formative years as a teenager, where Id set out for my first job as an estate agent and where I'd returned for sporadic breaks between stints of acting in my twenties. The house looked completely worn out and abused now. And I had inherited it.

This had happened by default. My mother and father had come to an agreement that anything she had to leave would come to me and anything he had would go to his sister, Enid, who was known to have been having a bad time with her husband.

I wasn't surprised, though, to find that Dad had died intestate and I was his next of kin.

Enid needed somewhere to escape from her marriage, a home in which to look after her autistic daughter, Cathy.

I had squandered most of what I'd inherited from my mother on Michael Slater's aloe-vera farm and that didn't look as if it would ever be a productive venture. I didn't want that to happen again, so once my father's ragged property and effects had been sold, I aimed most of the proceeds Enid's way.

And there I was at forty-nine, an orphan. It was a strange feeling, being at last cut loose to drift through life without the anchorage your parents provided.

My mother had died at sixty seven, my father at seventy-two. I was very conscious of my own mortality at the time and I couldn't help wondering if my own death might not be so far in the future.

To add to the grief I felt over my father, my third marriage had broken up quite harshly, I had just lived through two years of an extremely volatile and destructive relationship that had also gone badly sour, and now I'd been orphaned – all in the space of three years.

I needed a drink, badly.

But before I left Sunnybank on that day after the funeral, I was having a last look through what was what, when I found an old ARP box tucked away in a spare room wardrobe. In it was a letter from my mother to my father, written about fifty years before. In it, she begged his forgiveness because she had strayed and had become pregnant. She had no idea how to tell her father, because he would have been scandalized.

I tried to piece together what might have gone on between them.

They had met and had just a brief and, I suspect, fairly unphysical liaison before deciding to get married right away because, with the looming threat of a Nazi invasion, there might be no tomorrow.

What I read into this was that Mum had become pregnant by another man.

The man I had called Dad was not my father.

Or, if he was, either my mother's pregnancy was terminated or she'd had the child, given it away and I had a half-sibling somewhere.

These were possibilities but nevertheless, suddenly everything was making sense to me. My father's persistent hostility towards me could simply be due to the fact that I was not his son.

This startling revelation was knocked on the head, however, when I found my parents' marriage certificate and, as they say over the pond, did the math.

They had been married in October, 1941, in plenty of time for me to have been conceived and born by August the following year.

After running a gamut of emotions in a very short time while I sat on the spare bed, clutching and rereading the salient documents, I finally convinced myself that I was indeed my father's son, and my mother's escapade must have happened *before* I was conceived. What had come of the earlier pregnancy and any resulting child, I had no idea and never discovered.

Chapter 8
Miami Twice

I was still shaking off the trauma of Dad's death when I had to fly off to work in the States – not to make a movie in Hollywood, but to film a two-part *Only Fools* Christmas special in Miami.

Miami Twice – The American Dream and *Oh to be in England* – was by far the most ambitious project Sullivan and Gareth Gwenlan had undertaken.

John Sullivan had decided that *Boycie* and *Marlene* would go to Miami on holiday. There, after a chapter of accidents, they would bump into *Del* and *Rodney* being chased by a posse of Mafia goons in the Everglades.

Sue and I thought ourselves very lucky, being the only members of the cast to go to the States along with David and Nick. We promised all the other seething members of the cast that we'd send them a card when we got there. We flew out to be greeted in Miami by David and Nick, Gareth Gwenlan and Tony Dow, as well as quite a few familiar members of the crew, especially the doughty Sue Longstaff.

The whole wheeze looked a lot more fun than we expected, when were told there were union problems relating to the shoot, and we might have to stay in Miami for more than the three days scheduled. *Oh no!*

It turned out that the BBC, in a fit of economizing, had decided to use key staff of their own while filming in Miami, hiring locals only for the more menial functions. The Teamsters' Union of America were not happy about this. 'This is the US of A, buddy, and we do things big out here.'

Gareth tried to explain to a Jimmy Hoffa character that this was the BBC and we had a limited budget.

'Well, buddy, this is the Teamsters and unless you employ more of our people, you don't do the movie at all... Period.'

It seemed they had the power to institute a heavy picket around the unit, although they were only concerned about our unit's drivers. Delicate negotiations dragged on while Gareth grew more pallid and hollow-eyed by the hour. In the end, half a dozen Teamsters were taken on to replace some of the owner-drivers the BBC had hired. On the whole, they sat around all day doing nothing but making a dent in the BBC's already strained budget – although John Sullivan assigned one of them to himself and spent a lot of time picking over US labour laws as he was driven around Miami.

I would be lying if I said I minded the forced delay. Sue and I ended up staying in Coconut Grove for a week more than we'd expected. We didn't think it too awful to go up to the Grove each morning to have our all-American breakfasts, flirting with the tide on Biscayne Bay, or plunging into an empty hotel pool. Evenings offered the option of drinking a skinful of margaritas in downtown Miami, or having a little something to eat on the waterfront, before returning to the all-expenses paid hotel for a well earned rest after an exhausting day doing nothing. This of course is the upside of the business, when you feel the luckiest people on the planet, and you make the most of it while it lasts, albeit at the BBC's expense.

Finding unexpected time on my hands I looked up an old acquaintance, whom I might otherwise have overlooked – a Scotsman whom I only ever knew as Jimmy. He harked back to the time when I'd been with my second wife, Debbie Arnold. She'd had a great friend at the time called Leanne Robinson – daughter of Cardew (*The Cad*) Robinson, a radio and variety turn I remembered from my youth. Jimmy had been Leanne's man.

Jimmy had always had a harsh, brooding side to him and here in Florida he'd gone native – inasmuch as he was heavily into guns. He told me with great gusto that although he didn't have a licence to carry, he could keep a weapon at home which meant that he could keep one in the car.

He took me to a shooting range, where he checked out a mean and ugly pistol with which he blazed away at targets in the form of cardboard cut-outs of enemies of Uncle Sam – the Ayatollah Khomeini, Fidel Castro, and bizarrely, Charles Manson. Jimmy who'd always been a fan of the martial arts and other aggressive 'sports', used his weapon with disturbing relish. I had a go, too. Strangely, I was deemed quite a good shot, although I was frankly uncomfortable toting a 9mm Glock in my hand and feeling the thing buck as I loosed off.

Jimmy also liked the girlie joints and took me to one on the appropriately named 'Strip' one lunchtime, for God's sake! I hadn't seen a lunchtime stripper for years, not since I'd once been hauled off to a pub in Battersea which fielded a few not very sophisticated striptease artistes during the Friday lunch hour in order to build up a base for the weekend trade. There, on a small, rickety stage and a carpet sticky with spilt beer, an unwholesome, bored-looking girl waggled her ample buttocks at a largely unresponsive crowd in the bar. Looking for a laugh, a punter yelled out, 'What's them spots on her bum?'

Another wag picked up the challenge. 'That's not spots,' he shouted back. 'That's her price in Braille.'

It didn't make my pint taste any better.

The Miami girls writhed around with extravagant lasciviousness, taking their tops off and winking at the ogling audience with unsubtle suggestiveness. It didn't do much for me but Jimmy loved it and eagerly thrust small wads of dollar bills into any adjacent G-strings. He seemed to know one of the girls and she came and sat with us.

'I... er... Do you do this sort of thing often?' I spluttered primly.

'As often as you like, honey,' she pouted beneath eyelashes like a pair of yard brooms.

She did a dance especially for us, which had me crawling with embarrassment and Jimmy howling with raucous laughter.

When at last Gareth had settled terms with the Teamsters, shooting started for us up in the Everglades National Park, a swampy wilderness in which I would never choose to get lost.

Boycie and *Marlene* were assigned an Everglades airboat – one of those huge floating skidoos, with a socking great propeller on the back. Our driver, Wayne, was a very obliging fellow who wore a red bandana over a mop of dark blond curls and loved his work. He flew a Confederate flag from the mast beside the propeller as he powered us across the water, through the beds of reed and water hyacinth.

With a lot of 'Yee-haws' going on and Wayne thinking his job was solely to entertain us, riding the thing didn't feel at all like any work I'd ever done.

Eventually, as part of Sullivan's surreal plot *Del Boy* and *Rodney* appear, crawling from warm soupy water draped in dripping vegetation and *Boycie* observes at his most supercilious, 'Good God, Del Boy – you smell like a vegetarian's fart!' – a line which I was sure would become a classic, if only John had kept it in the final cut!

It's worth interrupting the narrative flow here to mention again that John Sullivan consistently wrote and shot more material than an episode ever had time for, and some scenes, however good, had to go. The scenes that stayed were selected on their relevance: what was most germane to the plot survived while anything ancillary was cut until the show fitted the time slot assigned to it.

In fact, throughout the whole run of the show there were stacks of out-takes and sometimes whole finished scenes that were made but never shown. This sort of extravagance can be helpful, as many authors know – the more you can cut out any extraneous or weaker material you may have written, the tighter and more focused the finished product article will be. There just aren't so many serial TV directors who have that luxury. John was a perfectionist and he demanded this latitude, with the result that there are very few, if any, dull, lifeless or pointless padding scenes throughout all the episodes of *Only Fools*.

The frustrating result of this was that scenes which had been fun to make and certainly worked in their own right and of which an actor might be quite proud, often ended up on the cutting-room floor and in the case of our show, securely chucked away in a bin to be disposed of permanently, never to see the light of day in *Auntie's Greatest Bloomers*.

A pity really – given that there was probably enough rejected footage to make half a dozen more episodes, but John didn't want his out-takes seen because he didn't want his actors to look stupid, or make fools of themselves.

In Miami some classic bloomer footage was shot of one of the animal stars employed for a scene, an angry amphibian with the moniker *Al the Gator*.

It was supposed to come rushing up a bank at *Del Boy* and *Rodney* as they tried to find their way out of the swamp while escaping from a Mafia gang. This unlikely scenario had come about because *Del Boy* evidently looked very like the local Mafia Don. The gang had concluded that if *Del* was caught, killed off and found dead, the cops would stop looking for his doppelganger...

The alligator came with a 'wrangler' – a hard-looking nut called Sean. He had set things up so that on the call of 'Action' the beast would be released and scuttle up towards a large bowl of food (invisible to the audience, of course) laid out for it fifteen feet in front of the camera, where Sean the wrangler would leap on top of it and subdue it.

Sue and I watched, intrigued, from the sidelines and at a safe distance and as far as we could see, rehearsals went well and according to the script. However, when it came to the take, *Al the Gator* was evidently bored, hadn't read the script and was no longer so peckish. On 'Action!' he rushed off in the right direction but, completely ignoring the food, hurtled straight on towards the cameraman, his crew and the sound and lighting men, who all legged it like Usain Bolt on amphetamines as soon as the rampant reptile by-passed the food.

The camera was left running and caught the real action when Sean with a superb swallow dive, landed on the alligator and amazingly managed to wrap duct tape around its snapping jaws and a blindfold over its eyes – I say 'its' because I had no idea what gender this beast was, and I've seen human beings of both sexes behave in a similar way from time to time.

Sue Holderness had already got her video-cam out to film the action but in her terror, when the 'gator charged, she lost control and only got shots of upper branches of trees and a deep blue sky.

In making *Miami Twice*, John Sullivan also indulged his penchant for putting celebrities on the show. *Only Fools* had a wide range of fans and there was no shortage of willing victims. As *Del* and *Rodney* set off from Gatwick, they had an encounter with a grinning Richard Branson, who kept corpsing and required several takes to get his lines out. In Miami, Barry Gibb, who had a home there, was easily talked into making a brief, slightly self-conscious appearance. John used to love this and when it happened, it probably did help to bring an extra fizz to the show. Tony Dow, our director, was less keen. He thought it cheapening.

There were several others over the years, like Jonathan Ross playing himself in one of the last episodes of *Only Fools, If They Could See Us Now*, and much later, in *The Green, Green Grass*, Ricky Hatton, the boxer appears, shaking his head in disgust when a fight breaks out in the local pub, while Fiona Bruce was persuaded to appear in a story that involved the *Antiques Road Show*.

I said goodbye to Florida at the end of our wrap party somewhere on Miami Beach, where, I have been told, I danced with a palm tree and with Sue Longstaff, although I couldn't have told the difference, they were both such good dancers. I finished up standing in the back of a stretch limo with Nicholas Lyndhurst, both our heads poking through the roof, raising several glasses to the United States in general, Coconut Grove and, in particular, Hooters, the famous bar where the waitresses' skirts were short and the cocktails were long.

Back in cold grey London, as the Christmas Special was finished off in the studio, I started rehearsals for my first pantomime. If you can brace yourself for the rigours of a panto season and generally deprive yourself of booze over the festive period, you soon become convinced that panto is such a quirky, British tradition it can be a lot of fun. There's nothing quite like being in a good, slick production, with a great script, fresh jokes (rare) and wonderful, over-the-top costumes, playing to full houses of genuinely appreciative audiences.

However, this first one, *Cinderella*, nearly put me off for life. It was a ramshackle extravaganza put on at Guildford Civic Hall by Tony Cartwright, a Liverpudlian who thought a producer's job was to wander around backstage, drinking champagne and spending a lot of time in the dancers' dressing-room.

The stars of the show included Maggie Moone, a chanteuse who had made her name as resident singer on *Name That Tune* and Bob Carolgees. Bob had a brilliant act with his hand puppet, *Spit the Dog*, which was clever, anarchic and horribly funny, although it was clear that Bob was bored with the dog he'd created and was beginning to hate it. He also hated being 'down South'; he felt that his patter, designed for the Northern club circuit where he'd been born and bred, meant nothing in the cosy Surrey countryside.

Maggie was a magnificent *Prince Charming*, with great legs, lavish boots and a glint in her eye but the show was a shambles from the start. The wardrobe department was in chaos because the costumes had arrived late and fitted nobody. The set looked as if it had been put up by *Harold Steptoe* and there was no script – just a few lines of rambling guidance between the songs, like *'John Challis (Boycie) enters and does his thing for five or ten minutes.'*

When I first saw it I was appalled. Did they think I was a stand-up comedian or what? Didn't they *know* that actors liked to work with a script? I was almost ready to abandon the show but the money wasn't bad and my name and mugshot were already out there, writ large over the theatre entrance, so I couldn't easily walk out on it.

I thought I'd better stay and see what happened.

Astonishingly, although we had strong competition from a much classier production at the town's *Yvonne Arnaud Theatre*, our *Cinderella* did tremendous business, beating the *Arnaud* hands down. I guess we had names that were better known to a panto audience, and there was a certain amount of flash and glitter to our cobbled-together effort. In the end I enjoyed myself, and this turned out to be the first of twenty-one consecutive pantomimes for me.

For the run of *Cinderella,* I'd been commuting to Guildford from my flat in Sheen Lane. Since I'd got back from *Boycie's* outing to the Everglades, I'd seen more of Carol and I was relieved to find how much I'd missed her and how I enjoyed being with her after this short time apart. In fact, we spent Christmas day together at Peter and Myra Egans' and found we were getting on better than ever. But I was still reluctant to accept that I was back in a full-blown relationship. I suppose that I was finally learning to be a little more circumspect in the way I approached these things.

At the end of an uproarious and inebriated Christmas Day party, I found around my neck a string of pearls, which carried a lingering scent I recognized as Carol's and a pile of walnut shells around my plate, all cracked open by her, just for me!

Chapter 9
Hawaii Five O

By the time 1992 arrived, Carol and I were practically sharing my flat in Sheen Lane. While I'd been in Miami, I had commissioned her to make some cushion covers and curtains for me, which we installed together. She showed me what she was made of, too, when she had to perform a feeding of the five thousand: not my disciples, but a large gang of my tennis friends, whom I'd asked round for a party without checking that I had any food to give them. All I had in my fridge was a chicken that looked like it had just been kidnapped from someone's back yard and a few bits of elderly salad.

I called on Carol for her help and from these unpromising ingredients she managed to produce an astonishing chicken salad that satisfied the whole gang. It was little short of a miracle and an achievement that made a lasting impression on me.

Even so, I was still dragging my heels in accepting that I was in a relationship again. I had no confidence in my ability to survive it. There was, I knew, nothing I could find wrong with Carol – quite the opposite, in fact. As far as I could see, she was everything a man like me could have asked for.

She was funny and beautiful, a brilliant needlewoman, an excellent, resourceful cook and the chemistry between us was magical. Despite all this, I was still reluctant to embark on yet another path that might go nowhere and I resisted all the voices inside me urging me to ask her to move in with me permanently.

To take my mind off this conundrum, I agreed to take part in what looked like another shambolic, out-of-control show, *Noel Edmonds' House Party*.

Noel, his show and his compadre, *Mr Blobby*, had come in for quite a bit of stick and generally hostile criticism but I rather enjoyed them. It was one of the first truly populist shows in which the public, who came to see it recorded, were fully engaged.

Contestants were involved in some remarkably silly competitions, and paid the price of losing with a nasty soaking with some beastly-looking liquid. Most of the jokes were at the expense of someone's dignity but I guessed if you didn't take yourself too seriously, you should be able to live with that.

All this silliness took place in a bogus medieval manor house in a make-believe folksy village called Crinkly Bottom. Most serious actors would have had major misgivings before agreeing to appear in it.

I overcame my misgivings. I thought it might be fun and, in any case, I was going to look after *Boycie*, so I insisted that he would only appear at the door and be involved in a formalized sketch.

When I was first on the show, I'd forgotten about *Mr Blobby* – a large, round, pink cartoon character, who would appear unexpectedly from anywhere, to barge around anarchically and usually finish up sitting on top of Noel.

I found him hilarious. Was there something wrong with me?

I ended up doing four of Noel's shows and met an eclectic bunch of people– Frank Carson, David Seaman (the Gunners' goalkeeper), Joan Collins and Spike Milligan.

David 'Safe Hands' Seaman reckoned that the goals he saved in the European Championships were nothing compared to being on Noel's show. 'I've never been so nervous in my life,' he told me.

Joan Collins walked in like the Queen Mother. Everyone duly genuflected slightly when they spoke to her. She sat in the middle of the BBC make-up room, beneath signs warning of dire retribution for anyone caught smoking and lit up a king-size Marlboro Light, in an elegant cigarette holder, without a flicker of regard for the rules. Nobody said a word. I was impressed.

She gave it her all on the show and I ended up dancing with her at the end, which made it worth the visit.

Spike Milligan had been a hero of mine since I used to listen to the Goon Show with my Dad as a teenager in the '50s. I loved it that his anarchic and surreal meeting with Noel on the show bore no relation whatsoever to the rehearsal script. I had to tell him afterwards what a pleasure it was to be in the same show as him and how he'd had me glued to the radio as a kid and ever since.

'Oh, you poor fool,' he quavered and to the room in general: 'This man needs treatment!'

It was part of the show's energy that the audience never knew who was going to come in through the front door. I couldn't believe the deafening reception I got when Noel opened it to me. I felt as if I'd just hammered the ball into the roof of the net for the Arsenal winner against Spurs in the Cup Final!

It was fun but four shows were enough. I was asked to do more with Neil Morrissey, perhaps because they found actors better at sticking to the script, but I didn't want to get too identified with the show.

By way of contrast, in February I was back at the Mill in Sonning, for my third appearance there, in a serious Ira Levin play called *Veronica's Room*, directed, once again, by Myra Egan. Levin was already deservedly famous for his story, *Rosemary's Baby*, a movie starring John Cassavetes and Mia Farrow. *Veronica's Room* was another dark piece that blurred reality with fantasy, leading to obsession and murder.

Two middle-aged retainers of a great plantation house in the Southern States lure a young couple into the spooky old place because the girl looks very like Veronica, the deceased daughter of the last owner of the house. One of the retainers turns out to be Veronica's sister and persuades the girl to pay the role of her dead sibling.

She has no idea how to reproduce the woman's fantasy version of Veronica and can't do it. As a result she is smothered on stage.

In our production, the pathological sister was played by Mary Peach, a '60s screen star, whom I had admired a lot, particularly in *No Love for Johnnie*. It seemed that Myra was deliberately reawakening my past with her choice of leading ladies.

I fell back into the stagecraft of role playing with great relish – it took me back once more to my repertory days, where I loved escaping into my character and being someone else for a while.

However, I was brought down to earth with a rude thump one night in *Veronica's Room*.

The play opens in a fusty old nineteenth-century attic, with dust covers draped over the furniture. Everything you could discern through the gloom was from a past time – no one has been up in the attic for years.

A sliver of light shows under the door; muffled voices are heard, the door creaks open, two dimly-lit characters appear. Mary Peach and I, the middle-aged retainers, shuffle on, wearing shabby old clothes.

I uttered the first line of the play in a well-rehearsed Southern drawl. 'We should never have come up here.'

In the silence that followed, you could have cut the tension with a knife.

After a few moments, a woman in the front row leaned in to her neighbour.

'That's him!' she said in a clearly audible whisper. '*That's Boycie!*'

I guessed she had been studying her programme, which gave the cast in order of appearance. The curse of episodic television had struck again.

Veronica's Room had not been an easy play for the cast. For one thing, the girl's murder on stage was quite harrowing for us and there were no laughs to counteract the gloom. Tom Hughes, who ran the theatre, was also concerned that it played to only 85 per cent capacity. A West End theatre would have killed for that sort of figure but Tom was used to closer to 100 per cent. 'That's why we don't do this sort of play very often,' he said. 'Bloody good acting, though!' he added ina tactful afterthought.

While *Veronica's Room* was going on I could work in London during the day and had an enjoyable session appearing as a voice on the phone in one of my favourite TV comedies at the time, *One Foot in the Grave*, with Richard Wilson as *Victor Meldrew*. I was playing a burglar who had broken into the *Meldrews'* house and stolen a video recorder, which, once he'd got it home, he couldn't operate and he was ringing *Victor* to ask him how it worked. A nice little scene, which evoked, inevitably, the famous Meldrew cry – 'I don't *beleeve* it!'

I had to admire the way Richard had been able to endow the grumpy old *Victor Meldrew* with such a strong, inimitable personality.

When *Veronica's Room* was finished, they must have liked something about my performance as I was asked back to do a fourth play at the Mill within a year – a record, I was told. Alan Ayckbourn's *Season's Greetings* was being put on a month or two later, directed by Ted Craig (who ran the Warehouse Theatre in Croydon).

My part was that of *Bernard*, a limp, ineffectual doctor, who has devised his own puppet show. He is asked round each year at Christmas by the same family to give a performance of, in this case, *The Three Little Pigs* for the unseen children in the play.

His show is beset by a string of cocks-ups and misfortunes. *Bernard* is bullied by the grandfather of the family and the show falls to pieces as a result of the barracking and an incompetent assistant. It is heart-rending, typical Ayckbourn, as he strips his characters bare for us to laugh at, then reveals all their weaknesses and insecurities, making us feel guilty about laughing – bittersweet, middle-class English comedy at its finest.

Whether one likes it or not, one's fiftieth birthday marks a key stage in life. After that point has been reached, others only refer to you as 'Young Man' in a spirit of irony. As a twenty year old, I perceived people over fifty as past their sell-by date, committed only to a downward slope and definitely 'old'. But when I reached my half-century, I found it almost impossible to grasp that it was over thirty years since I'd set off at the wheel of the Argyle Theatre for Youth's Commer van, to play twenty shows of *Pinocchio* each week all over the country.

In gloomier moments I asked myself what I had learned since then – how much had I progressed? The answers I gave myself weren't encouraging... but at least I could now risk a few optimistic thoughts about my love life.

So far, in the months since I'd met Carol, it looked faintly possible that I might one day find myself in a satisfactory relationship that didn't involve a neurotic, a psychopath or an egomaniac (apart from myself). And I certainly didn't feel old.

Being fifty didn't seem to me like a reason for celebrating on a lavish scale, especially as it was an event which I was in half a mind to ignore, so I compromised by marking the occasion with a party for a dozen close friends at The Depot, a terrific restaurant at the bottom of White Hart Lane in Barnes.

Carol was there, to be at my side, with Keith and Madeleine (who had been so loyal during my mad Inge phase), Bob Hankinson and other members of the Coach & Horses community. Terry Booth, who was in *Season's Greetings* at the Mill, came with Carla Wansey Jackson.

After that, and once *Season's Greetings* had ended its run, Carol and I seemed to have reached a tipping point in our relationship. I was beginning to realize it was time to get off the fence, or lose the impetus of where we'd got to by then, and I was ready to be receptive, when she subtly hinted that we might go halfway round the world together to visit the Hawaiian Islands.

Carol had told me a lot about Hawaii and how she'd found her spiritual home there. She'd first been ten years before, after reading about the place and being strongly attracted by what she'd learned.

On her first visit she'd met Tom Selleck and his cronies, while he was there making his TV series, *Magnum PI*. She had fallen in love with the islands and the kind of life they offered and was determined to go back as often as possible. By seriously concentrating her resources, she'd managed to go back no less than eight times since her first visit. I was impressed by her enthusiasm and the pictures she showed me, shots of her looking bronzed, fit and magnificent on the beach at Waikiki, surrounded usually by suitably handsome men and resplendent in front of the Outrigger Canoe Club, with her Canadian friend, Dorothy, a dolly-drop, trolley-dolly who looked like a girl in a 1940s ice-cream ad.

I'd never been anywhere like these Pacific islands and, just as Carol had been, I felt drawn to them. And although she and I still didn't know each other well, we felt, 'What the hell! Let's go for it and see where it leads.'

We flew via Los Angeles, where the riots were in full flow, even producing threats to shoot down 747s landing at LAX. Unscathed we carried on and touched down in the tropical heat of Honolulu, where I had to adjust to the alarming idea that we were adrift on a few small blobs of volcanic outcrop in the middle of the Pacific, two thousand miles from the nearest continental land mass.

Carol took me everywhere she knew, from island to island – finding the spot where Captain James Cook was murdered by disgruntled natives in 1779, seeing the sun rise on the volcanic moonscape of Haleakala on Maui, exploring the sulphurous crater of Kilauea on the Big Island and sitting on the beach for sunset at the Colony Surf Hotel in Honolulu.

Carol captured a part of each place we went with dozens of photographs... of me. In every single one, I appear to be in some kind of Victorian photographic pose – sitting with elbow on knee, looking into the middle distance, or shading my eyes with one hand, and the other curled on my hip, or lying on my side with my chin leaning on my hand. It was as if I had some kind of affliction that made it impossible for me simply to stand there and look normal, as if I were just enjoying myself.

It was something that I did instinctively. It certainly wasn't part of a plan to have me photographed like a nineteenth-century cricket player all over the Hawaiian Islands. It was, I guess, the old actor's defence of simply covering up and becoming someone else when not so sure of my position with the other party.

Beside us on the Colony Surf beach were the Outrigger Canoe Club and the Hau Tree Restaurant, on whose wall was posted a notice: 'In case of Tsunami, keep calm, pay your bill, then run like hell!'

On this beach, Carol introduced me to Tom Selleck. *Magnum PI* was over, after a long run, but Tom had grown to love the islands so much that he'd bought a place up the coast from Diamond Head on Oahu and still liked to come down to the exclusive Outrigger Club.

Tom was lounging on the beach, looking like a god, and holding forth in a curious, high-pitched voice. He was a charming man and, it seemed, bewilderingly attractive to almost everyone he came across. He was keen to hear about my work in England and sympathized when I told him I had no idea if *Only Fools* would continue into the '90s or would just run out of steam.

'Tell me about it!' he said. 'It's hell! I have no idea what I'm gonna do next.'

It was hard to believe. Here I was sitting in paradise, talking to a major American TV star about being out of work.

He seemed to be coping, though. When he was ready to go, he leaped to his feet with a friendly wave, 'Later, John,' and ran down the beach to hurl himself into the ocean. He swam in a strong, steady crawl for at least a mile before emerging to run back up the beach to change for the evening.

I shook my head. Did that really happen?

Our three weeks in paradise were cut short by a summons to London to feature in Marks and Gran's *The New Statesman* with Rik Mayall. I played a grenade-festooned Che-Guevara type whom *Alan B'Stard* had to bring to the table with his tribal enemy (played by Don Henderson) to be manipulated for his own b'stardly ends.

Apart from the sheer wonder of being introduced to the islands of Hawaii, I was reeling from the joy of spending so much time with a woman who seemed so close to me in spirit. I had never met anyone with whom I had so much in common – so much that it almost overwhelmed us both and seemed almost too good to be true.

We soon realized, though, that it was true. It was inevitable that, when we arrived back in London, we decided to live together. Carol sold her basement in Chiswick and squeezed, with all her paraphernalia, into my flat in Sheen Lane.

As we were both six-footers and needed a lot of space, it was pretty obvious that this place wasn't big enough for the both of us and we started looking for somewhere more spacious.

Before that could happen, I was in rehearsals for a stage play, *Jack's Out* at the Bush Theatre in West London. Whenever I'm in that part of London, I think of the *Evening Standard* headline: MURDER HUNT IN WEST LONDON: POLICE COMB SHEPHERD'S BUSH– or was it a spoof?

The Bush Theatre at the time was run by Dominic Dromgoole, son of Patrick, who later went on to be artistic director at the Globe Theatre on the South Bank. *Jack's Out* was written by a promising young writer, Danny Miller, and directed by Ken McClymont. Like *Brighton Rock,* it was based around the Brighton underworld, and my character, *Frankie*, was a gay Catholic psychopath, who is reacting to the news that *Jack* – a big cheese in the local gangland – has been released from jail eight years earlier than expected, seeking retribution against those who have transgressed in his absence.

Frankie was a fascinating and complex role, which aims to convey the man's deeply embedded sense of accountability, set against his own self-righteousness and close 'personal' relationship with God.

The play worked, but only in parts, and in some ways *Frankie* was just too dominant a character. There were also a number of practical difficulties in the production. At a point in the action, my character had to exit at the back of the set, to re-enter later through the audience entrance at the front. In the Bush Theatre, the only way to do this was to go out through the emergency exit into the street and walk round the corner to the front of the theatre.

There was usually a fairly motley selection of characters lurking around Shepherd's Bush of an evening and invariably as I made my exit in full make-up from the building to the street, I would be accosted by members of the public for one reason or another – a light, the price of a cup of tea, to see if I required any ganja.

One night a small Cockney geezer stood his ground in front of me and grabbed his mate. "Ere, look – it's old Charlie! 'Allo, mate, how yer doin'? Let's 'ave a drink.'

'No, no,' I muttered, trying to step past him and anxious to get round for my re-entrance. 'I'm not who you think I am. I'm in the middle of a show. I'm an actor,' I added, perhaps a little unconvincingly.

The little feller looked at me quizzically for a moment. 'Well, we're all actors, ain't we? You wanna see how much acting I 'as to do to sell me cucumbers in the mornin'!'

After that, my entrance as the revengeful killer with missionary zeal whom I was supposed to be portraying wasn't easy, as I couldn't stop giggling.

On another occasion, one of my tennis-playing mates, Peter Jones, had come to see the play. A big bluff Welshman, he arrived late having booked a seat in the front row. Owing to the extremely intimate nature of the Bush Theatre he was crouching low so as not to be noticed as he scrambled along between the front row and the stage to reach his seat, until he found himself face to face with me during one of my soliloquies to the Almighty, begging forgiveness for my mortal sins. It was a tricky moment for both of us. Peter spent the rest of the show with his head down, hardly daring to look up at me. We're still good friends, though.

We had some positive reviews for the play but as usual they came too late. The *Independent* loved it and the *Evening Standard* thought it powerful, with a 'stand-out performance' from John Challis, who came over as a 'sort of low-grade Robert de Niro', which I took as a compliment.

Towards the end of the two-week run, I was handed a note backstage from someone called Christina Shepherd, who had recently started up a new agency and was looking for clients. If I were interested, would I get in touch?

At the time, Tim Combe was my agent, which he'd been almost since the start of *Only Fools*. Being an ex-BBC man, he knew all the ins and outs of Auntie's labyrinthine methods and had done a fine job negotiating all my contracts over that time. He had also looked after Buster Merryfield for some years, so he was almost part of the team. But the world and the business were changing. Tim had started to downsize and his partnership with Carey Ellison, who'd started the actor's directory *Spotlight*, belonged to a gentler age.

Christina was from a new generation, with a thrusting attitude, which I thought suited the times, so I signed up with her. Later I introduced her to Ken MacDonald, who was unsettled at his agency and he joined her too. I stayed with her for the next few years and through several *Only Fools* specials.

After *Jack's Out*, I had the next *Only Fools* Christmas special looming. There had been no regular series during 1992 but the feeling seemed to be that there was still life in Nelson Mandela House and I was very happy to be back with the team again. It was a year on since the *Trotters'* brush with the Miami mafia and *Del* seemed temporarily to have run out of motivation.

While he's clearing out his grandad's allotment (at the orders of the council) he digs out a couple of old chemical drums which, with help from *Trigger* and *Denzil*, are disposed of during the night.

In *Mother Nature's Son*, John Sullivan, always alert to new trends, is tapping into (forgive the pun) the bottled mineral water racket. *Del* has found a dribbling hose in the overgrown allotment and has a sudden, misguided *Del Boy* inspiration. He has recently visited a successful organic food shop and recognizes what's beginning to happen with the natural-food movement. Its a short leap for him to conclude that he has just discovered a source of natural mineral water in the allotment. He manages to wangle a certificate of purity for the water coming from the old hosepipe and has it bottled. He markets it as Peckham Spring Water, and starts coining it in.

In the money once more, *Del* and *Rodney* go off on holiday with *Raquel* and *Cassandra* to Brighton, where they are rung up in a panic to be told that there is a serious problem with the Peckham Spring Water. It's glowing in the dark and is thought to be badly contaminated. When they get back to deal with the crisis, they also learn that the local reservoir has been polluted by the chemical drums which they'd chucked into it. It was a classic *Only Fools*, screened on the evening of Christmas Day, 1992, and for the first time, it was watched by over twenty million viewers. Twenty years on, bottled Peckham Spring Water is always a best seller at the *Only Fools & Horses* conventions that are still held around the country.

Chapter 10
That's Entertainment

At the beginning of 1993, my friend, Bob Hankinson, a foundation stone of the Coach & Horses in Barnes High Street, entered a radio quiz based on knowledge of Zimbabwe. The quiz had been set by an organization called Tusk, a charity dedicated to conserving the African wildlife that's being eradicated at an alarming rate by poachers seeking elephant tusks and rhino horn. In this modern scientific world there has been an extraordinary leap in demand for rhino horns which, in ground form, are seriously believed to increase a man's libido. It's an absurd idea with no rational basis to it and presumably only the coincidence of the shape and texture of the horn could be perceived as having any connection with male sexuality. At the same time, the international trade in ivory has rocketed and elephant tusks are fetching huge prices.

Bob, who tends to know a lot about most things, also had a great interest in Zimbabwe, and particularly the Hwange National Park, where I'd been with him a couple of years before with Inge. He won the quiz – answering correctly the gestation period of an elephant – and his prize was a safari for two with Tusk.

He was asked if he would like to bring a wife.

'Whose wife? I haven't got one. Can I bring a friend?'

He was told he could.

He asked me.

'Can I bring my friend, too, if I pay for her?'

'Oh, no! Not another woman!' Bob wailed, remembering the awful time I'd had on the previous visit with Inge.

'This'll be different,' I quickly promised. 'Carol is an entirely different *kettle de poisson*.'

Bob knew Carol a little. He'd had dinner with us once and he was used to seeing her in the pub. He was impressed that she could sit down at the bar and knock off the *Telegraph* crossword, while all the men around her were talking bollocks. She would only stay as long as it took her to finish it, which wasn't long, thus curtailing my own drinking time quite severely. We soon agreed that the three of us would go to Zimbabwe together.

We had one of the most exciting trips ever. We'd been asked if we minded roughing it and we'd said we didn't. Having reached Harare, we flew north and landed in the middle of the Mavuradonha Wilderness. Mercifully this was devoid of human beings, who had hunted out 90 per cent (yes, **90 per cent**) of the larger wild animals that had lived there.

We explored it with the help of an ex-Rhodesian bush-fighter turned tobacco farmer called Nick O'Connor. He made it clear that he was very interested in Carol.

'I could do with a long strong blonde like her!' he told me, which was a little nerve-wracking, though not as alarming as riding the ex-polo ponies he'd produced to carry us out into the bush.

Carol, of course, although she hadn't ridden for years, was the daughter of a long line of Dorset hunting folk and soon found her seat. Bob who wasn't really constructed for this kind of thing, found it very uncomfortable and mildly terrifying. I did a little better, although I had difficulty staying on the first day we went out.

We had to cross a raging torrent that was carrying monsoon rains from the high ground. My pony, a wiry beast who knew exactly who was in control, had a change of heart about leaping over it and galloped off towards a stand of trees with long low branches.

'I've seen this in the movies,' I thought, as we approached them. 'You just sway to the side.'

I swayed, but I kept on going, straight out of the side door. The pony stopped, turned and looked at me pityingly.

A little further on, my handsome bush hat got picked up by the wind and flew off behind me. I made an instinctive grab for it and went straight out the back door. The pony stopped, looked, and turned away in embarrassment.

When we got back and I was congratulating myself for only falling on soft ground, I went to dismount, left one foot in the stirrup, flipped over and fell flat on my face. The pony didn't even bother to look.

The next day I was given a deep-seated Western saddle with a nice big pommel to hang on to, and remained on board for the rest of our safari.

Bob was too uncomfortable, and anxious not to miss out on useful drinking time, so he excused himself from further sorties by horse.

But Nick, who was a master of bush craft, took Carol and me out on a different route every day to special secret African places. He showed us some wonderful things – bat caves, ancient rock art, tumbling waterfalls and some rare sable antelopes.

Nights at the camp were fairly hairy too. The latrine – a unisex ten-foot hole in the ground, surrounded by flimsy canvas walls – was 50 yards by torchlight through the bush from our sleeping quarters. The thought of that journey was made more daunting by tales of the 'kasi snake', waiting for the chance to strike.

And one night, sleeping in our open A-frame huts, we were woken at 2am by the horses fidgeting and playing up. This was accompanied by a very strong odour of cat – big cat! We got some comfort – not much – from having remembered to sleep with our back packs behind our necks, because we were told, lions have a tendency to drag you out by the head.

While we were at the camp, we experienced a very violent storm that took out the whole of Nick's tobacco crop. Although in many ways, he was an old-fashioned colonial and had no time for President Robert Mugabe, he was very well thought of by the locals in his district, where he was responsible for employing a lot of people and was known for putting in schools and churches and encouraging the people to preserve their wildlife and treat it as the valuable tourist resource it represented.

This aspect of the Zimbabwe bush had been picked up and developed by Tusk in their endeavours to save the rare species from extinction.

Our next destination was a conservancy near Kwe Kwe, a place where twenty years before, in the former Rhodesia, I had toured with a production of a British farce, *Move over Mrs Markham*. From there we went to Bulawayo, Zimbabwe's second city. It had changed almost beyond recognition since I'd last been there.

The bush seemed to have crept into the town and was taking it over and it looked more like one of those dry, dusty one-horse towns that my old heroes Jimmy Stewart and Henry Fonda used to ride into. Weeds grew through the paving, once-thriving hotels were closed and there was an air of despair about the place.

In the Midlands, where we went next, we saw a lot of game, this time from the back of a Land Rover. Stately giraffe galloped across the veldt, mingled with antelope, wildebeest and warthog.

With the help of an African tracker called Clever we found a rare and magical black rhino wallowing magnificently in a mud hole just yards away from us.

We were downwind of the beast, which was good, but our host, Ken told us to stay absolutely still, as the black rhino, blind as a bat, will happily charge at any sound it doesn't like. Clever, who had quite a record for being charged by rhino, was less sanguine and skirted round to the other side of the mud hole to be well out of the way.

Ken shrugged. 'Clever's just superstitious. He thinks the rhino's got his number but he's right, if that rhino does charge, he's much more likely to come this way. If he does, just climb a tree.'

I looked around wildly. 'There are no trees.'

'Then just lie still. He can't see a bloody thing.'

This was not reassuring. The thought of just lying still with a two-ton rhino thundering towards us at 30 mph did not fill me with glee.

We nearly fainted when the animal suddenly heaved itself out of the wallow and cocked an ear at us.

The next moment, he wheeled around and charged off in the opposite direction, just missing Clever by a few feet.

From the Midlands we were flown by a young man called Clint Sparrow (oh yes) south east to the Lone Star Conservancy, close to the Mozambique border. Carol and Bob piled in the back of Clint's Piper Cherokee while I had the wonderful experience of sitting up front, watching the extraordinary African landscape unfold, several thousand feet below, with animals, like flies on the sand, running from our approach across the bush.

The patches of rain in the distance, apparently tendrils of cloud reaching down to the earth, began slowly to build until suddenly we were confronted with a massive bank of cloud.

Clint didn't like the look of it. He leaned forward and flipped the switch on his radio. 'Harare, Harare, this is CJ188, heading south east for Lone Star. Permission to descend to five thousand feet. Come in!' There was no reply.

His voice grew more urgent as he tried again. There was still no reply.

The cloud was still building but Clint spotted a gap between two banks of cumulo-nimbus and headed straight for it, like a surfer riding the barrel.

I thought we'd made it but as we got there the cloud closed right in and we were tossed about like a shuttle-cock in a gale, with sheets of rain hitting the windscreen, as if a Romanian car-washer were hurling buckets of water at it.

Clint's jaw was set, his knuckles were as white as bone as he gripped the controls. I was transfixed. I knew I was going to die but I felt strangely calm. What concerned me most was which kind of animal would eat my mortal remains.

'I hope it's not hyenas,' I said to myself. 'I don't like them. Cheetah, leopard, lion, maybe even wild dogs, but please, not hyenas.'

Suddenly, the sky lightened, the sun burst through again and we were on the other side of the clouds.

Harare were answering our call at last.

'CJ188. Harare here. What was your request?'

Clint turned to me and grinned as we shared our intense relief.

Carol sat up in the back. 'Are we nearly there?' she asked sleepily. She'd been out for the count for the last hour and had missed all the excitement.

The Lone Star was much more of a reservation than anywhere else we had been and a lot of work had been done to arrange safaris to finance the costs of conservation.

We saw a leopard for the first time – a young female sitting on a rock at night, blinking at us. We found a lioness with her cubs. She glared balefully at us while her offspring gambolled around our Land Rover. We set out to find a small herd of elephant with a tracker to help us, although we did pretty well just following a trail of large mounds of dung, which, bizarrely, were covered in butterflies.

Our tracker was certain the animals were close but there were no sounds or visual clues to help – a little like trying to find the wife in a supermarket. We never did find the herd.

Later we were paddled in a canoe down a primeval-looking lake, through a drowned forest to the site of an ancient settlement. It was in a perfect defensive spot, hidden from all sides by boulders forming a natural crater.

You could imagine the people sheltering in the small caves that had formed, or clustering around a circle of boulders that might have been their fireplace. Although it can't have been inhabited for centuries, it gave out a sense of still being occupied. It must have provided an incredibly secure home, surrounded by fruit trees, with an endless supply of game roaming around. I had strong feeling that this was a place that might have been occupied by the very earliest *homo sapiens*, long before the human diaspora from Africa.

After Lone Star, Bob Hankinson went off to see his brother in Johannesburg, where Inge and I had stayed once. Carol and I had more places on our wish list and I wanted to show her the Victoria Falls – the most impressive natural wonder I'd ever seen– which I'd visited during the Stoppard tour in 1977.

The falls were as grand as ever. I guess it would take a lot to change them. We saw them from beneath, on foot at the top and from the air and Carol was as excited by the 'smoke that thunders' as I had been. So aroused were we by it, that, quite madly, we decided to go white-water rafting on the river below.

Before we got on a raft, we had to sign an indemnity which stated, more or less, 'If you die, it's not our fault.'

We looked at each other. 'Great,' we said, already high on adrenalin at just the thought of it as we watched the mighty Zambezi roaring through the gorge, fierce, unpredictable and full of crocodiles.

We were a little alarmed to find that we were the oldest on the raft by about twenty years – the others were all bubbling with the exuberance of youth, bronzed, fit, full of confidence – pains in the arse.

Our pilot, Cephas, a young Zimbabwean, gave us a quick course in raft management, to get us scuttling around the craft. 'To the left, to the right, to the front, to the back. Oh dear, what am I going to do with you?'

Carol and I, being taller and relatively heavier were assigned to the two front corners of the raft, with the task of leaning right forward as far as we could when the raft came down the rapids and hit the return curl of water at the trough. It was this curl that could force the front to lift and, in extreme cases, flip it up and over in a somersault.

Cephas sat himself up at the stern to steer with a single long oar and we set off calmly enough, passing under the bridge which was the border with Zambia, festooned with baboons and bungee jumpers, until we became aware of a growing roar, like a massive locomotive thundering towards us, as a faint line of spume came into sight, marking the start of the falling water.

Before you have time to get used to the idea, you're staring into the abyss. Then you know for sure – 'This ain't no fairground ride or health-and-safety-fied Disneyland thrill. This is where you are going to die!'

It was the second time on this safari trip I knew I was going to die but this time I knew what was going to eat me – I could see them, lining the banks, licking their chops at the prospect of all this easy food. For them it must have been like sitting at one of those sushi bars where the nosh drifts by on a conveyor belt, while you make your mind up what you're going to eat.

I took a final glance at Carol as we started our plunge. I felt so bad that I'd dragged her into this. We'd had such a short time together. That short time had been fun; it had been more than fun– there had been some sublime moments, but now it was time to say 'Goodbye'.

The raft hurtled down. I could see no way in which we could come out of this. The nose of the rubber dirigible hammered into the curl at the bottom of the trough and my side went straight under the water; it was as if the craft had been stood up on its edge. I felt the water boiling and seething around me.

'So, this is what it's like,' I thought, quite calmly. A battering by an angry river and then oblivion.

Nevertheless, I tightened my grip on the rope at the side of the raft. Abruptly, it righted itself and we were on our way again. The near-death experience had lasted no more than three seconds. I looked across at Carol, who looked like the figurehead on the front of a clipper ship – a strong, proud and determined Wagnerian heroine. This effect was only slightly marred by her ill-chosen white jersey shorts, which were soaked and had become completely see-through, giving the boys further back in the craft a great view of her womanly curves. I, on the other hand, looked like a hairy dog that had been through a car-wash.

It was massively exhilarating to have been through and come out the other side but this rapid had been only the first of sixteen. Clearly,

Cephas had lined us up wrong for the first one, which wasn't encouraging, with runs with names like The Mother, or Highway to Hell or even The Washing Machine still to come.

It was only as we passed two capsized rafts and another stuck in a side stream that we realized Cephas must have been pretty good at his job.

We ran seven more rapids in quick succession, sometimes sideways, sometimes backwards, but always with a flourish. We grew more confident as we survived short violent drops, long turbulent flows and threshing cross-currents; our own addictive adrenalin juices were flowing and we had begun to look forward to the next buzz, when we found ourselves in a placid pool, just floating dreamily. We had stopped for lunch.

We pulled the raft right up on to the bank, which turned out to be a good move when out of nowhere a violent rainstorm hit us and as we scrambled for cover, a tiny stream dropping gently down the side of the gorge became a raging torrent, creating a flash flood, which carried most of our lunch out into the very murky Zambezi. In the way of tropical storms, it was all over in a few minutes.

While we were waiting to set off again – enthusiastic now – the capsized rafters turned up, full of tales of survival against incredible odds. We never saw the ones from the marooned raft, who'd had to be rescued. After the deluge, the river had reached its maximum safety height and we had to forego rapid number ten, The Mother, as it was deemed commercially unrunnable, but we survived the rest of them and came through to the end of our run soaked, battered and triumphant. After climbing almost vertically out of the gorge, we clambered aboard an ancient bench-seated truck to bump and rattle our way back to the Falls.

Carol and I were so elated by our success that we immediately signed up for more adventures on the Zambezi, hiring two kayaks with pilots for the trip upriver from the Falls. I suffered yet another dunking and near-death experience when my pilot and I capsized and instead of wriggling out in the way I'd been told, I found my legs stuck inside the little, upturned craft. Fatalistic once more, I contemplated a hippo ambling up the river bed and finding me hanging upside down like a pheasant on a butcher's hook.

It was the thought of not seeing Carol again that prompted me to another massive effort in which at last I yanked my legs free and I struggled to the surface with a gut full of finest Zambezi.

Recovering over a fitful night, we decided that this was enough excitement and it was time to go home. The trip had been a big decider for me. It had confirmed to me how happy I was to be with Carol – we'd shared and enjoyed so much together.

It had also persuaded me that I wanted to do all I could to help Tusk. I was mightily impressed with the practical, pragmatic way they went about their aims. They knew that a lot of the poaching of these seriously endangered species was possible only through the bribery and corruption that reached right up into Robert Mugabe's government. As one of the Tusk guys put it, 'What we're dealing with here is state-sponsored poaching.'

Shortly after Carol and I had got back to London, a herd of forty young bull elephants broke out of the reservation and, following a natural instinct to roam all over the country, eating as they went, they had completely destroyed and munched their way through several thousand hectares of tobacco (which must have produced one of the most gargantuan nicotine hits in history).

The farmer whose land it was couldn't shift them, and seeing his whole year's income ending up as large piles of steaming dung (with or without butterflies) he issued an ultimatum – either somebody moved them, or he would shoot them.

A herd of young bulls like this was essential to the health of the elephant population in Zimbabwe and Tusk had to respond. They needed aircraft, earth movers to herd the great animals, Land Rovers – a lot of tackle to persuade the unruly elephant youths to move back towards the safety of the reservation. And this would need a lot of money.

I was anxious to do what I could to help raise funds and awareness of the bigger picture regarding the loss of these wonderful creatures. I was very happy to find that I could deploy the huge and still growing popularity of *Only Fools & Horses* to great effect. By 'lending' *Boycie's* character to the cause I was able to find plenty of platforms from which to get the message across and journalists like Richard Littlejohn of the *Daily Mail* were hugely supportive, giving me a lot of space. Richard was kind of enough to say that although he'd seen plenty of 'celebrities' fronting up charity appeals, he thought I showed a true missionary zeal, which I certainly felt, about my tusked and trumpeting nicotine munchers.

I was immensely impressed by the way Tusk had responded and solved the problem. From then on, I became a committed supporter and I still am. As a charity they had been cleverly proactive by creating the individual sponsorship of particular animals, like mine of Edo the Elephant in Tsavo. Once people have been told what huge problems have been created by the reduction by human agricultural activity of the elephants' formerly vast territorial range, they are eager to respond, and helping to achieve this became and remains a part of my life, attracting several dodgy headlines over the years: BOYCIE'S OUT OF AFRICA, ELEPHANT BOYCIE and WHAT WOULD DEL AND RODDERS SAY ABOUT THIS DOWN THE NAG'S HEAD?

In fact, *Mike*, the landlord (Ken MacDonald) and *Trigger* (Roger Lloyd Pack) helped me out on several occasions, once, memorably, at London Zoo – which produced the headline – ONLY FOOLS AND TUSKERS.

Later that year, my agent had a call from Lee Dean, who'd been involved in the production of *The Rivals* when Sabina and I had appeared in it at Windsor. I was excited to be offered the chance to get back on the stage, this time in one of the great plays of the '60s – Joe Orton's *Entertaining Mr Sloane*. I loved the arch, sexual ambiguity of Orton's writing. I knew the part was right up my alley and something I'd always thought I'd like to do. I'd admired Harry Andrews' brilliant playing of it in the film version, with Beryl Reid and Peter McEnery. For this production, *Kath* (the Beryl Reid part) was to be played by none other than the legendary and much loved Barbara Windsor.

Before it was confirmed, I had to meet Lee Dean with Barbara and the director, John David at Joe Allen's in Covent Garden.

I hadn't met Barbara before but I found her very easy to get on with, as well as John David, and I went back to East Sheen to wait impatiently for my agent to call and say I had the part. Nothing happened.

I was astonished and a little devastated. Usually I'm philosophical about these things. I just shrug my shoulders, and try to move my focus on to the next prospect. This time I didn't. I really wanted the part; I was sure it was something I could do well. I rang my agent to ask her what had happened.

The response was deeply frustrating. She said they'd felt I was absolutely right for the part but thought an actor from *East Enders* would get more bums on seats.

I was mortified that the decision should be made like that. Besides – *Only Fools v. East Enders*? No contest, I thought. On the other hand, *East Enders* was on all year round, six days a week and had massive viewing figures, against maybe six or seven outings a year for our show (albeit sometimes with even bigger viewing figures.)

I gritted my teeth and tried hard to shrug my shoulders – a bit like trying to pat your head and rub your tummy in a circle. Quite apart from the acting required to play the part, it seemed a pretty tacky way to cast a show.

'But, hey! Gotta be a mango tree around here somewhere!' as they said in *Apocalypse Now*.

I was sitting with Carol in a fashionable coffee house in Covent Garden when I had an urgent call from my agent. How soon could I get to Bromley Theatre, she wanted to know. There had been a crisis with *Sloane*. The *East Enders* actor had had 'artistic differences' with the director and had left the production. Could I take over?

Could I? I was in Bromley by lunchtime!

Barbara looked mightily relieved. She said I had been her first choice all along.

'But you know,' she went on, 'It's all run by accountants these days.'

'More's the pity,' I agreed.

But the accountants needn't have worried. Barbara was such a national treasure in her own right that she packed them in – everyone, not just the chaps who remembered her bra flying off during PT sessions in *Carry on Camping*.

With Christopher Villiers as the wicked *Sloane* and Kenneth Waller who had been in the hit series *Bread*, as *Grandad*, we had a great cast and it remains one of the happiest jobs I've ever done.

Although throughout the run of the show Barbara was going through a dire emotional crisis at home, we swept 'em away, from Crewe to Brighton and back.

That's Entertainment

Reviewing the play in Brighton, Jack Tinker, well respected critic of the *Daily Mail*, described me as 'the most Ortonesque of all the characters', an ambiguous comment which I was happy to take as a compliment.

I received another compliment from an unlikely source when we played Croydon. After the show Barbara told me she wanted to meet a friend of hers in the bar afterwards. When I got there, she was talking to a short, stocky man with a pony tail and a bit of the gypsy about him. It was Charlie Kray, the only one of the three brothers still at large. It would have been a little unfair if he hadn't been at large, since, at that stage he hadn't been accused of anything.

Barbara, I gathered, went back a long way with the Krays. They loved being around show-biz and she, being from their bit of London, was considered almost one of their own.

Charlie looked up at me. ''Ere, you're a tall lad, aincher?' He looked as if he were measuring me for a coffin. 'We all love yer show, y'know. I'd like to buy you a drink.'

Although Charlie was generally considered to be the nicest, at any rate, the least evil of the three infamous brothers, I thought it probably not wise to refuse, although I found it a tad unsettling to picture him, Reggie and Ronnie with their mum, sitting around having a cup of tea and chortling away at *Only Fools & Horses*.

Our *Sloane* had been a good production with a great tour and now – the icing on the cake – it looked like transferring to the West End, just in time for the twenty-fifth anniversary of Joe Orton's death. However, before that could happen, with unkind irony, Barbara was offered the part of the landlady of the Queen Vic in *East Enders*. And I understood that for her, this trumped even a good play in the West End. I can't say I wasn't frustrated that one of the most satisfying shows I'd ever done should have been bracketed by disappoinment.

Still, as ever when Christmas was on the horizon, there was another *Only Fools* special to look forward to. Although we hadn't done a regular series for nearly two years and I had the feeling the Peckham saga was winding down, it seemed that John Sullivan was happy to concentrate on writing only the bigger shows that had become established in a regular Christmas slot. It gave him more scope to develop a plot, which he liked, but it could also lead to themes of a potentially dangerous complexity. *Fatal Extraction,* for example, strayed into the area of emotional domestic upheaval, with *Del Boy* and *Raquel's* relationship showing signs of cracking but somehow, John managed to keep all the threads together.

At the same time, David Jason wasn't so readily available. Not surprisingly, he had been poached by ITV, notably to play *Pop Larkin* in *The Darling Buds of May*, with Catherine Zeta Jones and Pam Ferris. *The Darling Buds,* based on H E Bates' hugely popular novels, was another big hit for David. With BAFTAS clogging up his mantelpiece, he had become the undeniable King of Comedy.

Reflecting on this, I was reminded of making an episode of *Only Fools* called *The Sky's the Limit. Boycie* had just acquired a new satellite dish, which he had installed in the back garden of his ersatz Georgian mansion in Peckham. In this scenario I not only had to deal with the dish, which was working independently of the remote, but also *Duke*, the Great Dane, who the script required to be galumphing all over the garden, while in fact he was completely comatose and could only be roused with the help of the furry microphone cover carried by the sound man. *Marlene* was there, of course, dressed in some animal print, pushing a pram in which sat the newly arrived *Tyler*, dressed in a miniature version of *Marlene's* outfit.

We had a lot of dialogue that had to be synched to the erratic movements of the satellite dish. It was going to be a tricky, nerve-wracking scene to do.

David, who always enjoyed a bit of a tease, drew up a chair beside the camera, rubbing his hands together in exaggerated expectation of a treat. 'This'll be good,' he announced with a smug chortle. 'I'm looking forward to this.'

'Thanks David,' I yelped, already pretty apprehensive, making it obvious, I thought, that I'd rather not have an audience at this moment. 'That'll be a great help.'

'No, no. I've got to be here. The John Challis School of Comedy – I might learn something!'

As we worked, I could see David looking at the monitors and making iffy hand gestures between takes. It was funny, sort of, and it was wicked – pure David.

By battening down our sensitivity hatches, Sue and I got through it. Now, looking back, I'm delighted he learned so much at the Challis

That's Entertainment

School of Comedy and went on to such great success. It's always gratifying to see one's ex-pupils do well.

Fatal Extraction drew only 19.6 million, half a million down on the previous Christmas's *Mother Nature's Son*, which some might have construed as slippage. In fact, it was still a monster figure and I was finding public recognition ever on the increase. I had by then become almost oblivious to the cries of 'Oi, Boycie! Where's Marlene?' from random members of the public. More challenging to deal with were persistent requests for *Boycie's* laugh, and I almost began to rue the day I'd invented it. It usually occurred in the show after one of *Boycie's* own jokes, like a short burst of machine gun fire with overtones of sheep in distress.

If I wasn't asked to do it, I often heard a version of it emanating from somewhere in the crowd at a football match or in a busy restaurant.

Most of the cast suffered from this kind of intrusion, but on the whole we took it light-heartedly – I certainly did, with an added sense of gratification.

Nicholas Lyndhurst told me once how he was walking down the High Street when a dodgy looking white-and-rust truck with a builder's stiff broom sticking up behind the cab had driven by, with the three lads in it hanging out of the windows, yelling, 'Oi, Rodney, you plonkah!' Next moment the truck ran straight into the back of a police car. That was fair enough, he thought.

After we had come back from our wonderful African trip, Carol and I had set about looking seriously for somewhere bigger to live. We soon found a semi-detached Edwardian villa in Deanhill Road, East Sheen that we both liked very much, while I sold the flat in Sheen Lane quite quickly and happily said goodbye to the remnants of my short-lived bachelor existence.

I needed to see the back of that period. Until Carol had become fully ensconced in my life I had been moving in bad areas after everything that had happened – divorce from Sabina, the stresses of life with Inge, the aloe-vera fiasco and my father's painful passing. I knew I'd been living badly but it took Carol's warm, steadying influence on me to find some kind of equilibrium again.

Carol didn't drink, for a start, which changed the shape of pub hours and my drinking habits completely. As someone once said: 'Pubs are full of women with a past and men with no future.'

The Coach & Horses, by far my most regular watering hole at the time, was usually full of seriously competitive drinkers. They might have come in for a couple with the boys before they staggered back to the wife and kids. Inevitably it was often more than a couple and the announcement of an early departure would provoke howls of laughter and unattractive renditions of the Stones' *Under My Thumb*. It wasn't healthy or, as Carol would say, a 'good look', and I was beginning to realize that I would have to excise this part of my life routine.

It didn't happen overnight and during the first couple of years of our relationship, I was guilty of some spectacular back-sliding in the booze department as the old habits found it hard to die.

After one particularly good tennis morning, to which I'd ridden on my bike from Deanhill Road, I went with my opponents to slake our thirst at the Bull, overlooking the Boat Race course at Barnes. The Bull was a jazz pub where I'd spent a lot of time in the old trad-jazz days. On this occasion they were showing an England v South Africa rugby international that was being played a few miles up river at Twickenham. After a tough match, England won. There was dancing in the pub, in Barnes High Street, all the way back to the Coach & Horses, which invited more celebration and the party carried on to a point where time had become meaningless.

Through a euphoric haze, I became dimly aware that I should have gone home for some reason – perhaps dinner – I couldn't recall. I did manage, though, to ring Carol on the pub pay-phone and say I'd be back in fifteen minutes – after all, I blathered, I wouldn't have to drive because, with astute foresight, I'd come on my bike.

I extracted a fellow tennis player, Jim, who had also come by bike and we tried to mount up. Neither of us could stay upright on our bikes and after falling off a few times, we gave up and wheeled them in the direction of Jim's house, which, it turned out, he had lost.

Luckily he recognized a pub near where he lived and we went in to ask directions to his home. It seemed impolite not to have a nightcap with him, especially as it turned out to be only seven o'clock. When I left him there twenty minutes or so later, I set off with my bike for home, not entirely certain of where I was.

By nine o'clock, I learned later, I had made thirteen phone calls home, offering profuse apologies, undying love, proposals of marriage and an account of an attack with my umbrella on someone whose views I had challenged.

Although Carol welcomed me back and laughed hysterically while she watched me trying to put my bike back in its shed, I knew that things would have to change. I was slowly coming to realize that there was something worth saving and looking after here.

I didn't stop playing tennis but I slowly managed to wean myself from the *craic* that followed and from a series of ancillary tennis, snooker and drinking trips to Dorset that one of my fellow players liked to arrange.

The great sober – or, at least, not entirely drunk – period of my life had begun.

Chapter 11
The Triumph of Hope

Just after New Year 1994, Carol and I were visited in Deanhill Road by two Nicks, Brooke and Mattingly, who had formed Baroque Productions, to put on theatrical shows. Brooke was a producer; Nick Mattingly I knew as the lighting designer at Sonning Mill, and he spoke very passionately of their plans for Baroque. Their first project was a musical called *Maria Marten*, a reworking of the Victorian melodrama, *Murder in the Red Barn*. In a glossy brochure they had included the outline and a few of the musical numbers. The story explored the possibility that the infamous *William Corder* had not murdered the breathless innocent *Maria*, but was, in fact, a scapegoat. It was mooted that the real villain of the piece was the local squire, who had much to lose in the awful scandal that followed.

They made me an attractive offer to play *Beauty Smith*, a rumbustious, larger-than-life character at the centre of the action.

Although I would have liked to have seen more of the finished product, the producers evidently knew what they were doing, and I was interested. I'd done the original play over 25 years before in Chesterfield with Jon Finch playing *Corder*. (I recalled him making an entrance at a tense and crucial moment in the story, when he announced: 'My name is William Corder, and what's more – I'm pissed.' But I digress.)

Brooke and Mattingly also offered Carol the job of wardrobe mistress, which was a good move and very much in her comfort zone. She had run her own costume business in the '80s that supplied mostly amateur companies with costumes for *Gilbert & Sullivan* shows – the same period as *Maria Marten*.

They explained that the writer, Trevor Pilling, was still developing the script and the final product would be something very special. They also had on board my old friend Jean Fergusson (now established in *Last of the Summer Wine*) and Nula Conwell who'd made a name for herself in *The Bill*. David Kelsey was to direct.

We both signed up to work together for the first (and by no means the last) time and drove up to Lincoln for the start of a six-to-eight week tour.

The Triumph of Hope

I was mildly alarmed to find that not a lot had happened to improve the script or the construction of the narrative of the show and we could see that David Kelsey was struggling with the material. He wasn't well either and was having trouble trailing up and down the hills of Lincoln, from where he was staying up near the cathedral to where we were rehearsing at the bottom of the hill by the river. Carol, trouper that she soon showed herself to be, did what she could to help him, doing his washing and feeding him.

The first sign that Baroque Productions was not a fit and proper organisation cropped up when, halfway through rehearsals, two thirds of the cast didn't get paid. For a number of the younger actors, this was their first venture after drama school and a rough introduction to the notoriously unstable world of the theatre. The problem was quickly resolved but it was an early- warning sign that the mechanism of the show was not running smoothly.

It was then that Martyn Rose, part lawyer, part fixer, part Rottweiler and part of the production team, appeared on the scene. Like his partners, he could talk the talk and said he was big fan of *Only Fools*.

'Don't worry, my son,' he quelled my suspicions. 'Everything's in place; all the theatres in the tour have guaranteed us our money.'

I relaxed. With guarantees in place, we couldn't run into too much trouble.

Shortly after we had opened in Lincoln, I was strongly reminded of how much *Only Fools* had become embedded in my life. Carol and I were having a final drink in a big pub after the show one evening, when an excited young man came up to us.

'This must be my lucky day!' he gulped breathlessly. 'I've just got hitched; this is the end of the party – we always finish up in the pub. Anyway my girlfriend – er – sorry – my *wife*, she'd never forgive me if she heard that! – She loves *Boycie*. Would you creep up behind her and say her favourite line? *'Stand aside, I am a doctor. Let the dog see the rabbit!'* If you did, she'd be made up!'

He was so animated, I couldn't turn him down. I raised an eyebrow at Carol and wandered over to deliver the line from a favourite episode, *The Chain Gang*.

I stood behind her, and as I got to '...*see the rabbit*,' she stood up, looked around, saw me and collapsed in a total faint. Unfortunately, on the way down, she hit her head on the table.

'Christ!' I thought. 'This only happens with people like Elvis!'

In fact, she was probably already quite drunk, and after much confusion and consternation, the poor girl was carried out, muttering incoherently.

A couple of days later, I saw the young man in the same pub and solicitously asked after his wife.

'She's fine, mate. Thanks for ruining my wedding night!'

Maria Marten, having got off to a shaky start in Lincoln, went downhill in the next leg of the tour at Southsea, in the King's, once a fine old Matcham Variety Theatre, now a sad reflection on the decline of live theatre over the previous 30 years. The King's Theatre was a magnificent, indulgent Victorian structure, with some handsome Edwardian embellishments. It was full of corridors, balconies, faded plush and peeling murals and could seat over two thousand people. However, the Gods had been closed for years and the place was only ever full for acts like Ken Dodd and then for one night only.

Our mish-mash of a musical with a few names off the telly arrived there and tried to fill it for a week and failed hopelessly, which was when the money ran out.

Nick Brooke and Martyn Rose came to me cap in hand and said we'd have to close unless somebody stumped up some cash to keep it going.

There is a golden rule in investment, which is never to put your money into failing ventures. In fact after my experience with the aloe-vera farm, I should have adjusted that to never put your money into any kind of venture.

But I couldn't bear the thought of the show closing and putting all the young hopefuls out of work in their first job. With a firm promise that I would be paid back, with interest, Frank Jarvis – another member of the company – and I came up with the wonga.

It probably goes without saying that I never saw any of the money again, let alone interest.

I did wonder at the time why Martyn Rose, who was keen to tell anyone how much money he had made as a lawyer, hadn't come up with the money himself. I guessed he'd had other things to spend it on since, when I heard he'd bought himself one of those 'Lordships of the Manor' you can buy on eBay, and styled himself Lord Rose of Asheldham.

We struggled on until the show breathed its last and was laid to rest in Poole, Dorset, where Matthew Kelly came along to see us and confirmed what we were no longer in doubt over – that the show just didn't work, and was probably beyond repair.

It was a shame because it had been the germ of a very good idea and, properly nurtured, it could have turned into something special. But that's often the way with rare orchids and theatrical musicals.

At least the absence of a show, or anything much else for the next few months, gave Carol and me a chance to bed ourselves in, as it were, in Deanhill Road, while I wondered what was going on with *Only Fools*. People were constantly asking me what was going to happen next. Was there another series?

I simply didn't know. There were rumours leaking from John Sullivan's camp and the BBC that it was going to end with *Del* and *Rodney* becoming millionaires and sailing off into the sunset but we were sworn to secrecy.

By this stage, anyway, Sullivan was busy writing a new series, *Roger, Roger*, about a minicab firm, which eventually went to pilot a couple of years later. David Jason was at Yorkshire TV having great success with *Frost*, a gruff, old-school detective, with just enough of David's personal idiosyncrasies to delight his many fans. Nick Lyndhurst was involved with Marks and Gran's *Goodnight Sweetheart,* which was also a great success and ran to six series.

The general feeling was that *Only Fools* had reached its apogee in the late eighties and the world had moved on, and so had we. We weren't, after all, getting any younger.

In 1995, before spring had arrived, Carol and I agreed we'd had enough of the English winter and we both wanted to get away for a while. I suggested we kill two birds by flying to Portugal, already warming up, to see what had happened to my aloe-vera investment.

This, of course, didn't really offer the right ingredients for a happy carefree holiday but at least it provided some justification for the trip. I'd had several phone conversations with Michael Slater, which hadn't encouraged much optimism. He had sounded shifty and nervous, and let slip that he and his wife Alison had split up.

That didn't surprise me. I'd always thought Alison far too much of a 'good egg' and genuine person for a devious philanderer like Slater. As a man, I'd usually found Slater good company, until you needed to rely on him for anything, when exchanges would be accompanied by the sound of scurrying feet and hastily closed doors.

Carol and I arrived in Portugal to find he'd been shacked up with a rich ex-pat in Lagoa, who'd soon rumbled him and thrown him out. He was clearly on his uppers and didn't look as if he were in a position to write a cheque for a tenner, let alone all the money he owed me.

After trying to winkle the truth from all his obfuscation and convoluted bullshit, I gathered that he had built up his own little consortium, with money from several of his mates, including poor Alison's father, and used that to buy his partnership with the Dutchman. Since then no divis had been paid to him or anyone else, and he'd been conned along with his investors. I soon learned that the others had backed out and written off their money, while, according to Slater, the Dutchman had organized the whole thing so that only he knew where the money was. I went to see the Dutchman myself. He shrugged his shoulders quite a lot, while shaking his head with regret. He said he had no idea Slater had borrowed all the money he had put in. I wondered what difference that made.

Slater claimed that he had started legal proceedings against his 'partner', but was looking at years of frustrating litigation, Portuguese law being a notoriously lethargic beast.

It was some measure of his own desperate straits that he was seriously trying to become an actor. To this end, he told me, he had joined a local amateur drama group. I went to see him in a show and suggested afterwards that a thespian career might not be the quickest way out of his hole. In the meantime, although very wary about being sued by anyone himself, he agreed to let me have a legal confirmation of the amount I had invested through him. I didn't think it would help much. I never received it anyway.

We saw him a couple more times, at a distance in Lagoa but he ran away before we could catch him.

I shrugged my shoulders. While we're in Portugal, I thought, I may as well show Carol around some of the quaint and beautiful places I got to know on my previous visits, and, as always, we got the most out of our time together there, although the trip won't go down as the jolliest we've ever had. Back in England, snippets of unhopeful information continued to dribble back from Portugal. Slater was under suspicion of being involved in an art theft; he'd had his passport confiscated.

After the trip, I'd bitten the bullet and mentally written off the money I'd given him and put it down to a little life education.

My sense of loss, anyway, was diminished by the early summer, when I found myself doing two jobs at the same time. The first one came about through Nick Angell, who ran Angell Sound where I'd been doing voice-overs for years. He and a BBC producer had heard that Auntie was looking for presenters to fill the well-named graveyard slot – 4.00 to 6.00 am – on BBC Radio Two. Nick immediately thought of me, he said, although that was probably because I was the next person to walk through the door.

He put it to me. Idler that I am, I loved the idea of sitting in a studio for maybe two hours a day, playing all the music I liked, chatting to interesting hand-picked guests and generally offering my thoughts and views on anything I liked to millions of enthralled listeners.

Nick and the producer put together a short demo of me doing the job, JC - DJ. We cobbled together a few ideas, with a bit of *Boycie*, a call on the appropriate music sources and produced a ten-minute sampler. We sent it off, without any great hopes – at least on my part – and didn't hear anything until a month or so later, when we got a call. 'Yes, we like it. When can you start?'

That was a shock. I hadn't thought at all how I was going to fill two whole hours – even at that ungodly hour of the morning.

For a start, although I'd gamely volunteered to choose all the music for the show, I soon realized that most of the stuff I wanted to play was miles from Radio Two's play-list. Besides, I was a technical moron and hadn't a clue how to deal with all the knobs, faders, dials, woofers and tweeters. I'd no idea what I was going to talk about but the next thing I knew, we were on. Luckily, Nick Angell was as excited – more so, in fact – as I was. It would be, after all, an Angell Sound production. We got down to work, with Nick picking me up at three in the morning in his Porsche Carrera and we hurtled through the deserted London streets like a couple of late-night hell-raisers, to arrive at Broadcasting House, nodded in by surprisingly alert commissionaires – old soldiers mostly, I was told – even before the rosy-fingered dawn had got a grip on Upper Regent Street.

I wasn't a natural, though. At first I was terrible; being an actor I tended to 'act' what I thought a real DJ would say and do – like Tony Blackburn with added syrup – and was hopelessly naff. When I came 'off script' and started improvizing, I found myself rambling around in circles, which drove the producers mad as they waited vainly for their cues. But quite quickly, I sort of got the hang of it. The *Boycie* bits worked well enough and some of the features we'd invented zipped along – an up-the-garden-path competition, a tongue-in-cheek sports feature, and a slot in which I talked to other people who were up and about at that time of the 'morning'.

The trouble was that it wasn't really working in conjunction with the other job I'd landed, appearing in two plays running in tandem at the Regent's Park Open Air Theatre – a summer festival always including a Shakespeare play and usually a musical of some sort. I was to play *Lord Stanley* in *Richard III*, directed by Brian Cox, a well-regarded Scottish actor who was also starring as *Harold Hill*, the main role in Meredith Willson's *The Music Man*, directed by Ian Talbot.

It was hard enough during preparation, working at the Beeb from sparrow-fart to six, then rehearsing all day, and worse during the performances, doing the shows at night then getting up a few hours later to go back to work as a DJ.

Theatre in the open air can be wonderful, and I expect it was in ancient Greece and Rome where they went in for this a lot, but, of course, they had the weather for it.

In England, it's wonderful too, when conditions are right – mainly because that's so bloody rare. Working in Ludlow Castle, for example, when nothing is stirring inside the vast stone walls and the swifts are sporting across a cerulean, then rosy sky, is utterly magical: when it rains, it's hell.

The same applies to Regent's Park, with the added sporadic irritation of extraneous sounds of helicopters, lawnmowers and motorbikes revving around the Inner Circle, as well as occasional animal noises drifting in the wind from London Zoo. And in one instance, as we fifteenth-century barons stood in a group, planning our next coup, while the rain trickled down our necks, under our costumes into our boots, a trio of ducks waddled across the stage, quacking furiously.

Seasoned sado-masochistic watchers of open-air theatre would naturally come prepared with waxed ponchos and hats or – less elegantly – black plastic rubbish bags with Tesco bags for hats and would sit there steadfastly in a steady downpour, daring us to leave the stage. We would continue until a sepulchral voice from behind the audience intoned: 'Would the actors kindly leave the stage?'

'No love, not you. He said actors,' giggled the mischievous Harriet Thorpe, playing *Elizabeth Woodville*.

It was a good cast, with *Lady Anne* played by the very lovely Natascha McElhone, who went on to star in Hollywood movies and a major US networked sitcom, *Californication,* while Jasper Britton (son of Tony, brother of Fern) brilliantly played the eponymous *Dick*, with the help of a useful limp he'd acquired in a road accident a few years before. It says something for Carol's trust in me that she had (at least, expressed) no objections when I got into the routine of dropping Natascha off every night after the show. Carol was right, of course. I was untouchable, refusing any offers of coffee on delivery.

Alongside Brian Cox in *The Music Man,* the part of *Marian Paroo* was played by the classy Liz Robertson, who had starred in many West End Musicals. I played *Mayor Shinn,* a dyed-in-the-wool martinet who wouldn't allow anything remotely anarchic to interfere with his idea of how a respectable Iowa community should be run. The production was a great success and we took it on to Edinburgh and the Yvonne Arnaud in Guildford, while it transpired that my career as a BBC disc jockey had run its course after just eight weekly sessions, never to be repeated (although naturally, I live in hope – not!)

In June 1995, the Government had recently announced that marriages could now take place in venues other than churches or register offices. One of the first places to apply and be granted a licence for holding weddings was the wonderful Regency fantasy of Brighton Pavilion. The third wedding to take place there, on 2 June was between one John Spurley Challis and his bride, Carol Ann Davies, née Palmer.

It was, unlike my previous three marriages, a quiet, unrowdy event, witnessed only by my good friends Keith Washington and Madeleine Howard. They were almost as happy as me to see me married again.

Carol looked truly magnificent in a cream suit and whacking great hat that made her six inches taller than me. I was dark-suited, and bearded, due to being *Lord Stanley* in Regent's Park. There was another show that evening, so after a good lunch at Pinnochio's, an Italian restaurant near the theatre, we all drove back to London.

Despite the understated nature of our wedding day, it has turned out to be, without doubt, the most significant day of my life, which was completely changed for ever after by my own unconditional commitment to Carol and hers to me.

Remarriage is often referred to as the triumph of hope over experience and in my case, with three failures behind me, that hope had to be pretty strong – much stronger than I could have imagined possible four years earlier, when my life was running on empty and booze was filling the void.

Although, in theory, I'd always thought I valued the feeling of being alone and free of relationships and commitment, I simply wasn't good at it. Besides I also needed a chum, a mate to share my experiences. Up until now, though, I'd been very inept in selecting those with whom to do my sharing. Although it is often said that an actor without a wife or a mortgage is best placed to take advantage of all the opportunities that come his (or her) way, in my view, that actor would also miss out on a lot of real life.

For the first time in a long time, I could stand back, look at myself objectively and say I was happy. Of course, there are always things that actors think they should be doing and jobs they should be getting when they're not but I also knew that life couldn't have been better for me at this stage. Being with Carol had successfully hauled me right out of the doldrums in which I'd been floating for two or three catastrophic years. I'd enjoyed doubling up as a Beeb DJ while playing in Regent's Park and then at the Yvonne Arnaud, and, although *Only Fools* had been shoved onto the back burner, it was still on the stove and the rumours of a return and the eventual resolution to the *Trotter* brothers' perpetual frustration were stronger than ever.

I was sanguine about it. Being with Carol had made me more relaxed and circumspect. As far as I was concerned, marriage to her was an unqualified success. 'At last!' I sometimes said to myself, looking back on the three previous failures. Carol and I had so much in common and, very importantly, the same sense of humour. Once we had moved into Deanhill Road, we spent half our time happily beavering away tarting up the house and sorting out the overgrown garden. The other half of the time was spent working, for me, with voices (as usual) and a new production of Tom Stoppard's *On the Razzle* which those of you who have read *Being Boycie*, the first half of this little memoir, will know, I'd appeared in when it was first produced at the National.

This time it was to be at the Nuffield Theatre in Southampton and I was playing the lead, *Herr Zangler* (which Dinsdale Landen had played in the original show.) I was chuffed to be asked for my suggestions for some of the casting. I managed to find roles for Madeleine Howard and Beverley Francis. I could just see Madeleine in the elegant Viennese fashion of the period. Beverley Walden, as she was known, was married to Richard Francis, a silver dealer I'd got to know during the period when I was messing about with antiques with Sabina and her mother and she revelled as I did in Stoppard's lyrical joke fest. I also managed to wangle parts for quite a few of the cast from the distressingly flopped *Maria Marten*.

Doing *Razzle* was a joy, as it had been at the National but this time I had the part that drove the show. I made the most of it and it went very well.

Tom Stoppard's secretary came to see it. Stoppard himself followed this up with a letter, saying he'd heard great reports of Patrick Sandford's production and he was delighted to think of 'Zangler and co whooping it up at the Nuffield.'

I'd run into Stoppard earlier in the year in bizarre circumstances, which showed me how the few instances of closeness that he and I had shared at a critical time in his life in New York, (just before *Night and Day* arrived there for the first time and raised his stock to giddy heights), had subsequently dissipated.

Carol and I were waiting with a few rowdy friends in the foyer of the Hammersmith Odeon to see Bob Dylan in concert. I spotted Tom, in '*I'm not really here*' mode, lurking by the box office. The concert was a sell-out, and Tom evidently had some tickets he didn't need and was trying to dispose of them. This was a perfectly reasonable thing to want to do, especially with tickets going at a heavy premium but he looked very put out to have been found doing it himself.

I was certainly very surprised and reacted clumsily, saying something crass like, 'So, this is what you're up to now.'

One of my friends, already drunk, lurched over to us. 'Well look who we've got here,' he bellowed. 'Amazing who you find at a Dylan gig!'

I tried to introduce them but Stoppard had fled.

It was an embarrassing encounter all round and I was sad that the strong connection I thought we'd made when we'd been working together ten years before seemed to have had no real basis.

Bob Dylan, by the way, whom I'd never really liked, was a big disappointment. Even after all those years of practice, he still couldn't play the mouth-organ.

Chapter 12
Swan Song?

Part of 1996 was taken up with making two musicals for the BBC, a job which I got through David Kelsey who'd come in to try to sort out *Maria Marten* a couple of years before. First I did *Guys & Dolls* with Mandy Patinkin, Anita Dobson and Claire Brown. Mandy is often cited as the greatest interpreter ever of Sondheim. He asked me if I was happy with his acting.

'You're acting's fine,' I assured him. 'It's your singing I'm worried about.'

Luckily, he laughed. It was so great to be doing this show with Mandy, I could hardly believe I was doing it.

Then Brian Pringle and I played the two hoodlums in *Kiss Me Kate* and sang 'Brush up your Shakespeare' together.

Sadly, although I was really enjoying myself with this kind of work and I was in no doubt that I'd done the right thing in marrying Carol, I was still drinking too much. Maybe I just thought it was all too good to last. It was as if I were deliberately clinging on to the Old Me, the former philanderer, the actor who could go out and meet his friends for a binge whenever he felt like it, the free agent who needed no one's permission to be where he wanted to be. It seemed there was an old devil inside me which I thought had been exorcized when I'd married Carol but was still hanging on in there, demanding attention.

Now I found myself pouring a few stiff whiskies long before the sun was over the yard-arm, followed by a trip to the CD player for a few favourite rowdy tracks – The Stones' 'Honky Tonk Women', Ian Hunter's 'Once Bitten Twice Shy', or Three Dog Night's 'Mama Told Me Not To Come', always at full blast. I would stagger back to the kitchen in Deanhill Road to find Carol.

'Come on darling,' I'd burble. 'Lez dance!'

Carol wasn't impressed. 'You only ever ask me to dance when you're pissed.'

'Pissed? Me, pissed?' Don't be ridiculous! If you don't want to dance, I'll find someone who will! I'm going out...' I lifted an unsteady eyebrow... 'and I may be some time.' ...followed by exit through back door, trip over cat and flowerpots, blunder round garden, stagger back to door, slump inside and collapse on chair at kitchen table in state of gloomy self-loathing as I wondered why anyone would put up with this kind of behaviour and for how long. Thank God these last convulsions of my departing inner devil didn't last forever and became rarer, especially as the happy reality of life with Carol sank in.

Towards the end of 1996, Tony Dow and Gareth Gwenlam assembled the whole team to record what we assumed would be the last ever three specials of *Only Fools & Horses,* to be run on three separate nights over the Christmas holiday. It felt quite strange to be preparing a swan song, although we'd all accepted that the show had to come to an end some time and that it would be better to finish on a high, rather than let it trickle away into oblivion as our hair became more silver and our teeth less abundant. But it was damned hard to let go.

The show had come to mean so much to so many people and all the main characters had become household names. We'd all been part of making it what it was and wondered if ending it now would consign us all to the scrap heap.

'Sorry, love, the show's over. So is your career, by the way.'

It didn't feel like that, though. David and Nick, obviously, had had plenty of other starring roles during the fifteen-year run of the series, while Roger Lloyd Pack had had great success with his part in Dawn French's *Vicar of Dibley,* as well as innumerable acclaimed stage appearances. Ken, Paul and I all had other avenues opening up.

Besides, as Kenny MacDonald optimistically declared: 'Anyway, we'll *never* be off, son. They'll open a new channel called BBC No Choice and we'll be on non-stop – trust me! I'm an actor.' How prescient this turned out to be. Since the BBC's UK Gold arrived, we've been on practically every day of the year.

The three 60-minute specials, comprising a continuous story, were to be shown on 25, 27 and 29 December. The first of them, *Heroes and Villains* contains one of the great set pieces of the series, when *Del* and *Rodney,* dressed as Batman and Robin, run down the street, late for a party, and accidentally stop a mugging that's in progress. When they reach the party, they're greeted by a smirking *Boycie* who has 'forgotten' to tell them that the host had died that morning and the party has become a wake.

'Must have completely slipped my mind,' *Boycie* says, as *Del,* in shock, presses the button on his aerosol fun-foam can.

It was a sensational piece of comedy drama and John Sullivan reluctantly confessed afterwards that he thought he would never write anything as good again.

He may have been right. This was the episode in which everything came together – his hero, *Del* was a universal character with whom all but the most smug and self-righteous could in some part identify, with his struggle to be somebody, a winner, a significant man of affairs. He *was* a contender, not a bum, like Marlon Brando in *On the Waterfront*, and every time he got knocked down, he got up again and was in there, pitching away, never giving up. *Heroes and Villains*, shown at 9pm on Christmas Day, pulled 21.3 million viewers, the best we had ever scored.

The story continues with *Modern Men*, in which Rodney's wife Cassandra miscarries their longed-for baby. There's a much-loved scene in the hospital, in which *Del* tells *Rodney* to 'stand up, be a man and take it on the chin,' before bursting into tears himself.

Two days later the third and final part was shown. Everyone knew the series was going to end but no one knew how. The bookies, nearly always reliable in these things, made the favourite option that of *Del* and *Rodney* finally becoming millionaires, as *Del* had so often predicted.

But they didn't know how that was going to happen.

Naturally, everyone on the show knew but had been sworn to the strictest secrecy, as, indeed, we had been for the *Batman and Robin* sequence in the first of the three.

The press have their ways of discovering people's secrets (as Lord Leveson has discovered) but John Sullivan was taking no chances. He was desperate to keep everything a surprise for the viewers. Lookouts were posted and decoys deployed. While filming the scene in *Boycie's* showroom in Bristol, where *Rodney* buys a Roller for *Del*, the production team were worried about a sudden increase in helicopter flights. We all assumed that they were press, as they must have known we were filming something, somewhere.

John, as always, came up with a great, unexpected twist to bring the thing to a climax. He produces *Raquel's* dad, *James Turner*, played by Michael Jayston (whom I'd met at the RSC years before and subsequently played cricket with).

Mr and Mrs Turner come to dinner at Nelson Mandela House. It is not a great success, but the next day, when *James* comes back to collect his car, he finds *Del* and *Rodney* rummaging around in their lock up. *Mr T* is an antique dealer, programmed to seek and find hidden bargains and he is very impressed to find an unusual watch that the brothers had acquired in a house clearance some 16 years before. He realizes that it may well be the long-lost, incredibly valuable Harrison Marine Watch. *Del* and *Rodney* take it off to Sotheby's who authenticate it and auction it for £6.2 million.

Once the extraordinary truth has sunk in, the *Trotters* go straight round to *Boycie's* garage to buy a Rolls Royce and then to the Nag's Head. As they make their entrance into the bar, they are greeted by a moment's silence, until *Denzil* starts clapping, followed swiftly by everyone else, except *Boycie*. Eventually, even *Boycie* joins in and there is a wonderful moment as *Del* looks up at *Boycie*, who murmurs through gritted teeth, 'Well done, Trotter,' while *Mike*, behind the bar yells, 'Drinks on the house!' followed by a great scramble for the free drinks.

The brothers are ecstatic for a few weeks, but having got themselves big, plush houses and posh cars, they are soon bored, with nothing to strive and duck and dive for, until *Del* decides that with their new-found wealth, they can take on the big boys in the financial-futures market.

As they walk off into the sunset, *Del* is back to his old, optimistic self.

'This time next year, Rodney, we'll be billionaires!'

John Sullivan had made a grand job of this final episode, carried off with his customary ability to stay true to the characters, even in this fantasy sequence and everyone was left feeling very emotional.

We finished the studio scenes at the point where *Mike* has announced drinks on the house, after which, the audience rose to their feet and gave us a standing ovation... the only time this has been heard of at the BBC. We were overcome, and stood there awkwardly, not knowing what to do, whether to embrace or cry.

We men were disinclined to do either (this was, after all, back in the '90s) but there were plenty of damp cheeks among our female colleagues.

Swan Song?

Time on Our Hands pulled in an audience of 24.3 million – a new record for a comedy programme on British TV.

The evening of transmission, I was rung by several showbiz hacks for my reaction to this amazing statistic. I hadn't seen it go out, because I was otherwise engaged in another pantomime at Redhill in Surrey. This show featured Christopher Beeny, the original footman in *Upstairs Downstairs*, as director and dame, *Sarah the Cook*, along with Christopher Timothy, best known as *James Herriot*. My role was *King Rat*, another romantic lead in the popular *Dick Whittington*. *Dick* himself was played by Mark Speight, who couldn't sing, so had to have his numbers sung by another member of cast off-stage, as he mimed his intention of getting down to London with his cat.

It wasn't his fault – just a matter of lack of communication in the heat of the moment, when his agent had told the producer that Mark could *probably* sing, if pushed, but would rather not. This evidently got lost in translation and came out, 'Oh yes, he can sing!'

But in any case, Mark was very popular with the kids for his extraordinary talent for producing instant pictures with whatever was at hand – paintbrush, charcoal, or just pieces of material. I noticed that he seemed quite tense during the whole run of the show and didn't seem to be enjoying it at all. I was very sad, a few years later, to hear confirmation of his unhappiness at that time, and his eventual suicide.

The fifth 'name' on the *Dick Whittington* bill was *Nightshade* from the show *Gladiators*. This was, in theory, an interesting addition. However, it soon became clear that *Ms Nightshade* had the greatest of difficulty adhering to the simplest of theatre disciplines, like – for example – arriving on time.

Traditionally the cast always turn up to a show at least half an hour before curtain up in case some glitch has cropped up – like the *Principal Boy* drowning – and alternative plans have to be made.

Nightshade often arrived five minutes before the show started, however much she was begged to come earlier. By way of explanation, she said she was 'trying to have a baby,' which invited some vivid speculation.

My first reaction on hearing we were being joined by *Gladiator Nightshade* was that at least she would know how to fight. But no.

She couldn't, as they say, have hit a barn door with a Howitzer.

In a carefully-choreographed fight between *King Rat* and the avenging *Nightshade*, a battle using king-sized cotton buds, I had to improvise every performance as she always forgot the routine and exposed herself to serious injury – from me?

'What's it like battling with *Nightshade*?' a punter asked me after the show one night. 'Deadly,' I quipped in a fit of honesty.

Nightshade may not have been enjoying the show, but plenty of the punters were – one gang especially, the Boycie Appreciation Society, whose members had come from as far as Scotland and Swansea, all moustachioed and dressed in shiny suits with loud tasteless ties. They all held between thumb and forefinger an unlit slim panatella and carried an empty plastic brandy glass. They sat in the second row, cheering uproariously when *King Rat* appeared and booing vigorously at the *Good Fairy*. Apart from that, they behaved impeccably and when I met them afterwards they were tremendously polite, even deferential, promising not to bother me again. I was flattered that they had gone to so much trouble.

I told the story of the Boycie Appreciation Society to a hack from one of the tabloids who had come round seeking a quote about the *Only Fools* final viewing figures. It was met with open-mouthed disbelief. Now this kind of thing is quite common at big events – a gang of robed and bearded Osama bin Ladens showed up at an Arsenal game, after a rumour had taken hold that Al Qaeda's dear leader was a Gooner and had been spotted at Highbury's Clock End. And I was amused to see on TV a few years later at Glastonbury festival a large cohort of men wearing beards and cork-dangling hats mustering to mob up their hero, Rolf Harris.

Chapter 13
Fresh Fields

After the exertions of *King Rat* in *Dick Whittington* and trying to fight with *Nightshade*, Carol agreed that a change of scene, an easy time and a dose of Mr Sun would do us both good. Taking advantage of the fact that we always seemed to enjoy the same things, we booked ourselves a Swann Hellenic cruise on the *Minerva*, a rather beautiful ship which was sailing from Singapore to Colombo, taking in the surrounding islands and countries of the eastern Indian Ocean. After a cultural feast in exotic places previously unknown to either of us, and almost overstuffed with fresh knowledge, we returned happy but a little reluctantly to our home in the suburbs.

In contrast to the wide-open views of the Far East, our own surroundings in Richmond, although comfortable and convenient, seemed to be closing in on us. It had been announced that the parking in our bijou cul-de-sac was to be controlled, the Upper Richmond Road was made a 'Red Route' and the graffiti that had first started appearing at Mortlake Station was creeping down the District Line towards us. We recognized that the writing was, so to speak, on the walls, which seemed to be closing in on us. It was then that we began to feel twitchy and the idea of moving out of London first took root.

In the meantime, though, I had more work to do.

As I may have remarked earlier in these memoirs, one of the undeniable advantages of being in one of the most popular TV shows of all time is that quite a few doors are opened to one – at least, one tends to be closer to the thinking part of a producer's mind – in this case, early in 1997, in the active little bonce of producer/impresario, Paddy Wilson.

Paddy was putting together an interesting cast to tour Neil Simon's excellent play, *Laughter on the 23rd Floor* which had just finished a good run in the West End with Gene Wilder in the lead role. The play was a partly autobiographical piece by Simon, loosely based on his own experiences of being in a group of writers working for the American comic, Sid Caesar.

Caesar (Sid, not Julius) had a top-rated US TV show during the

'60s, and there'd been heavy pressure on the gag-writers to come up with an endless supply of good, fresh material. Simon had written a wonderfully funny account of how it played out in the Writers' Room.

Our *Sid Caesar* was the well-known and highly regarded Frank Finlay. Years before at the *Old Vic*, Finlay had made a lasting impression on me when I'd seen him play a disturbingly convincing *Iago* to Laurence Olivier's *Othello*. Also in our cast was Sandra Dickinson, bright, blonde and bubbly. Paddy had signed up one of Britain's best character actors, Peter Polycarpou, who'd been in some great musicals as well as Marks and Gran's *Birds of a Feather*. He was playing *Ira Stone*, who was approximately Mel Brooks, another of Caesar's scribblers. Then there was this bloke from *Only Fools & Horses*, playing *Milt Field*, probably based on Simon himself.

This production offered me a nice opportunity to indulge in snappy, New York patois. Frank produced a hilariously irascible *Caesar* and Peter a ludicrous, hypochondriac *Stone*, who nearly stole the show. He had some great lines: on one occasion, to *Milt* (for some reason – perhaps aping Tom Wolfe – always dressed in a white suit), 'Milt, will ya sit down; you look like the entrance to the White House.'

Despite these stand-out individuals, it was a team effort, with several members of the cast from the London production, who brought with them a terrific company feel. I liked that very much. I was missing that warm, reassuring sense of camaraderie, now that *Only Fools* appeared to be over.

Despite all these qualities, once we set off on tour, we didn't do great business. Although Neil Simon is one of America's most popular playwrights, and a great Anglophile, he seems to have limited appeal in Britain. The theatrically sophisticated and the Simon aficionados turned up to see us but not in big enough numbers, though with each new venue – Edinburgh, Newcastle, Eastbourne, Windsor – we thought, 'Now, they'll like it here,' but we never filled the theatre and, sadly, the tour didn't make money.

Nevertheless, I thought it was a great show, as long as Peter Polycarpou was happy with the furniture in his dressing room. One evening he burst into mine, saw that it contained a reclining chair, a TV and a sun-lounger, and accused me of stealing them from his room. In fact, in spite of his being a Spurs supporter, he remains a good friend to this day.

Once the tour was over and we'd settled down, Carol and I started thinking seriously about a new way of life.

Although our existence was very comfortable, I was getting more sensitive to the encroaching crush and racket of modern life in the South East of England. I'd spent two years as part of a group protesting against the extension of Heathrow Airport – the rate at which planes were passing over our home was already almost unbearable. And it wasn't just us – literally millions of families suffer from excessive aircraft noise near our international airports. However, I learned the hard way that in the end, you can't beat big business, in this case, the Airports Authority, BA, its shareholders and the construction industry – and I've learned it again since, in protesting, in vain, against the erection of massive wind generators across the top of some of the loveliest hills in the Welsh Marches.

Sitting in our garden in Richmond early one summer's evening, we had to stop our conversation for a minute or two because we couldn't hear each other while Concorde, looking very beautiful, cruised overhead with a shattering roar on its approach to land.
It was 'Time to split, Jack,' as Dennis Hopper said to Martin Sheen in *Apocalypse Now*.

Carol and I both enjoyed beautiful old houses and gardens and we had visited dozens of them since we'd been together. We began to fantasize about the possibility of finding an ancient house for ourselves that needed a little TLC, preferably with some land attached where we could create a garden.

I was conscious that I would also have to go on making a living, probably more than a living if wherever we found demanded a large amount of TLC and LSD (currency, not mind-destroying drug.) This effectively restricted our search area to places within easy striking distance of London.

We soon found that everything we saw and liked down the M4/M40 corridor was beyond our reach for one reason or another. We looked at plenty of nice Georgian houses in a quarter of an acre for £1million or so but I didn't have a million and a quarter of an acre was a pocket handkerchief as far as we were concerned.

But I had a friend, Jean Boht, with whom I'd worked in

pantomime. She'd also had a great success in the long-running *Bread*. Jean was a kind of train-spotter when it came to beautiful old houses; she had spent a great deal of time looking at such places that came up for sale, although I don't think she ever bought any of them.

In the course of her weekly scrutiny of grand and lovely houses for sale in *Country Life*, she had spotted a remarkable piece of medieval survival in the far north-western corner of Herefordshire. She rang me to tell me about it.

It turned out to be an abbot's lodging, a glorious, ancient and weathered stone edifice, sitting among a group of ramshackle farm buildings, which had once been part of a vast Augustinian abbey, destroyed at the time of the dissolution, four and a half centuries ago. Most of the main abbey buildings had been systematically knocked down and pillaged over the intervening centuries by locals looking to build a nice place for themselves. What little was left of the abbey church and its ancillaries stood in the five acres that surrounded them and came with the former abbot's gaff, now known as the Grange, Wigmore Abbey. We agreed that it looked absolutely wonderful, but we had to be realistic: we didn't even know where Herefordshire was, let alone Wigmore. I pulled out the map book to find them.

'By 'eck!' I declared in the dialect of my Sheffield forefathers, 'That's way out i't' blooody sticks.'

You could tell just from the map, the obvious absence of roads and the empty rising ground to the west on the Welsh border, that this was not a busy spot.

With a regretful shrug of the shoulders, we carried on looking for places nearer the metropolis.

Gradually we began to give less weight to distance from London and more to the nature of the house. We started a mild flirtation with an Elizabethan manor house, not far from Milton Keynes. We got as far as offering, and being soundly gazumped, thank God! – as it turned out. We were told later that the whole roof had to be replaced at a cost of £400,000.

Coincidently, having discovered where Herefordshire was, shortly afterwards, in autumn 1997, we drove up to stay with friends, Robert and Hyllarie Borwick, who lived in Bircher, a village near the small market town of Leominster, very near Wigmore. It seemed like fate.

We had to go and at least look at the Abbey.

The first thing we saw on our approach was a wonderful old half-timbered gatehouse. We drove slowly by, and turned down a farm track, which, we learned later, was the vestige of the Romans' second-century Watling Street West, a kind of forerunner to the M5. Peering through a hedge and a line of poplar trees, across an ancient meadow, we were transfixed.

A quarter of a mile away, through the autumn mist hanging in the air, we gazed at the eastern end of the house and to its right, a small mound on which stood a ghostly stone finger of the ruined abbey church, pointing up at the sky.

The house itself, surrounded by rampant elder, sycamore and great dark conifers, appeared a jumble of elevations and rooflines, as if the place had been put together as an afterthought from bits they'd found hanging about. Several towering brick and stone chimneys added to its somewhat eccentric air. The hairs on the backs of our necks were standing up. We had to have a closer look, right there and then. We drove back to the entrance and Carol boldly set off down the drive while I waited in the car.

She came back looking stunned. 'It's amazing!' she whispered.

The owner had come out and challenged her.

'I... we just wanted to have a closer look. It's a wonderful place.'

'It so happens it's for sale; if you're interested you can make an appointment and then have a closer look.'

We did, the next day.

It was the most extraordinary house, started in the twelfth century and added to, changed, botched, reinforced over the centuries that followed. The abbot's lodging had remained a dwelling after Henry VIII had ordered the destruction of all the monasteries in the land but it had shown signs of instability and had been suitably buttressed. In Victorian times, it had been strapped and tied with forged iron braces.

The gentle, melancholy old building looked like a badly-wrapped parcel but its stones and timbers gave it a sense of tranquillity and it seemed to breathe its eight hundred years of history.

It was still lived in and over the previous twenty years it had been 'modernized'. Where the plaster hadn't been replaced with hardboard panels, it was painted stark white. Some of the ancient oak balustrading had been replaced with varnished brown pine. In other parts the grey stone walls stood undressed, in rocky nakedness. They cried out for warm colours, care and gentle understanding.

The owner of the house, no doubt sniffing a deal, allowed us to wander around the house on our own. We took our time, finding on the walls of the panelled library some framed documents and coats of arms. Carol did a double take; she was sure she recognized the arms and when we found an inventory prepared for one Thomas Cockerham, of The Grange at Wigmore in 1763, she made the connection. The same arms and the name of Cockerham appeared in records of her own family.

Suddenly, we felt very much closer to this wonderful old hunk of historic masonry. We were standing in a stone-flagged corridor, looking past an ancient oak staircase, through a door into what was called the Abbot's Parlour. We walked closer; a shaft of light from a south-facing tracery window cast a gleam on a brass crucifix standing on a rugged table. At that moment, wisps of some ethereal entity seemed to be seeping up through the floor and swirling round the sunlit crucifix.

This must be some kind of sign of Divine Providence, I thought, although I kept the thought from Carol, who is less tolerant of this kind of fantasizing and in this case she would have been right; the owner of the house had just lit a fire in the undercroft beneath the parlour, no doubt to enhance its attractions when we came to inspect it.

Later, in the car, we did agree that it surely was some sort of a sign that seemed to reinforce Carol's family connection. We left the house in a daze. It seemed so right, almost pre-ordained and we were absolutely unanimous about it. We discovered with subsequent research that the Cockerhams, who had lived in the house for two centuries after Henry VIII had dissolved the monasteries, were indeed Carol's ancestors.

We drove back from Herefordshire, both in a state of quivering excitement about finding the house of our dreams. But in the glare of harsh London sunshine, we were bombarded with doubts. It was too big, it was too far away, it was too much of a wreck, it was too much money and it had been on the market for two years. But we had to have it. It was a huge risk but like the white-water rafting, we had to have a go.

We told our surveyor and showed him the details.

'Oh God!' he said, but agreed to have a look at it, shaking his head as we left.

We talked to John Rawstron, a school friend of Keith Washington's, who happened to be a conveyancing lawyer.

'Oh God!' he said, but agreed to handle it, 'if it comes to anything.' He shook his head sadly as we left.

As it turned out the survey was unexpectedly positive. For its age, apparently, the Grange was in surprisingly good shape. It had been re-roofed in the 1970s. Structurally, it was more or less sound, thanks to the timely Victorian cast-iron bracing.

Of course, a lot of windows needed replacing, walls needed plastering and there was a good deal of plumbing work to be done. Outside, the five acres of derelict ground that surrounded the house was in turn bordered on two sides by a messy farm that had become separated from the house a long time before.

Scattered around, random remnants of the great abbey complex still remained. A fragment of the ruined nave of the church stood in the farmer's rick yard, while the mill house, which had been part of the monastic set-up, also belonged to the farm.

All these problems we could live with, happily, if it meant we could live in this wonderful old place, so warmly inviting to us, and cosily wrapped in its own history.

We agreed that when a place that said so much to us had made itself known in such a serendipitous way, we had to jump in. We made an offer, we negotiated, a deal was done and an entirely new stage of our lives began.

It was not until all our possessions had been transported halfway across the country from South West London to North West Herefordshire and the house in Deanhill Road had been sold that we felt we had really moved into Wigmore Abbey and there was no going back.

When we arrived on 23 July 1998, a few months before Carol's Big 'L' birthday, we both knew we'd entered an entirely new phase of our lives, which we welcomed and were committed to, although, I found it very disorienting. Unlike Carol, I'd never lived in the real country before and I wasn't prepared, even for the more obvious differences. It took me a long time to get accustomed to the complete absence of street lighting, even in some of the villages. And while I was used to a certain amount of birdsong in the leafy purlieus of East Sheen, the racket a feathered chorus can kick up of a summer's dawn among the spinneys and hedges of this very rural corner of England came as a shock. I had to get used to the absence of traffic in the lane that passed our house. What little there was, was largely of an agricultural nature and I learned the hard way, with a few near misses, that single-track lanes with ditches, thick hedges or solid banks don't allow for errors of judgement.

From the moment we arrived there, I loved where I lived – the horizons of rolling, wooded hills, the daytime peace broken by the keening of buzzards wheeling in an empty sky, the air heavy with the aroma of grass, cattle and fox.

But it took me a long time to feel that I wasn't an impostor, or an incomer with no right to be there. I felt I was polluting this beautiful peaceful innocent country with my nasty urban, showbiz habits. I knew that this minor paranoia wasn't helped by my continuing drinking and I made a determined effort to curtail it. But it was a process of adjustment that had to be gone through and took some time. It was a good two or three years before I felt I had really bedded in and become a genuine part of my surroundings.

One of my earliest and most urgent tasks at Wigmore was rodent disposal. We found some enormous rats, mostly dead for some time, presumably poisoned, although the one we found behind an ancient fridge among a pile of prawn shells had probably just failed to read the 'best before' date on the packet.

We found a whole family of the little fellows, who had clearly seen better days, eking out a living from inside the insulating jacket of the clapped-out boiler we'd inherited. Carol was horrified and disgusted; I felt a little sad. A Sunday tabloid had once described me, in a banner headline, as a THREE-TIMING ROMEO LOVE RAT so I think I had a little empathy with them.

At the back of the Aga we found what we thought at first was a batch of ancient musty black cannon balls, although, on closer inspection, they were forgotten baked potatoes that must have carried on baking for years.

Around the rest of the house, small constructional horrors that had been rendered invisible by the rose-tinted spectacles we'd been wearing when first falling in love with the house started to appear – little holes in the ceiling patched up with Sellotape, hunks of loose, crumbling render, gaping holes in the ancient oak and elm floor boards and areas of devastation on beams brought about by hyper-active wood-worm.

Surprisingly, the plumbing, although medieval in appearance, generally worked and there were no obvious leaks in the roof. But we also began to see that the house, started in 1174, had been tinkered with on and off for eight hundred years – with builders telling the owners, 'If you was just to knock a bit off 'ere, no one'd know, and we could turn that door into a window, or fit another little privy between this wall and that stanchion,' sort of thing – eight centuries of bodging.

Of course, each new discovery represented another substantial future bill, but, perversely, we loved it. We had no children and, without the workings of a miracle, weren't going to have any, so we'd sort of adopted the abbey – it was now our baby and whatever it took, we'd make sure it was going to be all right.

We were glad that we hadn't been granted the benefit of hindsight, for if we had, we might simply have not been there. We had taken the place on with all its flaws and the open-ended responsibility that entailed. We had no knowledge whatsoever of renovating ancient properties – and they didn't come much more ancient than this; we hadn't even vaguely costed the job, or indeed, had any real idea of how many jobs were involved. It was a massive undertaking, totally impractical, and we were in our fifties. Not surprisingly, a lot of our friends in London and the new friends we were making in the country thought we were barking.

But moving to Wigmore Abbey wasn't about expediency or practicality, it was about the feeling we had for the building and our response to the bizarre chain of events that had led us to it.

Carol, who had grown up in deepest Dorset, had warned me that people in the country could be different, as if they were some kind of aliens. I soon understood what she meant. In fact it wasn't the people who were different, but the priorities, ground rules and terms of engagement, which were more old fashioned – generally in a good way, we felt. There were a number of underlying accepted tenets in country life, which, if one wished to blend in, it was sensible to acknowledge.

On the whole, people were more polite, certainly compared to the free-for-all back-biting bitch fest which the London thespian world could sometimes be. I felt as if I were taking a step back in time when going about the everyday business of catching trains, having a pint in a pub, shopping and buying food. Life here was lived at a much slower pace. Even in our nearest town of Ludlow, which offered a choice of four (very good) butchers, there always seemed to be time for a chat and catch up between shopkeeper and customer. Most people seemed interested in what we trying to do at the Abbey, delighted that some one had taken on responsibility for preserving what was left of an important piece of history. On the opposite side of the broad glacial valley from the Abbey stood the ruins of Mortimer Castle on a rocky tump, from where in the middle ages, Roger de Mortimer and his clan had wielded influence on the Marches, deep into Wales and ultimately, on the English throne. I soon found myself becoming an amateur historian and there was no shortage of people to teach and encourage me.

On the whole, the people we met welcomed us warmly, both in our nearest villages of Wigmore and Leintwardine and among the county set generally. I don't doubt that there was a little sniffy resentment that a chap from 'That down-market sitcom on the TV' had taken over such a distinguished old house but it seldom surfaced.

As a result of our occupation of the Abbey, we came across a surprising number of wonderful, beautifully sited 'Big Houses' in the Marches, still occupied by the families that had lived in them for centuries. Their owners understood very well the experiences and problems we faced and were genuinely sympathetic and encouraging.

Stanage, for instance, was the home of Jonathan and Sophie Coltman-Rogers. Carol had a previous connection with Jonathan, who was godson to a cousin of hers. The house lay just over the Welsh border and not more than five or six miles to the west of Leintwardine and they asked us over. It was an extraordinary looking joint put together in the eighteenth and nineteenth centuries and a lovely jumble of scatty fantasies that had made it the memorable star of the TV version of Tom Sharpe's *Blott on the Landscape*.

On the way there, we passed Brampton Bryan, a seventeenth-century house and twelfth-century castle, where during the Civil War, Brilliana, Lady Harley, had defended her house from a long siege by Royalist forces, and whose descendent, Edward Harley, still occupied the house and its rolling wooded park. Soon afterwards we met Edward and his mother Susan. Edward took an interest in all the ancient dwellings in the region and several years later became head of the Historic Houses Association.

Soon after we were settled in the Abbey, the Coltman-Rogers asked if we'd like to make up a table for dinner at a big charity bash, the Caribbean Ball, being held in the grounds of Acton Burnell, another big drum up towards Shrewsbury. Here we met a large number of the local great and good, most notably Ivor and Caroline Windsor – Viscount and Viscountess – of the Windsor-Clive clan – he a descendent of Clive of India, she of the family of the Viceroy, Lord Curzon.

Tall and patrician, the idiosyncratic Ivor Windsor was a firm Chelsea supporter, as you might expect, and a big fan of *Only Fools & Horses*. He had wandered up and introduced himself. 'Ah, Boycie! I heard you were coming. You must come to lunch and bring Marlene!' He became a great champion, introducing us to anyone who came into view with: 'Have you met Boycie?'

We would have to follow that up by telling them our real names, and explaining what I did – not so many were *Only Fools* fans – and what we were doing in the Welsh Marches. They were interested in the Abbey, but some of the tweedier, more rosy-featured men and women wanted to know where we were going to shoot and with which pack of hounds we were going to hunt. We explained that, although we didn't disapprove, we found it easier to get our meat from the butcher. But, townies that we still were, we were surprised to find how traditional country pursuits seemed to be absolutely the norm.

But we'd prepared ourselves for the change in culture, and didn't want to be intolerant or judgemental. In any event, there was no doubt that being a face 'off the telly' at least gave us novelty value and by moving into a large, ancient house, we found we had at least that in common with a lot of the landowning folk – the old money, if you like. It seemed that we'd earned some respect for moving in to the Abbey in its parlous, crumbling state and, as Ivor Windsor so elegantly put it: 'Having the balls to take it on!'

Ivor Windsor's family home, near Bromfield, lay on the south bank of the fast-flowing River Teme, surrounded by tranquil, oak-filled parkland and an estate which follows the river down to the very edge of the rocky mound on which Ludlow Castle was built eight hundred years ago. With views of the distinctive wedge of Clee Hill to the east, it must be one of the most beautiful pieces of country in England.

Soon after the Caribbean bash, we were asked to lunch there – *al fresco*, on a beautiful, stone-flagged terrace beneath two vast, overhanging magnolias, where we were introduced to more engaging locals.

We soon found that one of Ivor's particular habits was to create nick-names for all the people he came across regularly and he enjoyed using these obscure monikers in introductions. It was years before I knew the real names of some of the people I met with him – Chippy, Wedgie, the March Lioness, the Squire of Soddington, JJ and The Beast. He also introduced us to the Wrigleys, who lived in what he called Del Boy Hall – in fact, Delbury Hall.

Thanks to this great welcome, we soon felt that we were becoming part of the community and after years of living in aloof, sophisticated London, we were amazed how open and friendly everyone was, from David Griffiths, who ran the garage and general store around which life in Leintwardine revolved, the ladies in the Post Office, the chaps in the wonderful old Sun Inn in Leintwardine, where nonagenarian landlady, Flossie Lane, doled out bitter in jugs passed through a hatch, our farming neighbours, the obliging postie, the village coracle maker, and all the other colourful characters that are so much more visible out here in the distant sticks. It was, frankly, a far cry from all the competitive show-biz folk and bibulous tennis players I'd been spending most of my time with in London.

After a few months, Carol and I could take a deep breath and agree that we would be very happy here, and we knew we'd been right to choose the ridiculously risky, blind-fold plunge we'd taken in buying Wigmore Abbey and moving in to make a new life there. It was for both of us a major decision in our lives, second only to our decision to marry.

We also knew that our lives had changed fundamentally. We had to get used to a slower pace, where less happened but what did happen was somehow more vivid. Our lives were no longer London-centric; our everyday town was Ludlow, a fascinating and extraordinarily well-preserved medieval hill town. For bigger stuff we had to drive down the old Roman road to the compact, old-fashioned city of Hereford, with a cattle market, a cathedral and a population of just 60,000. Some Metropolis!

But before we could relax and enjoy ourselves, there was a lot to get through – a lot of building, bad judgement, disappointment, frustration, paperwork, harassment by officials with clipboards and dogmatic views, and wasted wonga.

Inevitably, the Herefordshire Council had strong views about what we could and couldn't do to the house. We were paid a visit by the listed-building department in a delegation led by a woman of military bearing, in practical clothes and sensible shoes. It soon became clear that they were thrilled to be there; the previous owner, we were told, had jealously guarded his privacy and had done all he could to discourage visitors, especially official ones.

They toured the house with a lot of disapproving coughing noises; they kicked drainpipes and instructed us to keep the drain gratings clear – as if we wouldn't. They gazed at the windows, deemed hopelessly inappropriate and took their photographs with sharp intakes of breath through gritted teeth. They looked squiggly-eyed at the concrete mortar used on the stonework of the extension made in the 1970s.

In principal, we agreed with their view that the house should continue to look as close as possible to the 'original'. But which original? There must have been half a dozen variations on the building over the previous 800 years and deciding at which point to freeze it in time seemed pretty arbitrary.

Luckily, the council was happy for the 1970s additions to be considered part of the existing building, as these hadn't been done too untastefully – externally, at least and, despite the 'wrong' mortar, agreed that a complete rebuild wasn't justified, which was good of them. Otherwise, they were pretty fussy. (One wishes that so much consideration to heritage and aesthetics had come into play when the same council started giving permission for avaricious farmers to plant hideous, inefficient windmills on sensitive horizons to generate sporadically paltry amounts of massively subsidized electricity.)

Three months after they'd been, we heard the result of discussions that had gone on among various county council committees about what we should be compelled to do with the house, including the treatment of our windows. The key problem was that when the place had been 'done up' in the 1970s, flat modern glass had been used everywhere, giving a dull lifelessness to what you might call the eyes of the building – the windows to its soul. We were told what size of diamond-leaded lights we should use and the type of glass. We were very happy with the result when they were installed, although we didn't think much of the cost involved.

By this time, we were beginning to get a clearer idea of what the whole thing was going to cost, although that could obviously be pretty open-ended, depending on how pernickety one was going to be in decisions about materials and quality of finish – in so far as the listed-buildings squad in the council allowed us much choice. One thing was certain, it was going to cost more than we had and my need for gainful employment was becoming more acute.

It was, of course, in line with the Law of Sod that as soon as the bigger bills came fighting their way through our letterbox, the phone stopped ringing and the work dried up.

I still had some useful stand-by voice-over work but with a six-hour round trip on the train to London, it was neither convenient, nor particularly profitable. I began to think that as far as most casting directors were concerned, I'd moved too far beyond the pale – out of sight, out of mind – while the old safety net that *Only Fools* had provided for the previous nearly twenty years was gone. In moments of characteristic paranoia, I had bouts of thinking that in buying Wigmore and moving out there I'd made the stupidest mistake of my life.

Most of the time I found myself oscillating between periods of euphoria and bouts of terror – joy at just being in this beautiful, uncluttered part of the country, occupied with such an historic house and fear of never working again or being able to pay for it all. As it happened, my buying the Abbey had generated a lot of media interest and as Sue Holderness and I had somewhat cornered the market in publicizing the continual showings of *Only Fools* and a plethora of merchandise that had sprung from it, we now found ourselves sitting on a lot of sofas in day-time TV studios, where I could easily be persuaded to talk about the extraordinary changes in my life and the pleasures of the rural idyll.

I think friends and colleagues were simply waiting for the novelty to wear off before we headed back with a huge sigh of relief to the safe and familiar surroundings of South West London, which we had inhabited for so long. But we never did and never have tired of being in Wigmore. We relished the glorious, unchanging landscape that surrounded us and coming back on the train from London, rattling north from the junction at Newport (one of the ugliest cities in Britain) up beside the mighty ridges of the Black Mountains, across Herefordshire and the Rivers Wye, Arrow, Lugg and Teme, to alight at the station in Ludlow, in itself a step back into a gentler time, always gave my heart a great lift, and still does.

A few months into our occupation of Wigmore Abbey, we got to grips with our most pressing tasks in repairing, restoring and making comfortable our own personal pile of medieval masonry.

The first big mistake we made was not to recruit local tradesmen to start the work on our house. They would have had a better idea of what they were doing, they would have cost less and it would have been the right gesture towards the small rural community we'd joined. In our defence, our choice of builder was made for thoroughly impractical reasons of philanthropy, in trying to help out a friend. One of Carol's oldest chums, Anna Hall, was married to a charming, handsome man called Nick Barley. Nick's current occupation was that of a London property 'developer', which meant, we discovered, that he bought rough old, cheap gaffs in dodgy, possibly up-and-coming parts of London, did them up a bit and flogged them. Things hadn't been going brilliantly for him, though, and he needed a decent job to help him out of the doodah. We weighed in with a promise to give him the contract for renovating Wigmore Abbey.

It was soon clear that this was a very silly decision. He imported all his workers up from the other end of the country. To start with they all lived in the house, with Nick trying to cook them greasy spoon breakfasts every morning in Carol's still ramshackle kitchen. That arrangement didn't work and was curtailed fairly quickly, when they all decamped to a pub, The Compasses in Wigmore, which gave us back some privacy but inevitably cost money.

Nick – soon to be divorced from Anna and taking quite a lot of her money with him – turned out to be a lot better at talking about the job than doing it. The idea that his experience of nineteenth-century jerry-built artisan houses had equipped him to handle a Grade-I-Listed twelfth-century stone abbot's lodging was, in hindsight, absurd, but we were naive, as well as kind-hearted. He managed to get the work started. A new boiler was installed and miraculously, all forty-two radiators were operational. Some plastering and a few repairs to beams were started but there was an amateurish air to the whole process and we soon started to worry.

While we were making stuttering progress with the house, we'd barely looked at the vestiges of the old and vast monastery that occupied most of the five acres of wild garden that came with our house. The ruins were under the aegis of English Heritage, altogether snootier than the local listed-buildings officials and the senior organization responsible for all kinds of historic sites and ancient monuments in England.

It turned out that they had been itching to get their boots on to the site for years, while successive owners had denied them access. Now we let them in: they came, they saw, they monitored. They gave good advice, oversaw some critical aspects of renovation and hinted at further help to come.

Luckily, they didn't use the services of our builder and self-appointed foreman, Nick Barley, from whom I can't imagine they had derived much peace of mind. It had become abundantly clear that he had no idea what he was doing and even the tradesmen he'd brought with him were looking perplexed at some of his instructions, and shaking their heads with heavenward glances when he was trying to tell them what to do.

Talking to the English Heritage chaps, he was embarrassingly unconvincing.

'My clients don't have a lot of money,' he told them, 'and I'm really

A publicity shot for a happy show

Sue and I dressed up for a Status Quo concert
in an episode of *Green, Green Grass*

Boycie and Marlene reaffirm their wedding vows

The Green, Green Grassers
Left to right: Ivan Kaye, David Ross, Peter Hepplethwaite, Farmer Boyce

A Hair-Raising Experience on Green, Green Grass

Holders of a proud record. Boycie and Marlene are the longest surviving marriage on TV

Moustache-less!

Halfway down the slipway at The Lizard Lifeboat Station at 'the most southerly' on my birthday, August 16th 2009

The Red Arrows Squadron. Second from left is Fl. Lt. Jon Egging 'The Egg Man' who died on August 20th 2011 during a display in Hampshire. It reminds me how fragile our grip on life is

Charity cricket match in aid of Help for Heroes.

Oi Freddie! Have you nicked my tie?! Andrew Flintoff's XI vs Boycie's XI at Downton in Shropshire, 2010

Image courtesy of Ian Sheppard

With Bill Wyman and Georgie Fame at a Rhythm Kings' concert in Cheltenham. I'd met the other half of the greatest rhythm section the world has ever seen.

Image coutesy of Jules Annan

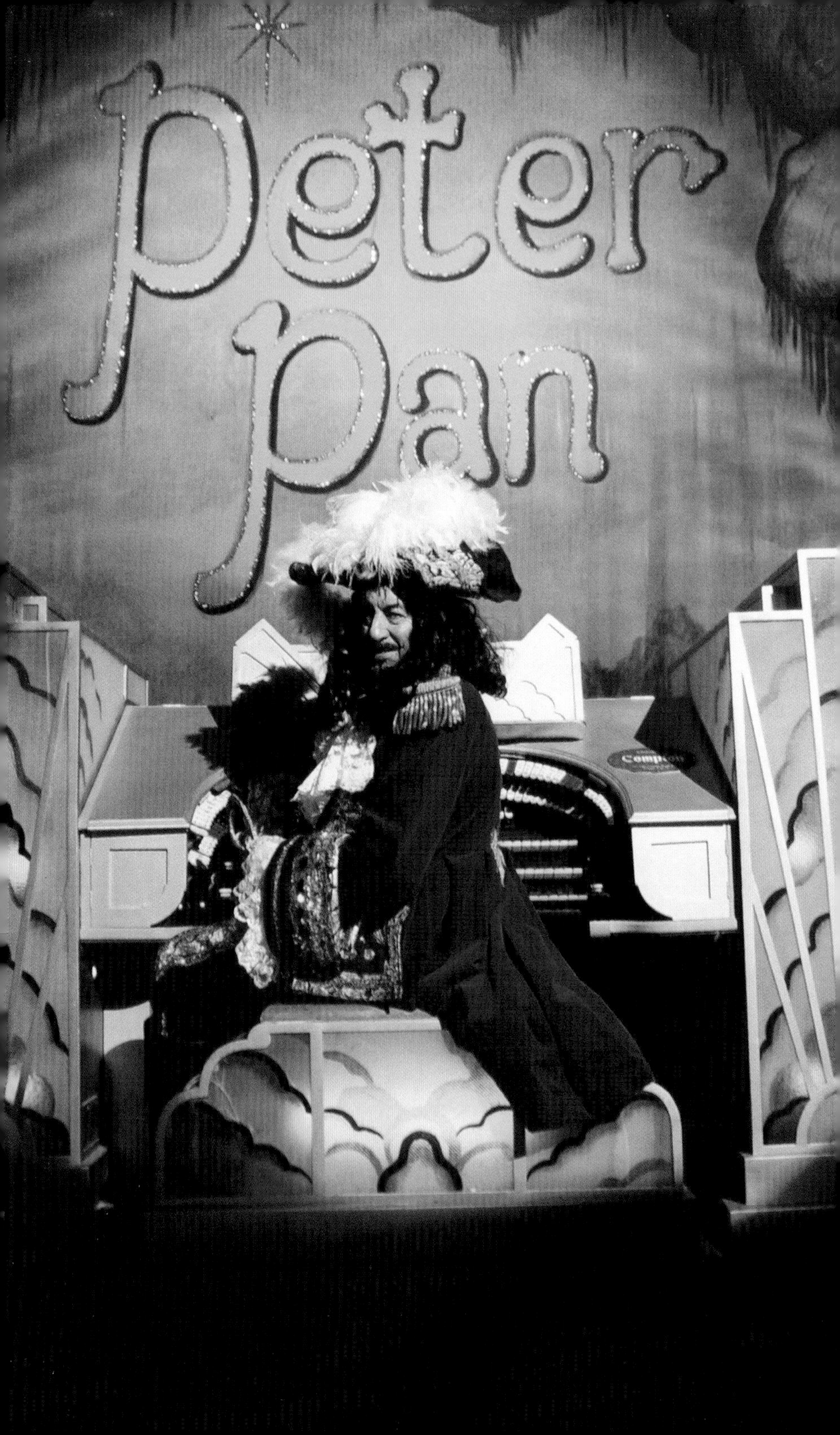
Peter
Pan

Left. Playing the organ at Stockport Plaza and above,
haranguing the audience in Swansea
Captain Hook my favourite role in pantomime

Snowbound with Mortimer

Wigmore Abbey, founded by the Mortimer dynasty

With Carol at Wigmore Abbey, Herefordshire, 2002

King Rat disguised as a pirate in *Dick Whittington*, Theatr
Cymru. At least the parrot appeared to be listening

Strangely moving, as
Malvolio in *Twelfth Night*
at Ludlow Castle 2011.
Image courtesy of Richard
Stanton

As Jeremy the jewel thief in *Last of the Summer Wine* with Jean Fergusson and Josephine Tewson "The lovely ladies"

going to have to kick ass round here to get the job in on budget. Now,'
he went on, 'let's cut to the quick...'

By the middle of 1999, having demanded and pocketed quite a lot of
our money for not always identifiable results, our drunken builder
parted company with us, and not on the best of terms. Soon after
that, he parted company with Carol's friend Anna, too, and moved
on, via rich new pastures, to a luxury re-hab clinic.

Fortunately we had by now done what we should have done in the
first place and discovered skilled local craftsmen who were properly
experienced in handling ancient, quirky buildings.

Master plasterer, Stuart Preece, for example, who came to look at
the job, sucked his teeth vigorously and did wonderful work on the
internal walls. Outside he re-pointed large areas of the stone-work
with proper lime mortar. Stuart left many reminders of his day's work
with dollops of plaster all over the floors, and limey footprints all over
the garden. He knew his job all right and had to be called in to show
TV builder Tommy Walsh, from *Groundforce* how to mix the lime
mortar that was always used in building, up until the nineteenth
century.

The roofer, Michael Morris, kidded us with a request for danger
money as our roofs were so high. I protested, 'That sounds like a
soldier asking for danger money before going into battle. After all,
that's what you chaps do, isn't it, clamber around at great heights?'

The man who came to sweep the chimneys with his own massive
tickling stick was called Ken Dodd and the boiler was installed by a
plumber called Trigger. He amused himself by signing the wall in the
boiler-room, 'Installed by Trigger.'

Progress was faster from then on; the house was becoming habitable,
and we didn't feel quite so mad to have taken it on. We were settling
into a manageable pace of life when we were delivered a big blow in
June 1999 – Buster Merryfield had died.

Buster had been ill with a brain tumour for some time and had
refused visitors for the past few months. The last time I spoke to him,
he said he didn't want his friends to see him 'in this state'. He was
79, and had first appeared in *Only Fools* in 1985, his first real
professional acting job, at the age of 65. That in itself was a bizarre

story, but he'd had a strange career – as a gunner in World War II, as an amateur boxer, and for many years as a banker, ending up manager of the Thames Ditton branch of the Westminster Bank. But he'd always lived for the theatre, and when he retired and decided to risk a professional career, he had got the job of replacing Lennard Pearce's *Grandad*. He had thrown himself with gusto and great charm into the job of being *Uncle Albert*, where he soon became one of the best-loved characters in the show. In private, he was a sweet, jolly bloke and an eternal optimist; I was very sad to think I would never see him sitting down at the piano again to bang out the old pub songs like he used to at the Nag's Head. A tear came into my eye, I don't mind admitting, as I watched Iris, Buster's devoted wife standing tearfully beside the grave, while the rest of us reflected on the friend and colleague we'd all lost.

Later that year, in life's eternal merry-go-round, Nick Lyndhurst was married to former ballet dancer, Lucy Smith. I was invited, and Ken MacDonald, but our wives were not, due to limited numbers at the venue. Ken and I went as a couple, though we could never decide who should wear the hat. It was a lovely laid-back wedding, but we all drank too much, and as a result, in the wedding shot of Nick, Lucy and the cast of *Only Fools*, which appeared in *OK!* magazine, they are demure and tidy; the rest of us are distinctly dishevelled. They flew away in a chopper to somewhere exotic (Luton Airport, maybe) and I won't forget Nick's excited boyish grin, waving to us all as they lifted off. In contrast to the last time we'd all been gathered a couple of months earlier for Buster's funeral, this was an event brimming with optimism, a new start full of hope and anticipation.

Chapter 14
House and Garden

Whether or not the dawn of the new millennium was as full of new hope as Nick's wedding is a moot point. While I don't subscribe to the gloomiest prognosticators who are convinced the world is going to hell in a handcart, there's no doubt that the human race has exerted a lot of pressure on the world we inhabit, and a lot of altruistic thinking needs to take place before we can safely say we have a sound future.

On the other hand, wearing my optimist's hat, it seemed to me that the departing century had seen the last of intra-European wars, and for the time being, a US-USSR conflict.

My strongest personal emotion on 1 January 2000 was relief. I had always wondered whether I would make it to that critical date; I shouldn't have doubted it, I was only 57 after all, but I'd always had a sense that I wouldn't. Neither Carol nor I were keen on New Year's Eve parties – parties for the sake of it, in my view, with no real point behind them – and though the invitations were there, we decided instead simply to plant an oak tree and have a quiet night in. Next day felt the same as any other winter's morning but our oak tree is still there, taller and standing proudly in the corner of our orchard, twelve years on.

When I'd bought *OK!* magazine for Carol to see the pictures of Nick and Lucy Lyndhurst's wedding, I leafed through the other articles about people's houses. On a whim, I contacted my agent to put out feelers to see if there'd be any interest among the glossy mags in featuring Wigmore Abbey. I didn't imagine it would bring in a fortune but it would cheer me if the house were to earn a little something towards its own keep.

We had a very quick response from *Hello!* who, in their breathless, gushy way told me they were 'over the moon' at being invited into our 'lovely home'. I'd been aware for some time of *Hello!*'s great success in terms of sales and guessed that their principle of not printing anything to upset or damage their subjects still paid off. In a sense, although always at the soft, cuddly end of the business, they were the trailblazers for the vast celebrity gossip industry that grew steadily during the '90s until in the new millennium, vicious gossip, with pictures to match, became an internationally traded commodity. It was, I suppose, no coincidence that as early as 1995, Rupert Murdoch must have seen value in this growth in intrusive journalism and appointed Piers Morgan – a mere gossip hack – as editor of the *News of the World*.

When they came, the writer and photographer for *Hello!* couldn't have been more agreeable. They took some great shots and the accompanying interview, we saw thankfully, looked at other aspects of our lives, besides the *Boycie* persona.

Perhaps the *Hello!* piece prompted someone's memory, because shortly after it appeared, out of the blue I was asked if I'd like to play *Malvolio* in a production of *Twelfth Night* for the Stafford Shakespeare festival. It was to be staged in the open air, among the ruins of Stafford Castle, hard by the M6 motorway.

Since I'd been in the play in Stratford with the RSC in 1966, I'd always wanted the chance to play *Malvolio*, one of Shakespeare's great comic creations and this seemed like a perfect opportunity. For this show I could commute (and I always prefer to come home after a gig if I can), it wasn't going to run for too long and it was quite well paid. I said yes.

Playing *Maria* was Jean Boht, who had first pointed us in the direction of Wigmore Abbey, and was, I think, partly instrumental in my being offered *Malvolio*. It was a terrific, very English set-up around the castle. Rather like a county show or equestrian event, there were canvas stands on all sides of a central stage and tents for dressing-rooms, wardrobe and facilities.

The good old English summer let us down, though, once again – it was cold, it rained pretty consistently, the west wind blew and the motorway hissed. However, the punters weren't deterred; six hundred at a time turned up. They'd paid, and they were bloody well going to enjoy it. The atmosphere was terrific, which relayed itself, as these things do, straight to the cast on stage, and a real company spirit developed.

After the show we would roll back down the hill with the audience, who were clearly delighted that we hadn't let them down. This reminded me of my earliest touring theatre days, when the fusion between players and audience could make them so much a part of the play.

Pantomime, too, was about audiences including themselves in the spirit of a show, which was essential to the experience. That was why I'd always loved it and was (by choice and not just for the wonga) still involved in pantomime at the end of every year, where it was as much part of Christmas for me as hearing Slade singing 'Merry Christmas Everybody' in the supermarket, Christmas pudding and slabs of turkey breast.

I had enjoyed playing a string of juicy, villainous roles – *Abanazar*, *King Rat*, *Fleshcreep* and the occasional *Ugly Sister* – although as soon as I was told I reminded someone of my mother, I abandoned the frocks.

Malvolio at Stafford had been great fun and a lovely challenge but without the security of *Only Fools* lurking in the wings and turning 58 that summer, I still felt very vulnerable about work. My agent, Christina Shepherd, who had been 'looking after' me since 1992 had found me a few odd parts in movies – the ghost of a dead train driver in *Subterrain*; a strangely obsessive bingo hall manager in *Five Seconds to Spare*, with Max Beesley and Ray Winstone and a sleazy beauty pageant promoter in *Dream* with Brian Conley. Most notably, I had a decent part in *The Tichborne Claimant*, which featured many of the cream of British character actors – Robert Pugh, Charles Gray, James Villiers, Stephen Fry, Sir John Geilgud, Robert Hardy and so on. I was the only one I hadn't heard of.

But by the time I did *Twelfth Night* in Stafford, this sporadic work was beginning to dry up. Christina had sent someone up to look at the show. It was dismissed as 'just a pantomime', which rankled. However, shortly after that, Christina was joined in the agency by a former actress, Lesley Duff, with whom I'd worked on *Get Back,* for Thames TV and also in *Season's Greetings* at Sonning. She soon made her mark at the agency and I found myself travelling up to Yorkshire to appear in an episode of *Heartbeat*, with the inimitable Derek Fowlds. But Lesley did confess to me that she had never dealt with an actor so closely identified with a role, as I was with *Boycie* and she was finding it difficult.

She soon left, in any case, to set up her own agency, and I was finding it hard to talk to Christina without an appointment and encountering a certain amount of indifference when I did. My thespian instincts (a type of paranoia) told me it was time to look for a new stable.

Barry Burnett had been Barbara Windsor's agent when she and I had worked together so harmoniously on *Entertaining Mr Sloane*. I was still in touch with Barbara and she suggested that I contact him.

The list of artistes represented by Barry Burnett was a roll-call of well-known names from all parts of the business. He was an 'old-school' agent; he had seen all sorts of changes in the way things worked and he had a realistic approach to the job. Early in 2001, I rang him, murmuring Barbara Windsor's name and we arranged a meeting.

Barry agreed to take me on. 'Your greatest asset is your availability,' he said. This was, I thought, a double-edged advantage. He added that he couldn't promise anything but he had a good feeling about our prospective relationship.

'Just get me some bloody work!' I wailed.

'How do you expect me to succeed where everyone else has failed?' he replied.

We have, I think, been friends ever since.

Barbara Windsor was not the only actress I knew on Barry's books. He was also agent to Sue Holderness, who'd played *Marlene* to my *Boycie* since 1985. Working for both of us now, he soon came up with the obvious suggestion that she and I could work together on stage, which we'd never done before.

Ever since I'd first worked with Sue in *Only Fools*, we'd liked one another and had developed a useful shorthand which allowed us to work together extremely well. The way we could dovetail our scenes in the Nag's Head had often been commented on. We luckily had a natural rapport, like David and Nick had in *Del* and *Rodney*, which made our scenes together very comfortable. It followed, although we hadn't thought of it before, that we could play husband and wife in other milieus. Barry quickly found a play for us, Alan Ayckbourn's *Relatively Speaking*, which we had both admired for a long time.

After two weeks rehearsal in London, we opened at the Devonshire Park Theatre in Eastbourne, where I'd last appeared with the Penguin Players in 1963! The play was a delight. Ayckbourn's dialogue, clever plot and beautifully crafted characters made the kind of thing you wanted to be doing all the time. The public quite rightly loved his work and it wasn't hard to fill the theatre.

We were having a great time, and I was as happy to be back on stage every night, as I had been ten years before in Sonning.

We were still in Eastbourne when my birthday came round in August and I came into my dressing room to find it decked out with balloons and ribbons and flowers. I thought back to the time when I'd celebrated my twenty-first, as the youngest member of the Penguin Players with a party at my landlady's in Bexhill-on-Sea, just down the coast.

What a lot had happened in the 38 years in between, and yet here I was, back on the stage, doing what I'd always loved, but now with a wonderful wife and none of the hideous uncertainties and vagaries that had dogged my love life for so long.

Carol went back to Herefordshire, from where she would call me every day to keep me up to date with what was going on at Wigmore. I'd finished the show one night and I was just getting changed when she called. I knew at once that something wrong.

Kenny MacDonald had died of a heart attack.

As Carol told me tears welled up in my eyes and I sat back down on the chair in front of my table, staring into the mirror without seeing anything.

Kenny had died on holiday in Hawaii. He was there with his wife, Sheila and their two children, Charlotte and Will. He was just fifty years old.

I'd worked with Ken since 1983 on *Only Fools*, and he'd become one of my greatest friends in the cast. Now I felt almost responsible for what had happened. Carol and I had set up the holiday for him and his family. Kenny had always told me how fascinated he was by the idea of Hawaii, mainly through watching the Jack Lord TV series, *Hawaii Five-O*. I'd whetted his appetite more with my own graphic descriptions of the beautiful islands and tales of meeting people like Tom Selleck on the beach at the Outrigger Club.

Carol, who knew the islands intimately, had insisted that a first visit should always be made to Oahu, with its twin delights of

Honolulu and Waikiki. We had stayed at the Colony Surf Apartments there and suggested that Kenny's family stay at the Kaiamana Beach Hotel, next door. We'd arranged to have a big bunch of flowers delivered there with a note, 'Welcome to paradise!'

They'd been there only a few days when Kenny went to Waikiki for breakfast. When he came back, he said he felt a bit strange, and suddenly collapsed.

Carol had phoned just after that, to make sure that they were happy with everything, only to be told the terrible news. She had, very considerately, held back from phoning to tell me until after our show.

When I told Sue, she and I just sat together in stunned silence. At first it was impossible to believe that we would never see Kenny again.

Inevitably, memories of him crowded into our heads, he'd always been such a presence in the show, especially off-camera. I thought of him sitting in the Nag's Head set before a take, having wedged a beer mat on his nose, shouting, "'Ere! Who threw that?' and the time when we were told before a show that our usual warm-up man had been taken ill. Kenny cocked his head like a war horse to a bugle. 'I'll do it!' he called out. And he did – at least, he tried, but he soon had to call for all of us to come out and tell our best jokes to keep the audience happy.

'I thought it went quite well, son,' he told me afterwards. 'I died a death!'

He had been a big fan of the quirky music-hall comic, Max Miller, and had put together a one-man show based on Miller, which he did whenever and wherever he could. John Sullivan went to see him do it. 'Bloody hell, he's got more front than Brighton,' he said afterwards.

During the '70s Kenny had tasted success in *It Ain't Half Hot, Mum*. He'd recently shown me a picture of the cast and had pointed out that at least half of them were no longer with us.

'See him,' he'd said stabbing a finger at one of them, 'brown bread, son! And him, he's been brown bread for years. Him? Next time I see him, he'll be toast.'

He followed this with a wheezy rat-a-tat laugh, which didn't stop before you were laughing with him.

He'd always been a big fan of the Kinks, too, and when he'd met Ray Davies he had tried very hard to persuade him to cast him in his new musical. He told me next time he saw me, 'Well that's it; I'm going in the West End, son.'

Nothing happened that time but he had been in the West End in the very successful *My Night with Reg*, which had led to the National Theatre and a part in *Guys & Dolls*. Earlier in his career he'd been cast in *Animal Farm* at the National, directed by the then head of the company, the very eminent Sir Peter Hall.

Aware of Ken's habit of dispensing with all normal protocol and approaching anyone and everyone with 'Hello, son, my name's Ken,' someone warned him of Sir Peter's imminent arrival at the start of rehearsals.

The assembled cast waited nervously as the great director made his entrance – all except Ken, who walked straight up to him. 'Hello, Sir Son; my name's Ken.'

This story was told at Ken's memorial held at the Criterion Theatre in Piccadilly. The place was packed with people who'd worked with him, or who'd just known him from a pub somewhere, or whose lives had been touched and brightened by him in some way. I was glad to be asked to get up and say something and, I hope, offer a little light relief by pretending that I'd never liked Ken and was somewhat embarrassed by his constant clinging on to me as a friend, as well as his annoying habit of ringing up to tell me what he was doing. 'Nothing much going on here, son. I'm going in the West End again; I don't know how I'm going to fit it in with the 12 part mini-series I've been offered in Paraguay. I've got so much money, I don't know what to do with it! Quiet for you as well, is it, son?'

He often rang up and said, 'I've heard we're on again, son.' Somehow, he always knew before anyone else if *Only Fools* was about to be repeated again somewhere in the tellysphere.

At the end of my eulogy I looked up at the seats in the gods.

'Wher*ever* you are, son, we're still on!'

He would have been proud of that, and it's been pretty much true ever since.

Ken had been such a part of my life since he'd first appeared on *Only Fools* eighteen years earlier, it took me quite a time to get over losing him. It was going to be very strange to be in the Nag's Head without him, if the rumours of an absolutely final splurge of *Only Fools* turned out to be true.

But life, as it does, slowly got back to normal, and there was plenty to do at the Abbey to take our minds off Kenny's going. A TV documentary series, *The House Detectives at Large*, wanted to make a programme about the house, how it had been built, its history and setting. Carol and I were thrilled; we'd both become enthusiastic amateur historians – it was hard not to be when you lived all the time in such an atmospheric, ancient dump.

The programme brought together experts in archaeology, architecture and mediaeval history. The producers also liked to find a little mystery on to which they could hang a narrative – in this case, the whereabouts of the mortal remains of Roger de Mortimer. Roger was the infamous Marcher baron who went off with Edward II's wife, Queen Isabella, put the king himself under house arrest and ruled England as regent from 1327. However, he got his come-uppance; he was apprehended by supporters of Edward III and hanged at Tyburn on 29 November 1330. The site of his burial, though, remains unknown. Was his body, as has often been surmised, buried in a field that we owned, alongside the great abbey, and was his head still with his body?

One theory is that Isabella took his body away and had it buried under what is now a supermarket car-park in Coventry.

Dan Cruickshank and Carenza Lewis who were presenting, had the task of telling the tangled history of the building and its connection with the Mortimer family, who ruled this part of England for four hundred years following the Norman Conquest.

They studied chunks of carved stone from the abbey which still lay all around; they were allowed to dig two small excavation trenches under the beady eye of Paul Stamper, the English Heritage chief for our area. At the end of our lawn, about seven feet down, they uncovered three different floor levels of the abbey complex, and sensationally, only seven inches below the surface of a field of ancient pasture, beyond the great stone finger that remained, they found the mediaeval tiled floor of a lady chapel.

I was given a role too, besides that of astonished, accidental owner of an ancient monument. I was cast as a thirteenth-century monk and dressed in coarse black habit, to illustrate the Seven Deadly Sins – I recall Lust and Gluttony with particular relish.

House and Garden

One evening, during a break in filming around dusk, I strolled out onto a long flight of stone steps on the outside of the building. A lone ploughman was driving his weary way homeward in his tractor. He saw me and seemed to stall. I waved. He did a rapid double take and his tractor dropped straight into a ditch. He struggled frantically to back his way out, drove out of the field, on to the lane and headed off towards Wigmore as fast as his tractor would go (28 mph, they tell me).

I thought it odd that he hadn't waved back as he usually did – until I remembered I was still wearing my monk's habit, with the cowl over my head. I heard afterwards that he had reached the village, jumped off his vehicle and rushed breathlessly into the pub, gabbling uncontrollably that he'd just seen the ghost of Wigmore Abbey.

For my day job, at the time, I was also performing with Sue Holderness in *Relatively Speaking*, which had gone well. Our partnership was working and the audiences who came out in good numbers didn't seem to mind that the characters we were playing bore no resemblance to the *Only Fools* characters for which we were known. After Eastbourne we had successfully transferred to Windsor and later went on to Bromley.

While they were making *The House Detectives* I was commuting every day down to Windsor and driving back after the show to Wigmore to carry on filming the TV programme next morning. It was lucky they were such different jobs.

Generally, with all that was going on, we seldom had a chance to listen to the radio or catch up with the TV news. On 11 September, I'd set off as usual after lunch to drive to Windsor. I didn't turn on the radio until I was nearly there and, unusually, tuned it to Radio Four, probably to hear a cricket score.

A very grave-voiced newsreader announced that some catastrophic disaster had happened in New York, leaving thousands dead and the massive Twin Towers of the World Trade Centre collapsed in a heap of rubble.

The Pentagon had been attacked, too and it seemed like the whole of the US was under threat.

For a few moments I could only assume that I'd just found one of those futuristic, experimental dramas that the BBC likes to put out on Radio Four, like the Orson Welles' *War of the Worlds,* which US

Radio had broadcast fifty-six years before. I fiddled with the tuner, but the same news story was everywhere.

I reached Windsor and sat in the car park by the theatre, listening in complete disbelief, until I realized a major world drama really *was* unfolding, and I started getting angry.

I knew the Twin Towers – I'd been up there. I had a lot of friends in New York.

Jesus! – I thought – we couldn't possibly do the show!

I rushed in through the stage door, spluttering incoherently. 'We can't do the show! It's out of the question! Fuck these people – whoever they are. We must show some respect for the people who have died. We can't do a fucking comedy! It's stupid and thoughtless!'

Everyone else had already been watching the shocking scenes for hours on TV. They'd had time to calm down and be more rational about it.

They understood my rage, of course, but pointed out that if we cancelled the show, the leprous rats that had done this horrible thing would have won. It was our duty to carry on, as normal, and say 'Up yours!' to Al Qaeda.

We went on, and received a standing ovation for our efforts.

On the long drive home in the dark, my rage turned to a feeling of dread for the future. Like a lot of people, I spent most of the night unable to sleep, unable to dispel from my head the horrors I'd seen on the endless loop of those ghastly events.

It's still horrible, at this distance in time, over ten years on and I still don't understand how anyone could ever be motivated to cause so much death and destruction. Whether or not our going to war in Iraq was the right response, I don't know, but I always felt someone, somewhere should have been brought to justice, and I wish Osama bin Laden had been put on trial before he'd been shot.

At the time, though, life grudgingly got back to normal. *The House Detectives* was edited and shown. Dan Cruickshank did a super job of explaining the house, both in his delivery and his narration. The programme generated a lot of interest – at least within our village, and, I hope, a bit beyond.

In the house, our new local decorators were laboriously painting the grand, high-ceilinged abbot's parlour in yellow ochre mixed with cow dung and lime, while Bill Kenwright had sent Sue and me off to Bromley with *Relatively Speaking*. On top of this, at last, the rumours of a final *Trotter* outing had come to fruition. John Sullivan and Gareth Gwenlan had persuaded the BBC that they should make three very, very last *Only Fools* Christmas Specials, to be broadcast over the next three Christmases but all made at the same time.

After much discussion, it had been decided that there should be a new end to the story. I'd always held the view, quite strongly, that the wheel should turn full circle for *Del* and *Rodney*, that they should lose all their new-found money and end up returning to live in Nelson Mandela House, happy to be back to their old life. If they hadn't the programme would have promoted the undesirable and erroneous idea that money was the answer to everything.

The seeds of this had been sown in the original 'final' episode, *Time on our Hands*, shown over Christmas '96, with *Del* sitting in the empty sitting-room, on the phone, working out a deal with *Monkey Harris*, and *Rodney* saying, 'Del, we don't have to do this anymore.' *Del* looks up with a look of disappointed acceptance.

We were, all of us, quite distracted when we met up for the read through. It had been five years since we'd all worked together. There was a little more 'snow on the roof' for some of us, although in David's case, his hair seemed to have got darker. There was no doubt that we all felt it just wasn't the same without Buster and Kenny. Kenny especially, as his natural chutzpah had always rubbed off on everyone, while David and Nick no longer had *Uncle Albert* to bounce off. We had *Albert's* funeral scene to look forward to, reminiscent of *Grandad's* back in 1985, when Buster had first appeared. Kenny's character, *Mike Fisher*, landlord of the Nag's Head was said to have been up to some chicanery, fallen foul of the authorities and disappeared.

John Sullivan surveyed us all. 'I really miss those two, you know. I thought it would be OK, but it ain't the same.'

It wasn't. I missed talking to Buster about parking, and his bouncing around on the piano stool. I missed saying, 'Kenneth, behave yourself!' which he'd always enjoyed, because it made him feel posh.

The first of the three specials, *If They Could See Us Now*, featured as a guest Jonathan Ross, playing the host of a quiz show.

Del, having lost all his and *Rodney's* money in dodgy Central American funds, has wound up back in Nelson Mandela House and on the quiz show, where he has worked his way up to the £50,000 question.

Quizmaster Ross asks him, 'What is a female swan called?'

Rodney surreptitiously waves a pen at him.

'A bic?' *Del* answers.

Despite losing two much loved characters, John Sullivan hadn't lost his touch. *If They Could See Us Now* was as good as any script he'd written for the show, and full of affection for the core qualities of the two remaining *Trotters*. It achieved 20.3 million viewers, which was amazing, given how long it had been since the last episode and the way the world had changed since *Del Boy* had first been introduced to the public in 1981 – twenty whole years before!

Following straight on from making *If You could see us Now*, we made *Strangers on the Shore* and *Sleepless in Peckham*, to be aired as Christmas Specials at the end of 2002 and 2003, which would bring the whole *Only Fools & Horses* saga to its very final conclusion. Although we were now certain we would never make another episode of the show, there was nevertheless great comfort in knowing there were two more major shows to be aired; it made one feel that that a key part of one's life had not yet entirely died.

There was still an enormous interest in *Only Fools*; the twentieth anniversary had passed but the demand for re-showings seemed, if anything, to have increased. It was now, unquestionably, a television phenomenon.

I was pleased too to be maintaining my acting partnership with Sue Holderness, which, of course, *Only Fools* had created. After the success of *Relatively Speaking*, Bill Kenwright, multi-faceted impresario, (ex-*Corrie* star) and famous for taking chances, had asked us to follow it up with another Ayckbourn play, *Time and Time Again*, also featuring Robert Duncan, well known from the hit comedy, *Drop the Dead Donkey*.

This was a pleasure. I knew the play well as I'd done it in 1970, and here I was, more than thirty years on, playing the same part. *Graham* was an intolerant suburbanite who possessed, as it happened, a number of *Boycie* overtones. I recognized only now that I had first ventured into this character's hinterland back then, and given him more flesh when I'd met the drinking acquaintance at the St Margaret's Hotel on whom I'd based *DI Humphreys* in *Citizen Smith*. *Humphreys* had then morphed into *Boycie*, the magnificent creature that now bestrides the cultural landscape '*de nos jours*', as *Del Boy* would have put it.

Like all Ayckbourn plays, *Time and Time Again* was a wonderfully constructed word-spinner, and an opportunity to explore the underbelly of surprisingly resilient, middle-class England. Sue and I dovetailed perfectly and had a lot of fun as a pretentious, *nouveau riche* couple, airing their paranoia while a cricket match was being played in a field beyond their garden.

The *Time and Time Again* tour led up to my next significant birthday, the LX, as I prefer to disguise it. Obviously, I'd watched it coming, since the Big Five-O, and I was conscious that I hadn't played cricket or tennis since coming up to live in the Welsh Marches. Up until then, every time I took to the field or court, I'd increasingly found myself pulling muscles I didn't even know I had, my reactions were not as sharp as they had been and I began not to enjoy playing either sport. This could have felt very tragic but I'd also found I had a huge amount of physical work to do in getting the garden together and under control.

We'd been living at Wigmore Abbey nearly five years by the time 16 August 2002 came around. Carol evidently felt we had done enough to the place to throw a party there with confidence. She and I had discussions about holding a smallish celebration, mainly with the local people who had been so supportive; we were, after all, a long way from our previous lives.

However, behind my back, Carol had been trawling through the address book and had contacted practically everyone I'd ever known and even a few I hadn't. Friends and colleagues from the distant past and long lost-relations were sounded out with the promise of overnight accommodation in outlying, friendly B&Bs to keep the whole thing hidden from me.

It was a major feat of subterfuge. I knew she was up to something when suddenly I wasn't allowed to answer the phone or look at the post, but, at that stage, I thought it was only our friends from the past four years who were coming.

The 16 August dawned fine and clear. I was woken at eight o'clock by the sounds of an army of people arriving to engage in manual activity. I was vaguely suspicious that something wasn't right when these noises were followed by shouted instructions, the clashing of iron against iron and bellows of laughter. I peeked blearily through the curtains of our bedroom and saw to my amazement canvas marquees being erected, chairs and tables being arranged in the garden and clusters of men and women milling around looking very busy.

I went to the top of the stairs.

'What the hell's going on?' I bellowed.

'What do you mean?' Carol's question floated innocently back up the stairs.

'What do you mean, what do I mean? There's a bloody great tent in the garden

'What tent?'

'What do you mean, what tent?'

'Oh that tent! That's not a tent; it's an awning.'

'What's a bloody awning doing in the garden?'

'Stop shouting and get dressed. It's your birthday.'

It was indeed.

The first people to arrive, mid-morning, were Keith Washington and Madeleine Howard. 'Oh, we just happened to be passing,' they lied. It was great to see them; they had been firm friends for ages, through many of my ridiculous personal crises, looking on like parents of a wayward teenager.

By lunchtime, I was astonished by the procession of people I simply hadn't dreamt would have come all this way, waiting in line to say warm, complimentary things while pressing into my palsied hands tokens of their appreciation that I had reached such an age and remained standing. I hadn't for a moment thought that anyone would bring presents.

I was frankly overwhelmed and not helped in this by having downed several large gulps of festive wine to deal with the trauma of it all. I could see even more people arriving and queuing up to remind me how old I was and I became very emotional when most of the team from *Only Fools* turned up.

David Jason had come, John Sullivan, Gareth Gwenlan, Tony Dow, Sue – of course, Paul Barber, sporting dreadlocks and a T-shirt proclaiming 'NORF LONDON', Roy Heather, who played *Sid*, the café owner, and Ken MacDonald's widow, Sheila.

So many people from my past appeared that it was difficult to get round them all. Most of the locals we had asked were able to come and gave a wonderful slant to what might otherwise have been just another show-biz party. The actors – or Max Factors, as a good Cockney might have put it – were all on fine form and engaged brilliantly with the locals. Paul Barber raced around talking to everybody, and Christopher Timothy, always a hit with the ladies, charmed anyone he met.

Pushing the party along were Richard Heffer, who had become a close friend since the emotional fall-out of *The Relapse* tour and Ray Lonnen whom I'd met at a commercial casting years before in my murkier past.

Sue Holderness and her husband, Mark Piper had stayed in the uplifting surroundings of the elegant eighteenth-century pile which was home to Ivor and Caroline Windsor. Lord Windsor had been more than happy to welcome *Marlene* into his home and was especially entertaining all day, regaling locals and actors alike with his good humour and tall tales.

There were friends from our nearby villages, from the local farming community, county types and long-lost relations from Dorset and Somerset.

David Jason, immensely famous now not just as *Del Boy*, but also for superb portrayals of the well-loved *Pop Larkin* and the TV detective, *Frost*, held court at a table just below the tottering stone finger of the ruined abbey. He dealt happily with his increasingly inebriated audience, unfazed by the unfamiliar tones and demeanour of the local land-owners and assorted rustic toffs.

He, Sue, Ron and Paul all joined me for photographs around another of Carol's brilliant ideas – a birthday cake decorated with the figures of *Del Boy, Rodney, Trigger, Boycie* and *Marlene* around the little yellow three-wheeler van.

There were speeches. In reply to Keith's generous words I became hopelessly emotional, mumbled and fumbled my way through an entirely unprepared effort. 'Imagine you're a pair of curtains,' I scolded myself, 'and pull yourself together.'

After, through a haze of gratitude and booze, I saw John Sullivan approach. 'I've had a bit of an idea,' he said. 'I'll get back to you.'

I sensed a hint of something exciting in the air, but couldn't quite focus on it.

After eight hours or so, quite a crowd were still in the garden. It rained, we rushed to cram ourselves under the awning until it stopped. Some couldn't be bothered and just sat there getting wet.

As the last stragglers meandered up the track to the field which our neighbourly farmer had lent us for a car-park, I was able to reflect on what a great day it had been – unexpected, glorious fun, brilliantly organized by the perfect hostess, Carol, who was now inside, doing the washing up.

I wandered through the garden, and stopped at table full of empty glasses and an ashtray overflowing with cigarette and cigar butts. Around the table were four chairs and I wondered who had sat there and what they'd talked about.

More or less sober now, I thought about being sixty. It was sort of disturbing but I didn't feel any different, and there was nothing I could do about it. It was a number, a milestone. Unlike *The Who*, I had never hoped to die before I got old. I was too scared of death, too uncertain of my own immortality and I remembered Kenny MacDonald worrying about dying too young. His father had died at 43 and Ken always thought he had inherited some condition that would mean the same for him. Perhaps he was right, poor soul.

I don't know why I was asked to appear in a celebrity edition of Anne Robinson's torture show. My grasp of a broad range of facts, especially the history of the Arsenal Football Club isn't bad but there are a number of large lacunae in my general knowledge. I had met Anne on less combative terms at the twenty-fifth anniversary of the Mulberry fashion company, where I had performed an impromptu sketch with Richard Heffer, an old friend of Mulberry founder, Roger Saul. (It was a great party, and Roger became a good friend of Carol's and mine after that.)

Quite sparky with a notably acerbic wit, as you might expect, Anne was also very friendly and entertaining. When I agreed to do the *Weakest Link*, friends gasped, shook my hand, wished me luck and referred to it as the *Bleakest Stink*, although I found I was rather looking forward to it. Needless to say, the idea was that whichever 'celebrity' won, being all sitcom stars off the telly, they obviously wouldn't need the money and would donate it to a charity of their choice. As it happened, I could think of a few old sitcom stars who were in pretty desperate need themselves.

The victims all gathered before the show, nine in all, including Mike Grady, from *Last of the Summer Wine*, Clive Swift from *Keeping up Appearances*, Ian Lavender from *Dad's Army*, Vicky Michelle from '*Allo 'Allo* and Lesley Joseph from *Birds of a Feather*.

We chatted, and told each other that as long as we weren't slung out at the first round, we didn't mind how we did (although we all wanted to win, really.)

In the first round of easy-peasy questions, poor old Mike got caught by one of those trick mathematical questions, in which you realize you're wrong even as you're blurting out the wrong answer.

Mike blurted, got it wrong, and we had to vote him off. I felt inexplicably disloyal in doing it; his face as he trudged off showed his shame and mortification and I felt much as I had years before when I'd watched my wayward dog, the Prune, go off when I sent him to the vet to have his nuts off.

The rounds went on, and I felt a stab of guilt for every one of my fellow sitcom stars I voted off. I was saved myself by Ian Lavender after a bad round and I was glad to be still there and in with a shout. The problem now, though, was that by the fourth round I'd run out of barbed witty ripostes to Ms Robinson's waspish sorties and I was feeling rather vulnerable.

But I did become excited when we were down to the last three – Lavender, Joseph and Challis. At the end of the round, Lavender and I both voted off Lesley Joseph.

Anne looked at me with a raised eyebrow and an off-the-shoulder smile. 'Why Lesley, John?' she asked sweetly.

All joked out, I could only think of, 'Because she's a woman,' but I knew that wouldn't do.

After a short pause I had an idea.

'I've never really liked her,' I said, deadpan.

Anne got it, and laughed.

Lesley didn't see the joke; she gave me a chilling look and wouldn't speak to me for about two years. My over-developed sense of irony had dropped me in it, again.

Lavender and I went head to head, to finish with a sudden-death round, when I got a question about show-jumping. I can't remember if I refused, fell off or knocked a pole down. Serves me right. Ian Lavender won. The money went off to his nominated charity and at least the taxman didn't get his claws into it.

Back at the Abbey, although we had used my birthday party in the summer as an incentive to finish off most of the lingering repairs to the house, the process of generally putting details right and adding stuff for reasons of both comfort and aesthetics was more or less ongoing and we seemed constantly to be setting ourselves new tasks. This was particularly difficult in a listed house like ours, as we had to get permssion from Herefordshire council practically to change a light bulb, and that permission could be withheld for the most specious of reasons. We had for instance, a brutal and entirely inappropriate lump of a stone fireplace that had been installed during the '70s in the most important room in the house, the abbot's parlour. The listed building people bizarrely considered it part of the 'history of the house' and it had to stay, although we soon had it dressed in a good thick coat of plaster and an ochre lime wash.

The fireplace took its revenge, though, a few weeks later, when Bonham's, the antique auctioneers, held a promotional jolly at the Abbey. Tim Hales, who with his wife Celestria had become good friends since soon after our arrival at Wigmore, was then the Bonham's local business drummer-up and he'd asked if he could use the house as a venue for the function.

We hadn't had a big party like this inside the house, and we thought it would be a good opportunity to see how it dealt with a large number of visitors. The centre of the reception was the parlour, and on a damp autumnal day, the great gaping hearth semed to be crying out to be filled up, to give a bit of live warmth to the high-ceilinged room.

House and Garden

I made a hefty tump of kindling and big split oak logs, put a match to it and waited until it started to burn. I noticed a little smoke seeping back into the room but I guessed it would be fine once the chimney had warmed up. Just then the phone rang and somebody turned up to deliver the drink for the evening's hooley. I was downstairs dealing with this for a while and forgot all about the fire. When I went back the great room was full of smoke, right up to its cruck-beamed roof.

Angry with the fire and myself for letting it get away with it, I opened all the windows and started frantically trying to bat the smoke out with a large piece of cardboard. As it started to thin I grabbed the large wrought-iron fire basket that held the glowing logs, managed to pick it up and rush out with it and hurl the logs into a skip that was semi-permanently parked outside. Luckily there was nothing inflammable in the skip. I rushed back to the room and looked at my watch; there was an hour to go before people would start arriving for the party. I arranged a new, unlit pile of logs in the iron basket as artistically as possible and carried on batting the smoke out of the window.

When the first guests arrived and came into the room, they asked me how I had managed to produce such a wonderfully authentic mediaeval aroma of woodsmoke. The house seemed to puff out its chest with pride and looked wonderful with all the candles lit. The sight and sound of people enjoying themselves gave us great encouragement for future activities there.

My sixty-first year was marked, at least, by the achievement of one small personal ambition. Over fifty years after I'd first set eyes on Douglas Wilmer playing *Captain Hook* in *Peter Pan* in London's West End, I was invited to play the part myself at the Grand Theatre in Swansea. I'd been playing a series of ogres and baddies in pantomime for several years and always enjoyed it, but I was more chuffed than I'd expected to be playing *Hook*.

I'd always guessed what a treat it would be to stride across the stage in a crimson frock coat with black lace trimmings, with a jaunty tri-corn in my head, boots up to my armpits and my sword flashing from its diamanté-encrusted scabbard at the drop of a titfer.

Apart from the novel experience of seeing *Boycie* bearded,

bewigged and playing *Captain Hook*, the Swansea punters also got *Mrs Darling* played by the inimitable Dora Bryan, although for her fellow players, working with Dora was the stuff of bad dreams. Despite Dora being naturally a very funny woman and a great comic actress, you could never rely on her to enter at the right time, or the right place, which some actors can get disproportionately angry about. In fact, it occurred to me that perhaps she used her own vagueness as an excuse for generating a little extra audience sympathy.

During one performance, I was on stage, standing in the wings and keeping an eye on her before our next entrance together, which was due in a couple of minutes. She was standing about chatting animatedly to a couple of stagehands, when I whispered loudly, 'Dora!'

She looked round, eyes wide with panic, and rushed past me, straight out on to the stage. She realized at once that she'd arrived too early. She wasn't fazed; she was too experienced a trouper. She turned to the audience. 'Oh dear,' she said in her cuddly northern accent, 'I've come out to too early, haven't I?'

The punters shrieked with laughter and she left the stage to a great round of applause.

She was chatting about it to the stagehands again, when she glanced at me and I nodded. She panicked again and rushed out a second time, about half a minute too soon.

She stopped and dropped her shoulders, turning to the audience once more. 'Oh Lor'! I've done it again!' She got a bigger applause this time, and scuttled off.

By almost physically hanging onto her, I managed to bring her on with me, this time, on cue. At her third appearance, the audience cheered and clapped even more.

Good old Dora, I thought, three rounds of applause in as many minutes, and all unscripted.

One night the punters had an extra thrill when *Peter Pan* got well and truly stuck on her flying wire for five minutes, which felt like half an hour, dangling thirty-five feet above the audience. *Captain Hook* and his *Pirates* swiftly became brilliant improvisers, though unheard by the punters who were gazing up in grisly fascination at the struggling *Peter Pan* all tangled in her wire.

House and Garden

Although Swansea lacks a reputation for elegant beauty and demonstrates a distinct lack of civic pride (pax, Swansea-ites, you probably love the place), it produced some fine audiences – and what more can one ask of a town?

I loved being *Hook* and have played the part no less than six more times since then.

The year ended on a high for me when the second of the very last three *Only Fools* specials, *Strangers on the Shore* was shown at prime time on Christmas Day and drew an audience of over 16million.

The following year, 2003, I set off on a fresh theatrical venture with Sue Holderness, another play by Alan Ayckbourn. *How the Other Half Loves* was produced, once again, by Bill Kenwright. Although I'd never appeared in it, I'd seen it in its first West End showing at the *Phoenix* in 1970, with Robert Morley in the lead role.

I recalled that the production had been fairly contentious, in as much as Ayckbourn had asked for his name to be taken off the bill because he didn't like the direction in which it had been taken. It had effectively become the Robert Morley Show, simply because Morley was such a big personality that his presence completely overbalanced the play.

At the Library Theatre in Scarborough, where, like all his other plays, Ayckbourn had first shown it, it had been an entirely ensemble production. But its values had been substantially changed when Michael Codron brought it to London and wanted a cast of bigger names in order to attract bums on seats in sufficient numbers.

Robert Morley was big in every sense of the word and, in Ayckbourn's view, utterly unsuitable for the part. Now Sue and I had the task of turning *Boycie* and *Marlene* into a scatty middle-aged, middle-class couple, with all the wicked observations of the type for which the author was best known.

The tour started well enough, taking in the usual venues – Windsor, Bromley, Malvern and so on, with the addition this time of Belfast, which was the first time either of us had appeared on stage there.

We arrived towards the end of August to stay at the Europa Hotel, which had the dubious reputation for having been, back in the 1970s, the most bombed hotel in Europe. Thank God, with the Good-Friday agreement and the burgeoning dialogue between the two sides to that awful conflict, it was as safe as anywhere now.

We were playing at the Opera House, one of Belfast's largest theatres (which had also come close to being demolished by a car bomb – accidentally, we were told), and somewhat to our surprise, we were doing goodish business. Not long into the run there, we heard that a local 'Mr Big', an 'entrepreneur' identified only as 'Sean', was coming in to see the show and had invited us to dinner afterwards at a new night club he owned, part of a recently-developed leisure and entertainment area down by the waterfront on the River Lagan.

The show went well that night and we were met at the stage door by yer man's 'representative', who showed us and the rest of the cast to three gleaming black Mercedes waiting in line on the street. The doors were opened for us by a trio of chunky-looking chaps in dark suits and shades.

Once in, we were whisked away at great speed, as if the vehicle we were in was immune from chastisement for traffic violations.

Just as I had when sitting with Sabina in a restaurant in Syracuse, Sicily, I found my imagination, driven by my ever-vigilant paranoia, creating ways in which we might be in jeopardy.

We weren't these people's enemy, as far as I knew, but I guess we were worth something on the ransom market. Trying to lean back nonchalantly into the leather upholstery of the limo, I began to speculate about the size of ransom they might demand for us, and whether or not there was anyone in the world who would cough up more than a few grand for me.

And we all knew what had happened to Shergar when his owner didn't pay! At least, we think we do.

The cars pulled up outside an awning that looked more like LA's Sunset Strip than downtown Belfast. We were ushered out of the cars into a swish modern building – no doubt a kind of holding pen before we were taken to our next – final? – holding place.

Once we were sitting in what I suppose was a designated VIP area (also a possible holding pen?) with champagne bottles open, it seemed we were being treated with some deference. It seemed these kidnappers knew the value of looking after their hostages. When Sean and his wife sat down beside Sue and me, and told us what great *Only*

House and Garden

Fools fans they were, I started to consider that we might not in fact be a source of revenue to a gang of post-troubles Belfast hoodlums.

Over dinner, with the compliments flying about our show that night, I relaxed, and began to believe that I would probably sleep in my room at the Europa that night.

There was though, a tricky moment when I suggested that we actors were entirely outside any aspect of what had happened here in Northern Ireland and we were well placed to play the part of some kind of ambassador for our country.

The suggestion that Brits should be ambassadors for anything didn't go down well with our host, because, he said, the Brits had killed his brother, and he didn't sound ready to be forgiving about it. The atmosphere was distinctly chillier and we were regaled with stories about the wicked anti-Catholic stance of the British occupying forces.

However hard we tried to see his point of view, he wasn't having it. None of us felt like dancing. We couldn't wait to get back to our hotel.

We did in the end, and were never ransomed, then or at any later stage in our visit to the province. I wondered if I should see a shrink about my rampant paranoia. I wondered if there were any shrinks in Herefordshire; I thought not.

Another minor adventure that befell me in Belfast to some extent redressed the discomfort of our session in the night club. Taking the rather bizarre 'Black Taxi' guided tour of the former trouble spots of Belfast (in what was still a segregated city) I ended up outside the Sinn Fein office deep down the Falls Road. The taxi driver beckoned us in; we weren't keen. I had no idea what we would find inside. Eventually, reining in the paranoia, I reluctantly agreed and pushed the door open, fully expecting to find Gerry Adams and Martin McGuinness standing there. 'Hello, Challis; we've been expecting ye.'

In fact, I found I was in a Sinn Fein souvenir shop, the part of the 'Troubles Tour' where this side of the former conflict got its cut. I doubt if many people refused the chance of buying a little memento. Like any pilgrimage destination gift shop, there were icons – statues of Gerry and Martin, rosaries, books about how to deal with Protestantism (*Protestantism – it's not Going Away*) and temptation (*Sin, Mortal and Imagined.*)

Boycie & Beyond

As I peered uncertainly at this merchandise I had the feeling I was being watched, perhaps on hidden cameras by people wondering what the hell I was doing here. I felt I must buy something to show my *bona fides*. I made my way towards the back of the shop where two middle-aged ladies sat behind a showcase counter. I tried a smile.

They beamed back. 'Well, now you're here, you'd better sign an autograph,' one said.

The other nodded. 'And can you sign one for my daughter; she's your biggest fan; she's got every single episode.'

In a daze of relief, I happily signed a few autographs, and left the shop unscathed, thinking it wasn't such a wicked old world after all.

Our production of *How the Other Half Loves* arrived safely back in England, having done well – well enough, at least, for Bill Kenwright to ask us to go out touring with another play the following year.

In the meantime, it was wonderful to get back to spend early autumn pottering about the gardens at Wigmore Abbey, which, after all, had been our main purpose in buying the place. The gardens by then were beginning to look like something to be proud of. The stone paths and terracing we'd started laying on the south side of the house two years before had settled beneath the pergola and rose-decked trellis tunnels we'd put up. In the centre we had placed a wonderful terracotta statue Carol and I had bought even before we'd left London, an elegant, beautifully proportioned figure, known as 'Joan' – after Roger de Mortimer's loyal wife and my late mother.

One visitor who came to cast her eye and some encouraging approval over the garden was the lovely horticultural writer, Mirabel Osler. She lives in Ludlow and came with her friend, Prue Bellak, who had also lived in the town for several years with the late, entertaining and controversial MP, Julian Critchley. We often met Mirabel with another redoubtable Marches resident Helen Osborne, widow of John.

John Osborne in the '50s and '60s was the *enfant terrible* who changed the face of English theatre, the Angry Young Man who had introduced the public to what became known as 'kitchen-sink' drama. With the encouragement of George Devine at the Royal Court Theatre in Sloane Square, Osborne had been reacting to the cosy, waspish, upper-middle-class comfort zone of the plays of Terence Rattigan and his ilk, which had dominated the London stage since the war.

In the drawing-room comedies and dramas of that time, the audience never saw a bedroom, let alone a kitchen, and especially not a sink. In Osborne's first play, *Look Back in Anger*, you could see the sink, the dirty dishes, the washing and the ironing board in a play that dealt directly with the seamier side of modern life, in which the embittered, cynical anti-hero *Jimmy Porter* railed against the iniquities of a decaying society. The play spearheaded a critical new direction for drama, and like most groundbreakers, was greeted with adulation and opprobrium in equal measures.

In later life, despite his colossal early success with other plays, *The Entertainer* and *A Patriot for Me*, Osborne had not been able to sustain his career and, after some marital disasters, had retreated, perhaps to lick his wounds, to more or less the back end of nowhere with Helen, his fifth wife, whom he'd married in 1978. Since 1985 they had lived in a Victorian pile called The Hurst, near Clun, where Shropshire pokes a westward finger deep into the belly of mid-Wales. In 1994, John had died there and Helen had chosen to stay and make the most of her time.

Among the people who welcomed us into their homes after we had arrived and settled ourselves in Herefordshire was a well-known artist, Jonathan Heale, and his wife, Mary, who lived a few miles down the road in the valley of the River Lugg at Aymestrey. It was at dinner with them that we first met Helen Osborne. I had the impression that since John had died Helen was still coming to terms with her loss. She was, though, a wonderfully erudite, clever, warm witty woman, and we loved her from the start. Luckily for us, she reciprocated and became a good friend and regular visitor to Wigmore Abbey.

She particularly liked Carol for being a strong, direct sort of woman and would often take her off to lunch with Mirabel Osler and Prue Bellak, on what they liked to call their 'Sketchleys Lunches' – to be enjoyed once clothes had been delivered to the cleaners and the rest of the day was free. These expeditions went far and wide, and might even involve train journeys to Abergavenny and a taxi out to the famous Walnut Tree. As the only husband extant, I was even invited to join them a few times, and for the only man at the table, they were a formidable gang.

Rather surprisingly, Helen, who was a former arts editor of the *Observer,* also became a loyal follower of my dramatic peregrinations. She would often come over to the Festival Theatre in Malvern if I was in a touring production there and she even came once to Birmingham to see me in *Aladdin.* This pantomime involved, as they often do, an eclectic mix of faces that would have meant nothing to her – Bobby Davro, as *Aladdin,* Amanda Barrie from *Coronation Street* and *Bad Girls,* and Melinda Messenger as *The Princess,* thoroughly professional and an impressive revelation for an actress who'd started as a Page Three Girl from Swindon (not to suggest there's anything wrong with Swindon.)

Helen admitted that until then, she'd never seen a pantomime but seemed genuinely to enjoy it, as she'd enjoyed the undemanding dramas of Alan Ayckbourn when she'd come to see me in them. She happily discussed these plays and why they had worked for her, giving them credit for making their point with a useful helping of humour, although she was, after all, from the heavier side of the business, a serious theatre and book critic of some reputation who had lived for a long time with one of our major playwrights. I think that now she enjoyed a little exposure to the kind of popular culture for which I was best known, and unstuffily was prepared to see the value in it. She would even watch the odd episode of *Only Fools* and tell me what she'd liked about it.

I guess it was precisely for this aspect of my career that she included me in a group of people she'd been asked to get together for a TV programme. The premise of the feature was the fact that The Hurst was to become a centre for new, aspiring writers, a boarding school for scribblers, as someone elegantly put it, and over lunch Helen's guests – all arts related – would talk about the motivation and impetus to write.

'Please come and help me out, darling,' she almost pleaded. 'I've got Maggie Smith and John Mortimer coming but the idea of the programme is so boring I need someone to liven it up a bit and nudge the conversation along. And have some fun, for God's sake!'

When it came to it, sitting in the vast Victorian dining room at *The Hurst,* surrounded by arts heavyweights was a fairly daunting experience. The room itself had become a kind of shrine to John

House and Garden

Osborne; the walls were covered with playbills, posters and shots of Osborne with assorted luminaries – Noel Coward, Laurence Olivier and Michael Caine, with whom Osborne had played the arch-villain in the great revenge thriller, *Get Carter*. Unflattering caricatures hung alongside unfriendly reviews, perversely enlarged and framed.

Somewhat to my surprise, the discussion went rather well. My presence seemed to provoke a debate about the validity of popular culture, in its broadest sense, as it related to writing. At some levels in the artistic world, 'popular' is still a dirty word. But among the more intellectually robust, the 'popular' is not always dismissed with the same elitist flip of a hand. The embedded notion among less imaginative, less creative thinkers that greater 'accessibility' is always an indication of lesser artistic value tried to rear its head, with even the clever John Mortimer finding it hard not to sneer at anything which appealed to large numbers of the working class – an odd stance for a prominent Labour supporter.

Specifically, we were asking: if you aspire to write, what should you write about? Should you aim at achieving the widest possible audience and couch whatever you want to say in the most easily absorbed medium – a musical, say, a Whitehall farce, a good, tense thriller? Would this devalue any observations about the human condition that might be found within it? Or was it more honest and valid to pare these observations down to an intellectually challenging treatise, to which only a small minority of readers would be able to relate?

Mortimer became quite sniffy about situation comedy in general, saying it was aimed at the lowest common denominator – in other words, it was widely 'accessible' – another dirty word, evidently. But he wouldn't accept that it was possible to write worthwhile drama in that way and at the same time put over new ideas and perspectives, as well as useful observations about human relationships and realities.

He himself had had a long-running TV success (and a good earner), with the help of Leo McKern, in his much-loved (and presumably intellectually justifiable) *Rumpole of the Bailey*, which made good use of a number of solid old sitcom tricks.

Maggie Smith on the other hand, was more *laissez-faire*. 'Look, darling, as long as it has some quality, I don't give a monkey's what it is. I've spent too much of my life wondering where the next job was coming from to be too picky.'

Helen told us that John Osborne suffered from severe writer's block over the years because he couldn't bear to write anything he didn't feel passionate about. Whether it was commercial or not was irrelevant.

It was a bizarre but stimulating session, which left me wondering if I'd really been there, like doing *Guys & Dolls* with Mandy Patinkin. It had been made special by Helen, who was one of those people you wish you'd met earlier in life but at least we did meet, and to this day, I can see her diminutive, spiky persona, in her little Lionel Bart cap, cigarette in one hand, drink in the other, flinging out the challenge – 'Isn't this what life's about?'

The TV discussion, as finally edited, worked pretty well, and generally left me with food for further thought, on which I've ruminated much in recent years, especially now as I try honestly, constructively – and *accessibly* – to write this account of my own chaotic existence.

After the pleasure of touring a good Ayckbourn play with a fine actress earlier in the year, pantomime 2003 was a bit of a come down. I was playing *Captain Hook* again, which I looked forward to, but it was in Croydon, at the Ashcroft Theatre, not my favourite venue. Named after the illustrious actress, Dame Peggy – a local lass, I was told – the theatre was part of an 'Arts Complex', the Fairfield Halls, an unattractive concrete construction of the early '60s Brutalist school and a council initiative which had deteriorated into more of a leisure centre – an unlovely venue for fading rock stars and tribute bands. The staff were well-intentioned but they were council employees, not theatre people and had no real concept of the priorities. It took two weeks to get the dressing rooms cleaned from the show that had preceded ours and this shambolic approach reflected the style of the production in general. It was cobbled together within just ten days. Little groups of performers rehearsed separately, the dancers doing their sweaty routines in one place and the principals in small private groups. Barnaby, the main comic, as *Smee*, and his pirates seemed to be in a completely different show.

Kirsten O'Brien looked as if she would make an engaging *Peter*

Pan. She was spirited away to rehearse with the children, which left me to rehearse with Julian Clary's sister, Frankie, who was cast as *Mrs Darling*, the children's mother. Frankie was an attractive and likeable woman, but she was basically a dancer, not an actress or a singer, both of which were required for the important role of *Mrs Darling*. I guess she had been cast in this arbitrary way simply as a means of getting bums on seats, without any consideration for her suitability.

It never fails to puzzle me when producers take these risks. Sue Holderness came across a similar piece of miscasting some years later, when she was touring a successful production of *Calendar Girls*, and Charlie Dimmock was cast as one of the key characters. Charlie Dimmock is a very nice person, and she's kind to animals, but she's a gardener, and not an actress.

This *Peter Pan* was full of these strange anomalies. The choreographer had decided that the girl pirates should behave like maritime pole dancers, which lent an inevitable air of vulgarity to the production. J M Barrie must have been spinning in his six-foot plot at this complete lack of respect for his original. Conceivably, as a chunk of the profits from any production is required to go to the Great Ormond Street hospital under the terms of Barrie's will, producers feel they can do what they want with the story, provided it pulls in the punters, and the wonga.

We also had to contend with the unsympathetic nature of the hideous building, which resembled an underground car park with an accidental theatre on top.

But despite all these drawbacks, the show did extraordinary business, so much so that we were asked to fit in extra performances in order to accommodate everyone who wanted to come.

It was, at least, good to feel wanted, and *Captain Hook* got an especially warm welcome after *Boycie* had appeared in the very last of the *Only Fools* Christmas Specials, *Sleepless in Peckham*. *Boycie* had featured in an engaging little sub-plot, in which it was thought by *Del* and his other chums that he had done away with *Marlene*, as no one had seen her for a couple of weeks. When he produces her at the Nag's Head, it is revealed that she has been away having her breasts surgically enhanced. The show ends with *Rodney* accepting that he is the son of *Freddie 'the Frog' Robdal*, and *Cassandra* finally having

a baby, a girl named *Joan*, after the *Trotters'* mother.
Once again, *Only Fools & Horses* topped the Christmas-Day ratings, with 15½ million viewers.

The following morning, on Boxing Day, when the news of the horrific Asian tsunami came through, it had the effect of unifying the company in the grief we all felt for the hundreds of thousands of people believed dead. I was asked to make a short speech after each performance, appealing for money to help the devastated populations of Indonesia, Thailand and Sri Lanka, to which the Croydon audiences responded with remarkable generosity.

Closer to home, we experienced a more personal sadness when we heard that Helen Osborne had died. I wasn't surprised; it had often seemed to me that, unlike most people, she didn't have that obsessive urge to hang on to life at the expense of all personal enjoyment, and had been quite prepared to die since John, her husband had predeceased her. I wasn't surprised but I was very sad about it; Helen was one of the warmest most engaging people I had ever met, and had helped very much to affirm our lives out in the sticks and we were both grateful for the friendship she'd shown us. She had been such an enlivening figure, so funny, so unstuffy and brave.

Chapter 15
The Green, Green Grass

In the spring of 2004 Bill Kenwright once again dispatched Sue and me on tour, this time with a great (but riskier) play, *London Suite* by Neil Simon.

The play depicts a series of events that take place in one particular hotel suite, each as a separate stand-alone drama, linked only by the room in which they take place. We had the stimulating task of playing three entirely different parts each night – just the kind of challenge and test of versatility I loved. Appearing with Sue and me were Sarah Crowe, a funny, striking woman, and the wonderfully tiggerish Mark Curry, famous for his innings as *Blue Peter* presenter.

We did a happy eight-week tour through most of the stronger provincial theatres. As we passed through Malvern, the nearest venue to home, I had a good show of local support.

We also did good business with the play at the Theatre Royal in Brighton and were delighted to hear from John Sullivan (a big Neil Simon fan) that for once he was coming to see us.

John was not alone among TV writer/producers in holding the view that theatre was a lot of actors shouting in long shot. I had once tried desperately to get Douglas Camfield, whom I'd done a few things for, to come and see me in a play where I was playing a sensitive dad with serious emotional problems.

'I know you'll be very good,' Camfield said, 'but on camera, when we spend so much time in close, we have to go with what you've got in your face – and yours is a dark face, however sensitive you might be feeling.'

This had become a familiar problem for me. As long as I was far enough away from the audience, it seemed, I could deal with most roles but close up on TV, it had to be hard-nosed coppers or hard-arsed crooks.

John Sullivan, though, saw me as neither of these. He had produced the bones and I had put the flesh on this creature from Peckham, who had bizarrely become an iconic character, celebrated in men's magazines, chanted about on football terraces and the toast of the second-hand motor trade.

As John had said, 'We've created this monster, and now it's got out of the cage.'

He had created another monster, of course, in *Marlene*. Once again, he'd had help through his own casting. His choice of Sue Holderness had been inspired. From what he'd given her, she'd been able to create in *Marlene* a wonderfully gross character, who could run rings around the pompous, self-inflated *Boycie*.

As a couple they were vulgar and tasteless but John had given them and their marriage an inherent warmth, with a firm sense of loyalty knitting them together. With these two strong characters, John had developed a relationship between the *Boyces* that had immediate resonance with a large number of people and had made *Boycie* and *Marlene* one of the most popular couples in British sit com.

John Sullivan had an apartment on Brighton front and he asked us over for tea – tiffin, as he put it – one afternoon during our run there.

Once we'd arrived, he came quickly to the point. 'If I was to tell you I'm thinking of a spin-off from *Only Fools & Horses*, featuring *Boycie* and *Marlene*, could you bear it?'

I felt my heart lurch and I stifled a gasp.

A spin off? From one of the most successful British comedy series of all time? With us in the lead?

I quickly got a grip on myself, sucked noisily through my teeth. 'I don't know John.' I shook my head. 'I'd have to look at my diary – I'm not sure about availability.'

I could see Sue on the edge of her chair, with her eyes popping out, not absolutely certain if I was having a laugh. She followed my lead; we kept it up for about ten seconds.

Then I burst. 'Are you kidding?' I gabbled, then more cautiously, 'or is this a wind up?'

'No, no, look. I'm sorry it's taken so long, but I couldn't think why *Boycie* and *Marlene* would want to leave Peckham. It was up at your party a couple of years ago, I got the idea of *Boycie* deciding to sell up and going to live in the sticks – a Peckham boy in the country – gave me loads of ideas. And it wasn't until I was watching some reruns and the *Driscoll Brothers* came on that I had the answer...' He paused. '*Boycie's* grassed them up... and he's on the run!'

I sat back slowly to absorb the idea. 'I think I'd have to see the script first, John,' I said.

'I haven't written the fucking thing yet,' John answered gently.

We were so excited we could hardly do our show that evening. It was extraordinary to be offered this when we thought we'd said our very final 'goodbye' to *Boycie* and *Marlene* with the airing of *Sleepless in Peckham* at Christmas.

It was as if *Boycie,* like Lazarus, had been awakened from the dead with a touch from Sullivan. Writers often boast that they give birth to characters in their shows; it seemed they could bring them back to life, too. I reflected that it was lucky that the last episode hadn't seen the *Trotters, Boycie, Marlene* and the gang going up in a gas explosion in Nelson Mandela House, which Sullivan might have thought was the only way to finish off the series for good.

Probably, he'd deliberately left a few doors open, and here was one through which *Boycie* and *Marlene* were being allowed to escape into a new life.

We realized a few years down the line that he'd left another door open in *Sleepless in Peckham*, which allowed him to bring back Nicholas as *Rodney's* dad, *Fred Robdal* in the 2010 *Only Fools* prequel, *Rock & Chips*.

When Sue and I had calmed down a bit after John's amazing announcement, we started to wonder how the hell would we do a spin-off and make a show of our own after a phenomenon like *Only Fools & Horses*. Spin-offs from big sitcoms were notoriously unpredictable beasts – *Frazier*, from *Cheers* worked fantastically; *Joey*, from *Friends* didn't.

But the idea gathered momentum. First, as is normal with these things, we had to make a pilot episode for the big wigs at the BBC to decide whether or not they wanted us. Sue and I were pretty committed for the rest of the year with tour dates and pantomimes for the 2004-2005 season, but we managed to schedule it for early autumn, in six months' time.

As the time got nearer, Sue and I became a little apprehensive that we would always be overshadowed by our mighty predecessor and the initial euphoria wore off a little. There was inevitably some reaction to the rumours now flying around about an *Only Fools* spin-off – some positive, some not.

But the script came, and we loved it. *Denzil* turns up at *Boycie's* bogus Tudor mansion in Peckham and tells him the *Driscoll Brothers* have been released from three life jail sentences. The police have relied on a supergrass to convict them but all the other witnesses have suddenly retracted their evidence, and it looks as if *Boycie* was the supergrass. He isn't, but he doesn't feel he'll be able to explain the misunderstanding. He's no hero and when he starts seeing a big black car cruising the road outside his house, filled with men in dark suits, he panics and goes out to buy himself an unseen pile in Shropshire, where he thinks the *Driscolls* will never find him.

He breaks the news to a startled *Marlene*.

'What is Shropshire?' *Marlene* asks.

'Good question,' *Boycie* answers, 'but that's where we're going.'

They pack up and leave Peckham in a moonlight flit, to arrive on a dark, stormy night at a rambling, creepy house hundreds of miles away in the middle of nowhere. Although *Boycie* has been told that the place had been empty for some time, they find various retainers already lurking on the property.

In the meantime we'd been asked by John and the producer, Julian Meers to look for a suitable house for *Boycie* and *Marlene* to escape to. We sent them photos of lots of local houses belonging to friends and acquaintances who weren't averse to having their places ravaged by a film crew. The location team came down to Wigmore to look at a few of the possibilities we had found – Paytoe, Wigmore Hall, Downton.

We were excited that the production team were keen to film in our area, and we hoped fervently that they would find what they wanted. Eventually the location people came back to the Abbey and told us they had found the ideal place – a rambling, run-down, spooky old dump.

'Great!' I exclaimed. 'Where is it?'

'Here. Your place,' they replied.

Just for a moment, I felt hurt on behalf of our beloved house, then I thought of the location fee, and maybe now we could repair some of the fifteenth-century plasterwork.

The pilot for the proposed *Boycie & Marlene* show was to be shot on location around Ludlow (where a suitable house for *Boycie's* Peckham residence was found), around the farm next door to us, in the surrounding lanes and fields, and at the Bridges Inn at Ratlinghope, deep in the Shropshire Hills, near Church Stretton. Although they were going to film around Wigmore Abbey from the outside, the interiors would be shot at Teddington Studios.

I was very used to the business of filming, but I experienced an entirely new feeling when the crew started to descend on my own place, in surroundings that were now my reality, among people I knew, liked and respected.

Sue and I met several times during the planning of it all; she was delighted that the shooting would take place in my home patch; it seemed somehow to give us a little extra say in what was going on. We knew we would have to be on top form, as leaders of the company, and although we'd met some other members of the cast, we couldn't yet tell if we would all gel satisfactorily into a cohesive unit that gives the best results.

Inevitably there was a lot of excitement locally, with everyone agog to see what would happen and how the process of filming worked. Everybody wanted to know if *Del Boy* and *Rodney* were suddenly going to pop out of the shrubbery. I had to say I didn't know, but I doubted it, and I hoped not – it was important, I thought, that the show should stand on its own.

Naturally the local press were in no doubt that the pilot would turn into a series, however much we tried to explain the uncertainty of these things. The truth was that, although John Sullivan's own track record was unquestionable, and *Boycie* and *Marlene* were already well established, iconic figures in the public's mind, there was always the possibility that one person in the upper echelons of the BBC wouldn't rate it and the whole thing could be binned.

Tony Dow, who had worked on *Only Fools* almost from the start and directed it since 1988 was directing our show too. David Hitchcock was the designer, and several of the old *Only Fools* team were on board as well. Another very welcome old face was Paul

Barber, as *Denzil*, who, sad to say, appeared only in the first part of the *Boyce's* new adventure.

Sue and I had to get used to the idea that we were in a far more crucial position than we'd been before. Where in *Only Fools* we might have just a couple of telling scenes in an episode, in this show we were driving the narrative in nearly every scene.

There were other minor worries, too. Living in the country with a superb cook, I had naturally put on a bit of weight since my last outing as *Boycie* had been filmed in 2001. As the episode featured *Boycie* apparently going off for jog after breakfast, I was a little sensitive about how this might look, knowing that I never cut an impressive figure with my knocked-kneed style of running.

I didn't have to worry too much when it came to it. *Boycie* simply trots around the corner, climbs into a waiting taxi and lights up one of his trademark panatellas.

Having kicked the dust of Peckham off his heels, *Boycie* tries to interest *Marlene* and the chubby *Tyler* in the joys and benefits of country living, although of course, he's there primarily to escape the aggressive attentions of the *Driscoll Brothers*. The *Boyces* have been welcomed to the house by the incumbent farm manager, *Elgin Sparrowhawk*, played by David Ross, who tells them that he and the staff are as good as fixtures and fittings, and *Boycie* reckons they aren't going to be disposed of lightly.

We had a lot of fun making the pilot, not least for the pleasure of filming around my own house and the country I now knew well. The studio audience loved it, and at the end of it, we thought, at least we've buckled down and made the pilot, given it our best shot, even if, in the end the BBC decide not to run with it.

Shortly before Christmas, not long after the pilot episode was edited and ready, the BBC announced that they wanted us. The series was to be called *The Green, Green Grass*.

John Sullivan was chuffed to smithereens; he was absolutely thrilled to have found a way to carry on what he'd started back in 1981 with *Only Fools & Horses*, after all, nearly a quarter of a century before.

Newspaper stories appeared: *Boycie and Marlene get their own series! What would Del Boy and Rodders think about that?*

The BBC also thought the pilot was good enough to go out as the first episode, which made us a little nervous; we couldn't help thinking that if we'd known it was the real thing, we would probably have done it better.

Still, there it was; we'd obviously done well enough, and we waited with high expectation for the rest of the scripts for the series – the first of many, we dared to hope.

On New Year's Day 2005, it was announced that John Sullivan had been awarded the OBE for Services to Entertainment. In my view there was no doubt that he had earned the honour. His writing had entertained millions in the way it so accurately and warmly portrayed responses to changing attitudes in society, using poignant humour and compassion.

John threw a party at the Dorchester Hotel for family, friends and the actors who had benefited so much from his talent. Throughout the evening's festivities, he wore the bauble around his neck with slightly apologetic but clear pride. I guess he couldn't be sure what his late father – a life-long Labour supporter – would have made of this symbol of approval. John had always done a lot in his writing to champion the common man, attacking pomposity, snobbery and the English class system. And here he was, being recognised by the Establishment which he professed to loathe.

He told us he'd thought about not accepting the gong for a while, before saying to himself, 'Fuck it, why not!'

It was here that Sue and I had thought we might hear what the rest of the *Only Fools* cast thought about our new series but not one of them mentioned it, apart from David Jason, who exclaimed when I came and sat down late for the speeches, 'I suppose he thinks he can do what he likes, now he's got his own series!'

Much later, as the celebrations continued late into the night at the Dorchester, in the bars, on the roof terraces, John's wife Sharon almost had to restrain him from booking rooms in the hotel for everyone who still had a glass in their hand.

We all knew how much we owed him, and this mighty piss-up was a fitting tribute to a man who had changed all our lives and given enormous pleasure to tens of millions of *Only Fools* fans all over the world.

We were scheduled to start making our first series of *The Green, Green Grass* during May and June, 2005. I had greeted the news that the BBC had already decided that they were going to use the pilot as the first episode of the seven projected with mixed feelings. On the one hand it was gratifying to hear that the BBC thought the pilot good enough (especially as it would save them around £400,000 in fresh production costs); on the other hand, Sue and I still felt we hadn't been quite ready for that first outing. As it happened, some scenes from the pilot had to be re-filmed to correct technical imperfections; I'd taken off some weight now, in readiness, and in the first episode of GGG that was ever shown, *Keep on Running*, close observers will notice *Boycie's* waistline fluctuating with changing scenes.

The BBC were also determined to save money when it came to hiring the 'talent'. My agent, Barry Burnett (AKA: Barry Brunette) was in the box-seat as he represented both Sue and me. He suggested a fee for us – which sounded like the fair, going rate – only to have it dismissed as 'ridiculous'. Inevitably that made us feel a little unloved, after we'd done 25 years in the most popular comedy series the BBC had ever produced. When they suggested that if we were going to ask that kind of fee they would find someone else, Tony Dow put his foot down, saying, 'Right – we'll get someone else but they'll have to look *exactly* like John Challis and Sue Holderness.'

We didn't know what kind of point they were trying to make in the casting department but it left a sour taste in our mouths as we started preparing for the series proper.

We also had to address the ticklish business of the location fee for the house. A rough schedule of the days on which the house would be required was produced. On the one hand, given that they were going to do a lot of filming there, and they'd chosen it, not us, we were inclined to get as much as we thought we could get away with; on the other hand, we didn't want to make it unattractive for them to do an endless number of further series there, and we didn't feel we should be too grasping – not yet, anyway.

The producer sent down a recce team to prepare the way. Our house became 'Winterdown Farm' and photos were taken of the rooms inside so that something similar could be produced for the interior studio recording.

Boycie was trying to become a 'gentleman farmer' in a place called 'Oakham'. Signs were already sprouting with 'Welcome to Oakham', a sign for the village hall appeared and the rickety old post office/general stores in Bucknell was identified as being suitable for the mythical village of Oakham.

Sue and I had a session with the rest of the cast for a read through at the dear old Acton Hilton which was increasingly becoming a storage facility for BBC wardrobe and administration. Everything was changing there; all the familiar studios and dressing rooms, make-up and wardrobe departments were being hired out to independent production companies, who then made the programmes which they flogged to the BBC for transmission.

John Sullivan had set up a new company named Shazam Productions after his wife, Sharon – known as Shazza. John's agent Tim Hancock was the other half of the company.

To begin with everything went swimmingly. We were confident that there were going to be some great characters in the show. For a start, there was David Ross's character, *Elgin Sparrowhawk*, whom he played with rustic relish; there was a large moon-calf of a stockman in the hands of Ivan Kaye; an affable, lumpen tractor driver, played by Peter Hepplethwaite, and the cleaner, *Mrs Cakeworthy*, who never cleaned but stuffed herself with an awful lot of biscuits and had a funny way of talking bucolic gobbledy-gook, brought memorably to life by Ella Kenion. Another regular was a rival farmer from Wales, *Llewellyn*, played by a rival actor from Wales, Alan David.

Boycie and *Marlene's* baby son, *Tyler*, had grown up into a tricky teenager, portrayed by Jack Doolan, who made a good start in the ensemble, as far as I was concerned, by announcing that he was an Arsenal supporter.

I found it strange at first to be in the position of 'leading man', and to be in practically every scene. A sense of responsibility descended on *Marlene* and me like a voluminous, heavy cloak. I wondered if David and Nicholas had felt the same in *Only Fools*.

Boycie had first to introduce his unappreciative family to the rolling countryside of the Welsh border country.

'Look at the view, Marlene!' he declaims from the top of a high grassy ridge, with hills disappearing dramatically into distant mid-Wales.

'Stuff the view,' *Marlene* comes back. 'Where's Debenhams?'

Tyler tries to skate his urban board down the grassy slopes below them and soon comes to a halt. 'I *hate* the country,' he moans.

The only happy member of the party is *Earl*, the family Rottweiler who bounds along excitedly, in reality desperate to get at the doggy treats held tightly in my hand to keep him interested.

Earl had replaced, *Duke*, the Great Dane that had been *Boycie* and *Marlene's* dog in *Only Fools*, since *Marlene* had first appeared in 1985. He should, in reality, have passed on to doggy heaven about seven or eight years before, but in any case, he wouldn't have survived in *The Green, Green Grass* as it was intended not to let the new show be seen simply as an add-on to its illustrious parent.

On 1 September, almost exactly 24 years after *Boycie's* first appearance on *Only Fools* in *Going West Young Man*, the first episode of *The Green, Green Grass*, entitled *Keep on Running*, was aired and achieved over nine and a half million viewers – an amazing result at the time.

This sort of figure, however, wasn't expected to last. And it didn't. As viewers who had been hoping that *Del Boy* and *Rodney* were going to be part of the action found they were not, we dropped about one and a half million for the second episode, *A Rocky Start*, eventually settling at six and a half to seven million. Under the new conditions of widespread multi-channel viewing, this was considered better than expected, and things looked very positive.

There was no doubt from the start that the series was going to be very good fun to make. In *Rocky Start*, it seems that *Boycie* had bought a 'gay' bull to cover his prize herd of three hundred Friesians. Clive Gurney, a farmer who was a neighbour of ours and a Parish Councillor agreed to provide one if his beasts to play the role of *Rocky*, a Hereford bull that was supposed to 'take guard well outside off-stump' and was apparently uninterested in any of his harem.

Clive was asked to get *Rocky* to stand in certain places and move off in certain directions at the appropriate time. In one scene, *Rocky* is supposed to spot *Boycie* and *Marlene* tentatively approaching, at which he was required to paw the ground menacingly and then charge.

We started the shoot, the camera rolled, and *Rocky* refused to budge an inch. He wouldn't even lift his front hoof, let alone paw the ground and charge. It was a stand off.

The cameraman left his carefully positioned camera and joined Tony and the rest of us for a strategy confab.

As if someone had just shouted 'action!' again, *Rocky* lifted his head, sniffed the air and charged like a steam train straight at the camera and up to the gate over which *Boycie* and *Marlene* were supposed to leap. It reminded me of the time *Al the Gator* in the Florida Everglades had charged at *Del* and *Rodney*.

We didn't know what had got him going but we were impressed. Clive went and got him back to his mark, the cameraman slightly altered the position of his tackle, Sue and I got on our marks and Clive did his best to ginger up the bull.

Once again, the bull simply stood there, tugging the odd mouthful from a nearby tussock, quite indifferent to any urgings, bored and uninterested in what was going on; he wouldn't move.

As soon as we gathered for another discussion, he was off, charging straight past us and up to the gate again.

This time the cameraman had stayed at his post and got the charge. All that was left was for *Boycie* and *Marlene* to run and leap over the five-bar gate, which we achieved with one take.

Rocky watched us, evidently bored to death now that we were doing something and put his head down to pick a bit more grass.

For the Christmas Special that was to wind up the first series, I was a little apprehensive when John told me he was writing the *Driscoll Brothers* back into the script. He had strategic reasons for doing it as he ultimately wanted them to track *Boycie* down in his rural hideaway.

It was of course, a long time since I'd anything much to do with Roy Marsden who had played *Danny Driscoll* in his previous appearance in an episode of *Only Fools* called *Little Problems*. His affair with Sabina, which had caused me so much distress when we were all working together in *The Relapse*, had happened 16 years ago.

I remembered the agony of indecision I'd been through, having previously arranged for him to appear in an episode of *Only Fools & Horses*, when John subsequently offered to write his part out of the script if I didn't want to go through with it. But I'd chosen in the end to let it happen; I felt that blanking out Roy would have been weak and petulant, and as a result, the *Driscoll Brothers* were introduced as Peckham's answer to the Krays.

They had never appeared again in *Only Fools*, but they had a key role in providing Sullivan with the only reason he could find for for sending *Boycie* off to the sticks, and thereby allowing *The Green, Green Grass* to happen. The supreme irony of this hadn't escaped me.

When I saw Roy for his appearance (albeit in a series of bad dreams *Boycie* was having), he was at his most charming. We were, I think, both aware of the change in our relative circumstances now that I was leading man in the show. In fact, given that I'd been happily married to Carol for ten years, I felt no rancour whatsoever that he had relieved me of Sabina and it was fun to see him again. We laughed a lot, and I was happy to see him when he appeared in two later episodes, having tracked *Boycie* to his rural refuge. I reflected on the old adage that Time is the Great Healer.

The episode went out as a fifty-minute special *One Flew over the Cuckoo Clock* on Christmas Day 2005 and did well. The BBC seemed happy enough with the performance of our first series of *The Green, Green Grass* to commit themselves to a second. We were sent John's scripts for the eight episodes of Series Two starting with *Testing Times*.

By June we'd finished making the second series, including another Christmas special, feeling that we had another good bunch of shows in the bag. Despite the amount of work involved as one of the leads in the show, I still had plenty in reserve and I was relieved that other work hadn't dried up completely.

One of the jobs I enjoyed doing that year was a great show on BBC Radio Four, *Love 40: New Balls Please*, written and produced by Mervyn Stutter.

Mervyn was a wonderfully talented, eccentric singer, songwriter and comedian, who happened also to be married to Moira Downie. I had once been close to Moira, as they say, when she'd helped me with my own play while we were touring South Africa in a production of Tom Stoppard's *Dirty Linen* for six months of 1977. I was glad to see her again, and I loved working with Mervyn. He wore colourful clothes and had an agit-prop background – this didn't necessarily make him a bad person and he'd had great success at the Edinburgh Fringe. He'd also been a founder member of the *Flying Pickets* band which had been very popular during the miner's strikes of the '80s. He had come up with an idea for a show in which a bunch of disparate characters, living in a kind of commune left adrift in the hippy aftermath, are trying, but mostly failing, to deal with the modern world. It was a great platform for Merv to rail against society's shortcomings – its iniquities and contradictions, its inability to connect to the common man. Merv used his talent for satirising to the full, using song and a bunch of great character actors, including Martin Freeman, Andrew Sachs and Tracy Ann Oberman. *Getting Nowhere Fast* became a cult hit on Radio Four and ran for four years, but although the audiences kept growing all the time, the BBC in their inexplicable perversity decided to take it off. I was very sad that my character, an ageing, mostly drunk actor laddie, *Dibden Purlieu*, was never heard of again.

I worked outside *The Green, Green Grass* with Sue, too, which we were very used to doing after all our theatrical touring together. But that year, for the first (and, as it happens, last) time we were asked to appear in pantomime together.

In fact, the promoters of *Jack and the Beanstalk* at the lovely Richmond Theatre, didn't really want us – *Boycie* and *Marlene*, despite leading their very own show, were deemed altogether too common for the respectable burghers of leafy Richmond. But the casting person, Scott Mitchell, was Barbara Windsor's husband and a thoroughly decent bloke. He had suggested us, and Kevin Wood, directing, had thought we would work brilliantly alongside his other star, Aled Jones, famed for his angelic recording of 'Walking in the Air'. These sorts of bizarre pantomime couplings crop up every year. (Can I remind you of my bizarre fights with *Nightshade* in Redhill in 1996?)

Scottie was pretty miffed when the theatre questioned his inspired casting choices. After much argie, and a fair bit of bargie, it was eventually accepted. 'OK, then – if we must,' was how it was tactfully relayed to us.

This may have been because we had already been booked by Scott, and the council would have had to pay us anyway, come what may. In the end, it was all agreed that the burghers of Richmond would have to put up with *Boycie* and *Marlene*, and Mrs Challis would take on the job of wardrobe supervisor – an arrangement we had often made which meant that we got to spend our Christmases together. We perhaps should have guessed that the little streak of grumpiness shown by the management was a harbinger of further disasters in the show.

It all started well, though. Aled as *Jack* was perfect casting. He was very masculine, had a wonderfully determined air about him, and, of course, could sing like a linnet. I was to play the revolting Figure of Hate, *Fleshcreep*, the Giant's henchman. Sue was cast as the *Good Fairy*, although she complained that she was very bad at being good.

From the lonely perspective of the pantomime villain, she was far too good and sweet, like Tim Vine was annoyingly good and funny as *Simple Simon*. The villain can never be sweet, or funny, or popular; it is his job just to be hated and booed.

Aled, on the other hand, never got to do the show at all. He had been given a spoof dancing scene, derived from the great success he'd recently had on *Strictly Come Dancing*. Rehearsals were going well, but close to the opening, he had slipped and torn his Achilles tendon. He was carried off the stage, ashen faced, and from the theatre, never to return.

Poor Carol, as wardrobe supervisor for the show, found herself at the centre of a fuss. As supervisor you tend to cop all the flak for naturally occurring problems arising from trying to get a big show on in too short a time. The hunt was on for someone to blame for Aled's accident and injury; the management stood to lose most, if not all their projected profits if Aled should decide to seek compensation for loss of earnings.

Aled had been wearing shoes one size too big during the rehearsal when he'd fallen. Carol had his correct size on order, promised to arrive shortly and had let Aled choose whether or not to wear the larger size.

After the accident, Aled still wanted to do the show, and a compromise was sought in which he would add a new twist to the traditional plot by playing *Jack* in plaster and crutches, with a kind of Stena beanstalk lift. But when he also developed DVT, any ideas like this had to be abandoned, and his place was taken by his understudy, Andrew Derbyshire, who in any case was already booked to do a few shows when Aled had other, older commitments.

The show went ahead with Andrew, whom the children adored and few of the people who had booked because Aled was on the original cast asked for their money back.

All this hassle hadn't kicked the show off in the best of spirits but these were lifted when quite a few friends and colleagues, historic and current turned up to see us.

My old mucker, Chris Lewis with whom I'd shared a house not far from the theatre, back in the early 1970s, came with his daughter. Tim Rice came. I'd met him at lunch at Lord Windsor's pile near Ludlow, and he had subsequently invited me to his box at Lords to see the Australians thrashing our boys in the first test match of the wonderful 2005 Ashes series. Tony Dow and several other members of our production team on *GGG* came, as well as Sheila MacDonald, Ken's widow.

An unlikely visitor was Christopher Campbell, political mover and shaker and opera buff supreme, who had been on a cruise on the Seine with us, learning about Impressionists. (He wasn't too impressed with my James Stewart impersonation in Monet's garden.) He admitted to me that, unable to stand the noise of seven hundred screaming children, he had left *Jack and the B* at half time, though not before I'd extracted a good laugh from him when as *Fleshcreep* I scowled nastily, 'You've heard of this charity, Children in Need? Well I've got a new charity: it's called Who Needs Children!' and was answered with a storm of boos and threats to my personal safety.

Over Christmas during the Richmond pantomime, a second Special episode of *The Green, Green Grass, From Here to Paternity,* was shown on Christmas Day and, as had happened before, it seemed to show in our audiences' reactions in the days that followed. I couldn't have been happier that *Boycie's* own sitcom still seemed to have legs. As 2007 opened, the feeling in our little *GGG* company was that we were here to stay and there was a lot of life in this particular dog.

Audience reaction to *The Green, Green, Grass* had been almost universally good, although one or two of the TV critics didn't get it, and weren't always kind to us. We accepted that we were never going to be *Only Fools & Horses*, but we were very happy with what we'd achieved so far.

We had at least gathered enough of a following and sufficient status that all the outside actors we asked to come in and make guest appearances, if they were available, had agreed to take part. June Whitfield, for instance, came in to play *Marlene's* Mum, *Dora*, four times and did it always with her customary panache – a worthy foil to *Boycie's* barbed criticisms. John Sullivan loved being in a position where he could get his favourite actors in to his shows.

Sadly my own relationship with John became a little strained for a while later on in the year when I was booked for a one-off appearance in another popular sitcom, *My Family*.

This show featured Robert Lindsay and Zoe Wanamaker and had managed seven or eight series since it was launched in 2000. It had American money behind it and was expensively shot, entirely on film, at Pinewood Studios. Like *Friends* and most of the American mega-shows, it was staffed with an army of writers who followed the action around, clutching clip-boards and constantly tweaking the script as the actors rehearsed.

I had a few second thoughts about taking the job; it was after all, on a rival series, although in my view, too American in style (and not especially funny). However, I was to play the *Ghost of Jacob Marley*, which was the sort of thing I enjoyed, and I wouldn't be recognizable, so I agreed. When I mentioned it to John Sullivan, he seemed unconcerned. Maybe he just hadn't taken in what I'd said, because when he was told about my appearance in *My Family* by a third party, he was very upset that a leading man in his show had taken a role in a rival comedy and, in particular, a show starring Robert Lindsay. Lindsay had starred in *Citizen Smith*, which had launched both John's career and his own twenty-five years earlier. John had wanted to do more *Citizen Smith* but for some reason, Lindsay hadn't, and they had never worked together again.

John, who was proud of his body of work and guarded it jealously, felt I was being disloyal, where I saw it as just another job for a working actor, in a role where I was heavily disguised anyway. Despite the slight spat this prompted, we made up and I lived to fight again another day and did another series of *The Green, Green Grass* the following year.

In the meantime, I staggered up to one of those regrettable milestones in my life that summer, when on 16 August 2007, I become an OAP! If I came round now to thinking: 'Hope I die before I get old,' it was too bloody late!

I may have been 'old', but at least I wasn't dead, and now I could reap the reasonable rewards of all the gentle bullying I'd been receiving for years from my friendly accountant, Alex Johnson. He had always reminded me that I should put something aside, keep up my NI contributions and not fritter everything away as soon as I got it. That advice now looked very sound. I had a decent state pension and a little pot I could draw on if necessary. It felt really grown up, even if the long white beard and zimmer frame were still some way round the corner.

But that didn't mean I was going to stop working, and after my efforts as the *Ghost of Jacob Marley*, I had a chance to frighten the kids again with a reprise of my *Captain Hook* in an independent production at the Theatre Royal in Nottingham. This *Peter Pan* was directed by the brilliant Nick Pegg, a multi-faceted thesp among whose more bizarre and continuing roles was that of a *Dalek* in the mighty *Dr Who*. Serendipitously – or perhaps as a result of meeting in a parallel universe, being thwarted by the *Doctor*, and deciding to cut their losses to cause mayhem in our galaxy – another *Dalek* was played by his partner, Barnaby Edwards.

The Nottingham show also starred Debra Stephenson, who'd had great success as *Shell Dockley* in *Bad Girls*, among other things. Debra, I discovered, was also a brilliant impressionist, which was useful when she had to pretend to do *Captain Hook's* voice on board the *Jolly Roger*.

The only discomfort I felt doing the show was as a result of the posters outside the theatre advertising a forthcoming attraction: *The Vagina Monologues*.

Beneath this rather unappetising title was the bright smiling face of my beloved screen wife, no less than *Marlene* herself, Sue

Holderness. I could only hope that the hordes of kids pouring in to be terrified by *Capt Hook*, weren't tugging at their grannies' sleeves asking what a monologue was.

We were struck every evening as we left the theatre by the extraordinary liveliness of Nottingham nightlife. We had to pick our way from the stage door back to our hotel through streets that seethed with gangs of pickled yooves and short-skirted, high-heeled teetering girls.

Back at our hotel we would watch from above as the bouncers and occasional bouncerettes tried to keep the young punters in order, with sporadic eruptions and interventions by the constabulary. Looking down on it, fascinated, I was put in mind of Fred Trueman, the famous Yorkshire fast bowler from another era, commentating on a pathetic display of batting by an England team. 'I don't know what's going off out there. Boot it'd never 'ave 'appened in my day.'

We ended the third series of *The Green, Green Grass* on 30 December 2007 with a Christmas Special and one of my favourite episodes, *The Special Relationship*.

I was thrilled when George Wendt, for years *Norm* who sat at the end of the Boston bar in the great American sitcom *Cheers,* agreed to come and star as *Cliff Cooper*, an American ex-serviceman who had been billeted in the farmhouse some thirty years earlier.

While he had been there, he'd had a relationship with a local girl who turned out to be *Mrs Cakeworthy's* mother. As he had also become a billionaire from manufacturing cookies, there is huge excitement when he announces that *Mrs C* is his daughter. Of course, it turns out that she's not but as he is driven away it dawns on him that *Bocyie's* dopey farmhand, *Jed*, might be his son. He decides to drive on.

George was a joy to work with, coming from the do-nothing-say-everything school of American acting. It worked perfectly, his phlegmatic economy contrasting with what he must have thought our larger-than-life way of doing it. I was delighted that an actor of his renown had wanted to come over and work on our show. He had been a great fan of *Only Fools*, which helped, and John decided to make a bit of a fuss of him. It was arranged for us all to go up to the new Wembley to watch an international match between England and

Germany. As George was of German extraction, John and I put ourselves under strict instructions to avoid any mention of 1966, or the war.

All was going well when Frank Lampard rifled one into the net in the first half but Germany came back and turned us over, 2-1.

'OK, let's mention the war,' John rasped.

George took it all in good part. In any case, he said, he didn't care much for what he called soccer.

It had, of course, been John Sullivan's initiative to get George. He'd always liked asking favourite stars and celebrities to appear on his shows. One of them, Jonathan Ross who'd been the quizmaster in *If They Could See us Now*, cropped up again in my life several years afterwards, when Sue Holderness and I were presenting at an awards ceremony that he was hosting. He told us what a fan he was and how much he'd enjoyed being on the show, although he didn't think he'd been much good.

'I've had that feeling for years,' I admitted.

'What! That you're not very good?' Jonathan asked, incredulous.

Quick as a flash, I replied, 'No, that *you* weren't much good.'

You don't often get handed chances like that and you have to take them.

I had an even better moment at that same awards ceremony. Across the not very edifying spectacle of my profession patting itself on the back, I saw Robert Vaughn, representing the cast of *Hustle* which was doing very well at the time, wending his way towards me.

As I waited, transfixed, he said: 'I love your show, *The Green, Green Grass*, especially that *Mrs Cakeworthy*. I hope you'll be doing some more.' He shook my hand warmly. 'Pleasure to meet you.' He wandered off.

I was speechless. The only surviving member of *The Magnificent Seven* liked my show!

After Christmas, we were slightly on tenterhooks. Another series, the fourth, had been discussed and in principle agreed with the BBC, but dotted lines on which to sign hadn't appeared yet.

We were aware that some of our show's strongest supporters had moved on. From the start, *The Green, Green Grass* had had a firm champion in BBC Controller, Peter Fincham. The previous year, while we were making the third series, he'd thought enough of the show to invite Sue Holderness and me to dinner in a Notting Hill restaurant to be part of a typically eclectic mix of the 'talent', as they liked to call anyone currently featured on their channels.

That evening Peter was joined by Gary Lineker, who seemed bored by the whole thing, Andrew Neil, as voluble as ever, Alan Yentob, an ex-controller and suitably enigmatic, Trevor Eve with a slightly superior air, Julia Bradbury, dark-eyed, intense, with a hint of the hockey-stick about her and *Boycie & Marlene*.

We felt, honestly, quite flattered to be in such company. We had a great evening and we left feeling confident that we had Peter Fincham's continuing support.

Unfortunately, a few months later a filmmaker in his department made a cock-up by cobbling together an edited misrepresentation of Her Majesty storming out of a photographic session. It had been done crassly – and dishonestly – to give a little edge to a documentary series they were doing. Peter hadn't been involved in any of the decisions leading to this but it had happened in his department and he was forced to fall on his sword.

Evidently, as a result, *The Green, Green Grass* wasn't viewed with so much warmth now. John Sullivan, wearing his producer's hat, announced to us, somewhat grumpily that the BBC were looking to slice his budget, which meant that he in turn would have to slice our wages.

However laid back one is about these things, it's always disappointing to be told, effectively, that you're worth less than you used to be. And it's not just about the money. But in the end, with our agent, Barry Burnett tearing his hair out, a compromise was reached and a contract drawn up for a further eight episodes, to be made in the second half of 2008 and broadcast the following year.

With no major commitments in the first half of the year, Carol and I were able to concentrate on things – the seemingly endless list of things – that still needed doing at the house.

Most importantly, after a long period of discussion, consideration and negotiation, English Heritage agreed to help with the fabric of the original abbey church.

The Heart of England English Heritage supremo arrived with an architect and an engineer to discuss the best way to shore up the one remaining crumbling arch of the transept, to ensure that it too, didn't end up as just another pile of rocks and rubble, to be raided for any local new build like the rest of the old monastery.

Their first suggestion was that a huge stainless-steel prop should be erected, to make it clear that this repair had been done in the twenty-first century. I was, frankly, not keen on a gaunt piece of steel jutting out of the earth and pointed out that as the shape of the original arch of which it had been a part was still detectable, perhaps we could simply rebuild the other side of it and avoid confusion among archaeologists in another thousand years, put up a little plaque pointing out which side was thirteenth century and which side twenty first.

They went away and produced some fine drawings which we loved. It was going to cost money, of course, but at least they would chip in a good whack of it and encourage any other grant-giving parties to do the same.

English Heritage in the end came up trumps and a piece of arch was rebuilt which acted as a kind of flying buttress, just as we'd envisaged.

The completion of the arch coincided with another notch in the tree of life, and for my sixty-seventh birthday, Carol suggested we take a gentle trip down to Cornwall to celebrate. Luckily, and not entirely coincidentally, we had some friends, Rob and Ros Woodard, who lived on the Helston River. In a previous life, Rob had been commander of the Royal Yacht *Britannia*. As a result, he'd been granted a property near Restormel Castle, where Sue Holderness and I had stayed during our *London Suite* tour five years before.

The night before we were to see the Woodards, we checked into the Budock Vean Hotel by the Helston River. I began to suspect that Carol was up to her tricks again when Richard Heffer and Belinda Rush Jansen 'happened' to turn up. Soon after that Rob Woodard walked in and insisted we all went back to his perch overlooking the river, further downstream.

Carol, of course, had organized a party with the Woodards and the Heffers and very jolly it was, with the added delight of the unexpected. What she had arranged for the next day was even more unexpected. After an inexplicable visit to Ann's Pasty Shop at the Lizard, purveyors of allegedly the best pasties in the world (with or without VAT) and a strange sojourn in the pub with everyone behaving very *vaguely*, until at what was clearly a pre-arranged signal, we all sauntered off. At this, I found myself in a state of amused detachment, ready for whatever fate was about to chuck at me.

After a short car journey we arrived at one of my favourite Cornish destinations, the Lizard Lifeboat Station, where the whole staff of the Lizard Lifeboat was waiting for us, including Carol's co-conspirator, Ned Nuzum. Coxswain Phil Burgess approached. 'Glad you're here, John. We've got an exercise today and we're a bit short of crew. Can you help us out?'

Could I? I couldn't wait.

Going out on a lifeboat was something I'd dreamed of doing ever since I was a kid. Rob Woodard looked on with a big grin as I was togged out in oilskins, helmet and boots. I was hustled on to the lifeboat in its little house and we were off down the slipway.

It was utterly thrilling – at least as exhilarating as the rides in Margate during the *Jolly Boys' Outing*. The English Channel was pretty calm but we still made a terrific splash. I realized why I'd been placed right at the stern of the boat when a plume of water shot up and hit me on the backside.

We turned to starboard (I think) into Mounts Bay, and I was given a go at driving, with some anxious tweaking from Phil as we veered too close to clusters of submerged rocks, of which, of course, I was blissfully unaware. It was a wonderful experience, and it was very good of the crew to let me do it.

We headed back and as we were winched back up the slipway, Carol, Richard, Belinda and Rob smiled benevolently at this well-known character off the telly, temporarily turned into a small boy let loose in a sweet shop.

Afterwards I was asked if I would become an ambassador for the Lizard Lifeboat in the RNLI's attempt to find funding for a new boathouse and a state-of-the-art replacement for the current craft. I was more than happy to agree and part of the proceeds from the sales of this book is dedicated to the RNLI.

In 2011 Carol and I were invited down to witness the launch of the new lifeboat, *Rose*. The band played, the people cheered and the sun came out as *Rose* smacked the water to begin her service in saving lives at sea.

Back in 'real' life, I was asked to be in an episode of *Last of the Summer Wine*. Unlike my outing with Robert Lindsay in *My Family*, there was no question of disloyalty in a guest appearance on the much-loved *Summer Wine*. I met up again with Jean Fergusson, with whom (those of you who have read *Being Boycie* will know) I'd shared digs in Harrogate in 1969, when we become good friends. It was a pleasure to work with her again in her role as *Marina*, a long-running (and cycling) character in the show.

Everyone had been thinking that *Last of the Summer Wine* was on the last of its summer legs. It had been running since 1973, but people kept watching it simply because there were so many wonderful old turns on it, still strutting their stuff – Peter Sallis, one of the only remaining original cast members, Frank Thornton, whom I seemed to have been watching since the flood, Burt Kwouk, revered as *Clouseau's* mad assistant in the *Pink Panther* and Brian Murphy who, with Yootha Joyce, had spun off from *Man About the House* to *George & Mildred*.

Also in the regular cast was Mike Grady, whom I'd last seen wandering disconsolately from the floor at Pinewood Studios under the steely gaze of Anne Robinson, after I'd voted him off.

Mike was philosophical about his humiliating experience. 'You fucking bastard!' he told me at the time. 'I'll never speak or work with you again. You've completely wrecked my career, my family have disowned me and after I've killed myself, you're next.'

I found myself in scenes with Jean Alexander – the immortal *Hilda Ogden* from *Coronation Street*.

The roster of famous old names that had appeared on the show went on and on but sometimes as we sat around under our umbrellas, waiting for the rain to stop, we would glance around at each other and wonder if this was, in fact, God's waiting room for actors.

Soon after that we were filming *The Green, Green Grass* again – eight new shows for broadcast in the first quarter of 2009. When they were in the can and the studio work completed at Teddington, I had been hoping for further news of a fifth series which had been discussed informally with John Sullivan and Gareth Gwenlan, still producing. The viewing figures for the third series as a whole had been respectable and the fourth series felt as tight and funny as ever.

In *For Richer, for Poorer*, the last episode, *Boycie* and *Marlene* are renewing their marriage vows. Their relationship had naturally come under greater focus and had been examined more closely in our series than in *Only Fools* and had developed in a very natural way. The affection between them had been more obvious and endearing in a way that gave the whole series an extra dimension. It was one of Sullivan's qualities as a writer that he gave as much humanity and realism as he could to his characters.

However, while we'd been making this episode, we'd all commented that it felt uncomfortably like a final, final one, although we'd been assured that this wasn't the case. Indeed, two weeks after we'd said our 'goodbyes' to everyone and wished them a Merry Christmas, John Sullivan was on the phone sounding highly excitable, to say that the Beeb definitely wanted a fifth series. I can remember now, putting the phone down and feeling things couldn't get much better. We'd all had such fun in the 33 shows we'd made so far, the public were watching loyally, the local community enjoyed their involvement and were proud of the fact that their little corner of Herefordshire featured so strongly.

John Sullivan and Dewi Humphreys, our director, had rightly celebrated the stunning countryside, full of quirky little corners, rambling villages, pubs, quaint old post offices and village halls. Local friends had become involved – happily appearing as extras – and nearby farmers had provided invaluable advice, livestock and farm machinery for the show; Wigmore Abbey itself had become an iconic feature as the Boyce's Winterdown Farm.

For Christmas 2008, my pantomime schedule took me back to Llandudno, the best seaside resort in North Wales, to play *King Rat* (again) in *Dick Whittington*. It was a nostalgic trip for me, as I'd had one of my earlier jobs in rep there in 1964, when I'd met Carol Robertson who became my first wife. Then I'd worked in the magnificent Palladium Theatre, which sadly is no longer a theatre, but was been well-preserved, nevertheless, as a J D Wetherspoon's mega-boozer. The Grand Theatre, where I'd seen my colleague, Ken

The Green, Green Grass

Platt, and Arthur Askey recording a BBC Light Programme Variety Show, was now the Broadway Nightclub and Disco.

Shortly after *Dick W* had finished its run in early 2009, the fourth series of *The Green, Green Grass* had started airing to good audiences, in spite of the newest planners at the BBC moving us around the schedules like a counter on a snakes-and-ladders board. I hadn't heard anything about the proposed fifth series and I was beginning to get twitchy, when I had another call from our producer, Gareth Gwenlan. 'Sorry John, they can't confirm the new series. There's a new regime here at the BBC and they're cutting everything.'

The global economic catastrophe that had emerged in 2008 was showing no signs of going away and, indeed, looked as if it would get worse. Within this big, gloomy picture, our show was shunted into a siding and we were given the impression that when things had settled down, *The Green, Green Grass* would get a green light. In the meantime, our fourth series was being put on directly after a floundering comedy show with Caroline Quentin and in the middle of two very popular reality shows on the independent channels. Our figures suffered, although not by a very significant amount. Six months later, the word came through that our show had definitely hit the buffers.

Perhaps it was mainly a matter of the new regime at the BBC, headed by Jay Hunt, simply not liking our sort of traditional situation comedy, where previously we'd had good support in key quarters. With that support removed, the odds had been against us. Gareth Gwenlan had pointed out that ours was not the cheapest of shows to make because John Sullivan was so keen – quite rightly in my view – on the strengthened reality offered by location shooting. And in this case we couldn't tell a story about *Farmer Boyce* trying to live in the countryside without showing the countryside. The job had been made comparatively cheaper by the designer building most of what was required in and around Wigmore Abbey. *Elgin Sparrowhawk's* shed had been created from the ruins of derelict farm structures in a rick yard just fifty yards from our back door.

The series had also been used to bring on new writers. John's own son, Jim, came up with some great ideas and scripts. Daunting though it must have been to follow in such a famous father's footsteps, Jim's offerings had genuine flair and originality. When we were told that all this was no longer required, John was incensed. We were in shock. We had been told at the end of the second series that ours was the BBC's flagship comedy; now, two years later, it looked like the flagship had hit the rocks. The final episode, *For Richer, for Poorer,* was shown in March 2009.

By that stage in my career, I'd learned that it's better for one's peace of mind and general wellbeing to be philosophical when things beyond one's control don't work out. Hard though it was, I took a deep breath and started thinking about the next project.

Chapter 16
Time for Reflection

The idea of writing an autobiography had first entered my head when we were making an episode of *The Green, Green Grass* the previous year in which *Boycie* decides to write his memoirs. In *I Done It My Way*, I was speaking into a recorder, relating *Boycie's* life as he saw it – full of triumph and free from disaster. Without any irony, he thinks he's generous, magnanimous even, a man to look up to, a pillar of the community. The episode was, naturally, peppered with clips from previous episodes, not just of *The Green, Green Grass*, but also scenes from thirty years of *Only Fools & Horses*, which offered a strong dose of nostalgia for a lot of people.

Boycie's absurdly deluded image of himself, started me thinking about how I saw myself – probably very differently from the way others did.

I was used to the business of writing. I'd often jotted notes – sketches, characters observed, snatches of conversation overheard and personal experiences, particularly at more critical moments in my life. When I'd written all my impressions of South Africa after the Stoppard tour in 1977, I had put them together as a play, *Cut the Grass, so We Can See the Elephants,* which was subsequently produced in London, Amsterdam and New York.

I'd had some help then organizing the material for the play and now I thought it might be wise to get an outside eye to look over what I was doing.

Tim Hales, a friend who'd held a party for Bonhams at Wigmore Abbey seven years before, was married to journalist and magazine editor Celestria Noel. Over lunch one Sunday Carol and I asked her if she could recommend someone suitable.

She suggested Peter Burden, who had worked with Leslie Philips on his autobiography *Hello!* and with the late David Hemmings on his book *Blow Up, and Other Exaggerations.*

I'd met David, iconic star of Antonioni's 1966 cult film *Blow Up* when we were both opening a jazz festival in Marlborough a year or so before he sadly died making a film in Romania. David's widow, Lucy was also a friend of Carol's chum, Anna Hall/Barley, and she agreed with Celestria's suggestion. As an added bonus, Peter lived just ten miles away from Wigmore Abbey in the middle of Ludlow.

Once he had seen all the material and had started to pull it together in some sort of shape, he suggested there was so much to tell, I should do it in two volumes – *Being Boycie* to lead up to 1985, when *Marlene* first appeared in *Only Fools & Horses*, and the book you're reading now. It turned out to be a great experience for me to try to relive and re-examine the stop-start progress of my chequered life. I'm sure it's only from the security of the wonderful marriage I now have that I could have looked at these things with something approaching objective equanimity.

With a little more time on my hands and the house and garden now in maintenance rather than development mode, I took the chance to relax and look around at more of the local culture that surrounded me and get involved in a lot of local activities and initiatives.

A local primary school threatened by a falling roll call asked me to help publicise the imminent danger of its closure. The local arts organization responsible for putting on an annual Shakespeare production at the long-standing Ludlow Festival approached me for support and a number of local clubs and organizations wanted to hear about what Carol and I had done at Wigmore Abbey, in the Abbot's Lodgings and in the gardens we had created.

One curious aspect of local culture that I wanted to have a closer look at was the trotting racing that goes on in the Marches of Mid-Wales. For reasons still obscure, a number of Welsh farmers in the 1930s developed a taste for racing their Welsh cobs in harness, from a two-wheeled sulky. As these races became more popular and competitive, ambitious trotting owners started importing Standard-bred horses from America, where the short-coupled breed is best suited for lateral trotting, a special ground-covering gait known as 'pacing'. Although trotting is a hugely popular in Canada, the US, France and Australia, it has never caught on in a big way in Britain. I don't know why, because it can be the most exciting variant of horse racing there is, from a spectator point of view.

My first visit to the trotters (no pun intended) gave us a good day's sport, with advice from the excellent landlord of the Lion pub in Llanbister, Ray Thomas (also a trotter owner and skilled builder).

The trotting fraternity, who unlike the point-to-point punters, tend not to wear a lot of tweed, were very welcoming and invited me to autograph their mobile bar – a first for me. I haven't bought a trotter for myself yet, but I'm thinking about it; even if it never won, the manure could come in useful for the dozens of rose trees that proliferate around our Abbey garden.

While pressing on with my book, I had to prepare once again for my annual pantomime. My more or less regular date with *Captain Hook* took place for the 2009-2010 season in the Sunderland Empire, a splendid old, 1,900-seater Thornton Moss Theatre. Carol came up to do wardrobe and we were billeted at the Marriot Hotel on the sea front at Roker where we soon settled in.

One night we got back from the theatre to find that all the furniture in our room had been changed. The familiar tables and three chairs in the bay window overlooking the windswept coast and grey, white-flecked North Sea, just down from where they'd dumped the bodies out at sea in *Get Carter*, the comfortable armchairs and sofa were all gone, and had been replaced by inferior substitutes. The bed at least seemed the same but we looked at each other and wondered if maybe we'd gone mad and we were in the wrong room or had got caught up in some kind of time warp.

I shook my head. Was I in an episode of the *X Files*? I thought I'd better go down to reception and ask. On the landing I encountered a man I hadn't seen before, dressed in an anonymous grey suit, evidently with other things on his mind and wires sprouting discreetly from one ear as he cursorily looked me up and down.

More apprehensive now, I pressed the button for the lift. Like any *CSI* addict I was expecting it to open to reveal the corpse of a young woman with no discernible cause of death and an aroma of something inexplicable, like liquorice.

The red lights winking above the door told the lift was on its way up: one, two, three, four – a pause, a rattle and the doors slid open. No corpse.

I tried to rein in my paranoia; I got into the lift and descended to the lobby. As the doors opened, I saw another pale-faced man in a dull suit peering at me from over his paper. This man looked distinctly suspicious. 'Good evening,' he said, continuing to regard me closely.

I made my way to the reception desk, where an unfamiliar young woman lurked.

'Excuse me,' I said, trying to disguise a nervous tremor. 'I notice that the furniture in my room has been changed and not entirely for the better.'

'Oh... Just a moment?' the girl said, with what I gather is called the interrogative upward inflection. 'Could I have your name, please?'

'Challis.'

'And how long have you been staying with us?'

'Several weeks.'

She tapped away on a keyboard and gazed blankly at the screen in front of her. 'I'm afraid I have no record of your credit-card details.'

'No, you wouldn't have. I'm here for the duration of the pantomime and it was agreed that you wouldn't need them for all that time,' I said, beginning to feel quite grumpy.

'Oh, no? I've been looking in the wrong place? We're all at sixes and sevens at the moment – you'll never guess – we've got royalty staying with us? Here at the Marriot?' Every sentence ended in the interrogative uplift, as if each was a separate question – very annoying to those of us who weren't brought up on *Neighbours* and *Home and Away*.

'The whole place is in a state. Some poor couple even had their furniture taken out to put into the royal room?... Oh my God!?'

So that was it. It wasn't the *X-Files*. Prince Edward and Sophie had breezed into town as Sophie had charitable connections in Sunderland. They'd decided to stay the night and had nicked all my furniture. This was outrageous, I told the girl.

Word of the outrage somehow got out, perhaps because I told the story so many times and the local press were on to it.

I was asked for a quote about the high-handed attitude of the young royals demanding the best possible treatment and probably raiding *Boycie's* room knowing full well he was tricorn-hatted and thigh-booted at the Empire to entertain the shoeless, ragged-trousered children of the under-privileged north-east.

My quote was simple: 'They are the Royal Family; they should have the best they can get. I am only too willing to help in anyway I can. I am a royalist.'

Oh well.

Carol, when I told her, was inclined to be a tad more assertive. Sophie and Edward were with us for a couple of days. After they'd left I quite missed their be-suited bodyguards in the lobby, on the stairs and the landing outside our room, with their faintly amused smiles.

Early in 2010, we thought that there could be an audience for a stage show featuring *Boycie* and *Marlene*. As I mentioned earlier, one of the pleasing by-products of *The Green, Green Grass* had been the opportunity to develop the relationship between *Mr & Mrs Boyce*. John Sullivan had made good use of this and portrayed an unexpected warmth and softness between the two potentially prickly characters. This had led to a greater interest in them as a couple, so the idea of *An Evening with Boycie & Marlene* was conceived.

We developed a script based on our two individual shows that we'd been giving sporadically on cruises which, while focusing on our TV personae, also took in other elements of our two careers. We illustrated the show with live 'clips' and archive footage, making use of all audio-visual gadgets available.

We had some fresh material and new gags added, some by Steve Walls, an experienced comic who'd played *Smee* in *Peter Pan* in Sunderland. We tried it out at Stockport. It worked well and we let it be known that we could be available. The great thing about a two-handed show like this was that it required very little by way of tack, set or anything else to put it on, so we ended up touring it quite extensively and it was fun to be back on the road with Sue.

More sombrely I became involved with celebrations of the Battle of Britain that were being played out to commemorate the seventy years that had passed since the RAF fought off the Luftwaffe offensives on London. I had been receiving communications from a Group Captain Patrick Tootal, DFC, inviting me and my spouse to the Battle of Britain memorial event in Capel le Ferne. Twice I had had to decline through other commitments, but in 2010 I felt it was something to which I should give priority.

Tootals' name was vaguely familiar to me, although I wasn't conscious of his identity until I remembered a boy of that name who'd been a pupil with me at Ottershaw School. This Patrick Tootal had been one of those boys who from the day he arrived seemed older and more mature than the rest of us. He always exuded a responsible air of gravitas and I recalled he had been allowed the keys to the ATC hut very soon after joining our fledgling Air Training Corps.

When finally I made contact with him over the Battle of Britain events, he confirmed that he was indeed the same Patrick Tootal. 'And, what's more,' he added, 'I made my first and last stage appearance with you at Ottershaw in *Two Gentlemen of Verona.*'

When Carol and I went to a moving ceremony at Capel le Ferne in Kent on Battle of Britain Day, we found Tootal looking resplendent in RAF uniform complete with lashings of scrambled egg, ribbons and medals. I hadn't seen him for fifty years; he looked much the same, apart from the medals.

Comparing notes, I discovered that about the time I was trying to get my African play on in New York, and being *Boycie* in *Only Fools* for the second time, he was a key player in the logistical nightmare of getting the RAF to the Falklands to protect all those sheep from the rampaging Argies.

In Kent it was a humbling experience to stand among the last remaining members of the 'Few' beneath a fly-past of Hurricanes, Spitfires and Lancaster bombers, under the very sky where it had happened.

Wanting to do my bit for the charity that looks after these old heroes, I made a sealed bid for a trip in a helicopter that was to be chased and harried by a Spitfire over the White Cliffs of Dover.

When Tootal announced that his old school mate Challis had won the ride, I went into a state of shock, suddenly remembering how scared I was of flying. My reverie was interrupted by Michael Aspel, former newscaster, MC *par excellence* and Antiques Road Show supremo arriving at our table complaining that I had outbid him. It was something he'd always wanted to do, he said plaintively.

'Why don't we share it?' I suggested, and we met up a month later for the flight of a lifetime.

As the Sikorsky chopper rumbled into the air and sped away from the anxious faces of our friends and families, I reflected on how extraordinary life could be. Aspel and I were like excited schoolboys. We had not met before our encounter at the event, yet here we were, bucketing over the Kent countryside being pursued by perhaps the most iconic aircraft of all time.

Soon, over the intercom, we heard: 'Bandits at two o'clock. After looking the wrong way for a while, I spotted the Spitfire drifting lazily alongside us, elegant but deadly, the tilted wings giving it a slightly balletic look. As we looked she suddenly ducked out of sight, and turned up on the other side. I suddenly knew how it must have felt to be the pilot of Junkers 88 in 1940 – bloody nervous! Then the show began.

The Spitfire did a slow roll, peeled off above us and swooped down from the opposite direction on our starboard side. It was their manoeuvrability at speed, according to the great ace, Geoffrey Wellum, that gave the Spitfires such an edge. All I wanted to do now was fly in one, and looking down at the White Cliffs, I could imagine what a beacon they must have been for the returning pilots, reaffirming the defiance of these brave men.

We felt very honoured after that, when we were also invited to the Battle of Britain Seventieth Anniversary Service at Westminster Abbey. At the reception afterwards, having been introduced to a few bemused dignitaries, we wandered over towards the band, which was playing appropriate mood music from the 1940s. As we approached the music slowed, the conductor paused, smiles broke out and the lead sax took his instrument from his mouth and nodded. ''Allo, Boycie!' A surreal exchange of greetings followed and the music resumed.

We were joined by Patrick Tootal's wife, Janet, a considerable opera singer, if you please, who introduced me to the Duchess of Cornwall, dressed in stunning pale lilac. Camilla's timing was immaculate, fitting us into a small pause as a queue fretted behind her – I felt as if I were crashing the line at Tesco's checkout. She was very sunny and, surprisingly, seemed to know who I was. She asked me about my connection with the Memorial Fund and if I had been to the Abbey before. I told her I hadn't but I was used to Abbeys, as I lived in one.

'May I introduce my wife, Carol,' I inquired, knowing what a wigging I would get if I didn't. I turned to where I assumed she would be, and introduced a completely strange woman as my wife. The next

few tortuous seconds were spent explaining ham-fistedly that this was not in fact my wife, who was actually over there...
There was a lot of sighing, and eyes raised heavenwards in the waiting queue. Carol reappeared at the last moment. I introduced her, she complimented the duchess on her frock, then those who had been waiting in line took over.

The highlight of the summer in the Marches for me was playing in a big charity cricket match in aid of the high profile, successful and thoroughly deserving charity, Help for Heroes. The match was played on a beautiful cricket ground, high on a hill overlooking Ludlow in the grounds of Downton Hall (no relation to Downton Abbey), owned by the Wiggin family (no relation to the Earl of Grantham).

As a former cricketer of little distinction I was persuaded by Peter Hayter – Ludlow man and *Daily Mail* cricket correspondent – to captain the home team against an XI led by none other than Andrew 'Freddie' Flintoff.

I was excited, but frankly more nervous about coming out to face Flintoff than I had been about any theatrical performance I'd been in for years. It was so long since I'd lifted a bat in anger, I couldn't find a box, and I'd almost forgotten how to take guard. I had to borrow pads, gloves (mine had been eaten by mice – why?) as well as a bat.

At lunch before the game, in a vast marquee over a cow pasture, we were joined by Sue Holderness and her husband Mark, Nick Owen, now heading up the BBC Midlands Newsdesk, with his partner, Vicki, and Peter Burden with vintage fashionista, Nina Hely-Hutchinson.

There was a brief moment of lost dignity when Peter, turning round, he said, to listen to a short rambling address I was giving, put one leg of his chair into a rabbit hole beneath the sisal matting that covered the grass, and toppled over backwards, taking Sue Holderness with him – not the most tactful thing to do.

Young Mark Wiggin's services as a butler at dinner were auctioned off and won by the auctioneer of the day, ex-racehorse trainer Charlie Brooks and his wife, former *News of the World* editor Rebekah, who had brought an entourage including a top Page Three Girl from the *Sun*. They were there, no doubt, to get a nifty paparazzo shot of Flintoff bowling a googly at the opposition skipper's unprotected goolies but they missed *Marlene* with her legs in the air.

When the time came, I stumbled out to bat in a silly-arse cap I had found and was immediately dumbfounded by the fact that every ball was a complete mystery to me. For a start, it was the first time I'd played in glasses, and my varifocals made the ball zoom in and out of focus in a most alarming way. Added to this was the disadvantage that the bowler was Vic Marks, an ex-England Test match off-spinner. He kindly gave me a couple of runs, but then had me completely tied down.

In the next over, when I was called for a quick single by a young blade in a Harlequin cap, I trotted up and fell over my borrowed pads halfway down the wicket. The crowd roared with laughter. Jim Carter, known most recently as *Carson* the butler in *Downton Abbey*, had gamely agreed to help the cause by commentating in his rich velvety voice. He now had the generosity to suggest that my falling over routine was a deliberate attempt to inject some comedy into the proceedings. Still, I got to my feet and reached the far end unscathed.

Facing again, I saw an opportunity to make something of the lollipop bowler at the other end. I charged down the wicket to hoist his next ball over the pavilion for six, missed completely and was bowled. It was, I knew, a pretty feeble performance but I trudged off to sympathetic applause.

Part of my brief for the day was to sit in the autograph tent and sign anything that moved or was waved at me in exchange for a contribution to the Help For Heroes fund. I assumed that my lieutenant, Derek Pringle – ex-England player – would look after things in my absence when our side came to field.

There was great disappointment among England cricket fans that my opposite number, Freddie Flintoff, was famously injured and had taken no part in the game so far. However, he was allowed to bat, as long as he stayed fairly still. He strode out to the middle to great applause and started to hit our bowlers all over the place. I knew this would happen, as soon as I was off the field things would start to unravel. Evidently, Pringle just couldn't handle it.

I loped out into the field, to be greeted at once by a thunderous Flintoff drive that headed straight at me like an Exocet missile. I knew how to deal with this – bend down and get everything behind it, to set a good example to my team. I wished I hadn't tried. I obviously didn't bend far enough; the ball pinged off the end of my fingers and hit me on the shin with a crack like a rifle shot.

'God, are you all right?' enquired my concerned team.

'No problem! Doesn't hurt a bit,' I lied through gritted teeth as a rasping pain shot up my leg. I didn't want to let the lads down.

After hopping around for a bit, the pain subsided a little. Meanwhile, Flintoff had got bored with slogging the ball out of the ground and obligingly holed out to a delighted long-off, giving a local lad a chance to go home and tell his family for the next fifty years how he had caught Freddie Flintoff.

My sturdy lieutenant Pringle congratulated me on my field placing and suggested I should bowl myself and win the game for Boycie's XI. This was quite a silly idea. I'd never been a bowler at the best of times, but it was for charity and I should show willing. I took the ball and decided to bowl leg breaks.

The first ball landed with a thud at my feet and gently trickled down the wicket towards the batsman, who sniggered nastily, swung, missed and obligingly picked up the ball to throw it back to me.

My second ball flew full toss over the batsman's head, and then the wicketkeeper's, to carry on for four byes. The third was tonked past square leg for a boundary, but the fourth by some miracle was perfectly pitched, turned nicely and hit the batsman on the pads – plumb LBW. There was a massive appeal, the finger went up, high fives all round. I had taken my first wicket in over twenty years, through an inspired piece of captaincy.

Unfortunately we still lost. I blamed Pringle, but it was a great day and we raised £30,000 for the charity.

I finished up with a wrenched shoulder, a septic leg and a promise to myself *never* to play again. It took me three months to recover.

I rounded off the year by donning the now customary full-bottomed wig, frock-coat, boots and hook, this time to pay the dastardly old varlet in the lovingly restored art-deco Plaza in Stockport. The locals give tremendous support to the charming venue, built in 1932 as a theatre and movie palace and we played to packed houses night after night.

Whilst I was there on 29 December, the BBC screened a Special episode of *Rock & Chips*, John Sullivan's intended prequel to *Only*

Fools & Horses. He had extrapolated the story from two *Only Fools* episodes, *The Frog's Legacy* and the very final one, *Sleepless in Peckham*, from which it was clear that *Rodney* had been born as a result of a liaison between the *Trotters'* mother *Joan*, and *Fred Robdal*. No doubt, Sullivan had spawned the idea partly to explain away the marked physical differences between the two brothers, and partly to leave the door open for just what he was now doing.

In this flashback to the late 1950s, *Rodney's* father, *Fred* is played by Nick Lyndhurst, and boyhood versions of some of the other characters appear as well, including a young *Del Boy* and a young *Boycie*.

It was an interesting idea and seemed to catch on. We heard that John was in the process of writing more episodes. I found it an extraordinary experience watching *Rock & Chips*, seeing Stephen Lloyd playing *Boycie* as a young man. It was difficult for him, too, I imagine, to know how far he should go in terms of impersonation. The *Only Fools* characters were so well-known that there was always the risk that people watching would think, 'No... *that's* not him. That's not how *Boycie* would have done it.'

The director, Dewi Humphries, who'd also directed us in *The Green, Green Grass* had briefed them, I was told later, to try and make the characters their own, with a few nods in the direction of the 'originals'. Stephen did a great job, and I was sure when I first saw it that *Rock & Chips* had legs.

It can't have been easy for John, either, seeing these people he had resuscitated in a time warp. I remembered sitting in one of the location Winnebagos with him during the filming of the epic *Batman & Robin* sequence in *Heroes and Villains*. I'd just told him that I thought it was so brilliant it would become a classic for all time.

'Yeah, you're probably right,' he said. 'I jus' worry I'll never write anything as good as this again.' He paused and sniffed. 'I really love those characters; I really *love* 'em.'

Perhaps in *Rock & Chips* he was trying to rediscover them, all over again.

Carol and I returned from Stockport to Wigmore to start 2011 with two big projects to look forward to – finishing and publishing my first book, *Being Boycie*, and playing *Malvolio* in *Twelfth Night* at Ludlow

Castle in the open air, for the town's venerable festival that summer.

Once we'd got through the bitter winter, which saw temperatures in our valley fall as low as -15C, we were looking forward, like the rest of the nation (and half the world), to celebrating the spring wedding of Prince William and Kate Middleton. Always an enthusiastic monarchist, I'd had a particular soft spot for William since, in December 2005, he'd volunteered to become patron of one of my favourite charitable organisations, Tusk, with which I had become involved after my trips to Africa, particularly with Carol in 1993.

Since I'd first been introduced to Tusk and its activities, it had been very well directed and was by now a major international charity under the stewardship of Charlie Mayhew. With Prince William as its committed royal patron, the future for all Africa's wildlife looks a little brighter than it did.

However, before the wedding happened, all of us who had ever worked on anything written by John Sullivan suffered a great blow when it was announced that he had died on 23 April, at the age of 64, from an attack of viral pneumonia.

It wasn't surprising that we were all hit so hard, particularly those who had been in *Only Fools* which had become such an integral part of our lives. John had been responsible for effectively hand-crafting these characters with which we had become so strongly identified. We all had enormous respect for his skill for observation, his ability to make those tiny twists that turn everyday activities into hysterically funny events. I had worked closely with several great writers and I was very aware of the different qualities they brought.

Stoppard used verbal pyrotechnics and a kind of intellectual conjuring; Marks and Gran had keen eyes and ears for satirical and edgy wit. Sullivan had something quite different – a compassion and empathy for the aspirational common man. He wrote about everybody's life, even the bad bits, with affection and an underlying pulse of humour. People could always recognize their own lives in his scripts. 'I've had that! That's happened to me!'

This is why, thirty years after they were written, they still resonate and *Only Fools* still plays endlessly on UK Gold and all over the world.

At John's funeral in Surrey a week later, almost everyone who had ever acted in or been involved in the production of John's shows was there to pay genuine respects. He had left behind a widow, two sons and a daughter, including, of course, Jim, who had worked with his father on *The Green, Green Grass*.

Four days after he'd died, the BBC screened the next episode of *Rock & Chips*, the last one he had completed. Who knows where he might have taken that.

In the meantime, we had decided that the book should come out in the following September, to coincide approximately with the thirtieth anniversary of *Only Fools & Horses*. We had formed our own publishing company, Wigmore Books Ltd, to put out *Being Boycie* in order to have more say in how it was done. Having seen so many 'celebrity' autobiographies spoiled by crass editing and bad publishing, I was anxious to retain control over the key aspects of it. I had offers from mainstream publishers but it made more sense to do it myself. Carol and I got a lot of satisfaction out of overseeing the whole process and now, a year on, I'm delighted we did it that way.

However, from the beginning of June, I had to drop everything else to concentrate on *Twelfth Night*.

As a patron of the Ludlow Festival, I had always let it be known to the committee that if there were anything constructive I could do to help, they had only to ask. This year, I was delighted that they did ask.

There had been a number of splendid Shakespeare productions at Ludlow over the years, particularly, in recent times, a great *Merry Wives of Windsor* directed by Michael Bogdanov. This time, with commendable courage, the committee had booked a fresh, new talent to direct. Charlie Walker-Wise, who had graduated from Sussex University with a degree in politics, went on to RADA to become an actor. He had appeared in Ludlow in the previous year's production of *Othello*. Son of Herbie Wise, who had directed *I, Claudius*, Charlie wanted to turn his attention to directing and was to make his debut with a regular festival favourite, *Twelfth Night*.

This was a good choice for me. I knew the play very well. I'd first performed in it as a teenager with my mother's drama group in Tadworth. I'd played *Feste*, clown and commentator – a cynical, more or less objective observer that Shakespeare often employed. I'd had a minor part in the Royal Shakespeare production at Stratford in

1966, when the great Ian Holm had played *Malvolio*, and I had played *Malvolio* myself at the production in Stafford Castle in 2000.

There was a lot of work involved for this production – four weeks rehearsal in London, with two weeks' performance, in the open at the castle. As is often the case in productions like this, the cast – all professionals and some with considerable experience – were working for the Equity minimum. I didn't feel I could ask for more and so offered to do it without fee. I wanted to help my local town and its festival. I was happy to do it on that basis and they accepted my offer.

I met Charlie and I was delighted to be working with him. When I arrived in London for rehearsals, his strengths were obvious from the first read through with rest of the company. He had cast the play well. All the others knew what they were doing and responded to his encouragement to bring their feelings and ideas for their character into play.

There was more analysis of text and character than I'd come across before, even at Stratford, and extensive reading of every note ever written about the play. This to some extent reflected current drama-school thinking and to begin with, I was a little wary of it, but in the end, it was clear that it did help everyone to deliver assured, convincing performances, even if not always in ways I would initially have chosen. Charlie also explained right away that he was going to set the action on the island of Majorca at the time of the Spanish Civil War.

I'd never been particularly keen about performing Shakespeare in modern dress, always believing that in the end, the text says it all. On the other hand, audiences have told me that it can make the dialogue more comprehensible. In our *Twelfth Night*, for example, in exchanges like the knockabout cross-talk scenes between *Sir Andrew Aguecheek* and *Sir Toby Belch* (brilliantly played in Ludlow by Paul Trussell and Patrick Brennan) watching them, hearing them deliver their sixteenth-century lines while wearing twentieth-century clothing of a Bertie Wooster variety made them sound completely modern and relevant and helped the words make more sense than had they been in doublet and hose.

The Spanish setting seemed to me less relevant, although I understood the sense in which it was conveying the idea of a decaying, outmoded society.

When it came to the performances, I was more nervous than usual, I suppose because I knew I was playing to a home crowd, as it were, and there would be a number of friends and people I knew in the audience, the vast majority of whom had only ever seen me playing *Boycie* on TV. There was bound to be some lurking doubt in some of their minds that I could pull off a Shakespeare. I didn't want to disappoint them with my performance, and I certainly didn't want to let down the festival. For that, I'd worked as hard on the part as on any I've ever played.

Malvolio himself was, and is meant to be, quite cruelly treated in the play. He is a universal character, a martinet who thinks he's always right, a neo-fascist in a sense, laughed at by the others for his Puritanical attitudes.

I already had a fairly good handle on the character in a way with which, luckily, our director concurred. He was as anxious as I that this should not be a 'comedy' performance, and wanted me to understate all the techniques of comedic acting that had become almost second nature to me, both on stage and on TV. I happily went along with this, even where it was hard to keep it under control. I'll admit that a couple of times in Ludlow when the rain came down – an ever-present risk with British *al fresco* theatre – I gave in to temptation.

There is a key scene in the play, in which *Malvolio* finds a letter (deliberately and malevolently planted by his enemies) that he believes is from his mistress (in the employer sense), *Olivia*, with whom he is secretly besotted. But *Olivia's* maid has forged her writing and the letter tells him that although *Olivia* loves him, she can never admit openly to it. In a key scene on which all the subsequent plot hangs, he reads it to the audience in mounting excitement, never suspecting that it's a fake.

During one performance at Ludlow, as soon as I'd picked up the letter and begun to read it, the rain started, and was soon bucketing down. Less sturdy members of the audience started to slink away. I wondered, with my normal paranoia, if I wasn't delivering this crucial scene as well as I should, while the letter itself started to disintegrate (perhaps it should have been laminated) in a very obvious way. Bits were falling from my hand and I had to pick them up to carry on pretending to read. The audience who had remained were loving it.

All actors are whores to some extent, and easily bought by the sound of laughter; I couldn't stop myself milking it, and was cut short only by the sombre announcement from the back of ancient stone inner bailey: 'Would the actors please leave the stage.'

We waited only a quarter of an hour before the rain eased, and the emergency copy of the letter had been found. It was dropped in place, *Malvolio* made his entrance and started to read it again. At almost exactly the same spot, the heavens opened again. The letter started to disintegrate as I tried to salvage it, and of course, the intrepid audience, now strongly bonding with the intrepid cast, howled wtih laughter. Cheap laughter, you may say, but very much appreciated by a bedraggled actor trying to deliver his key secne. This time the rain eased before we were called of and from then on the bond between the players and the audience who had remained was stronger than ever, and both sides benfited greatly from it.

On a fine night, though, Ludlow can be magical. The open stage in the castle comes into its own when the swifts come out to cavort over the battlements and the occasional pigeon lumbers across a sky turning gold, then pink and the sun shafts through gothic stone windows.

It was a wonderful place to be; it was an outstanding production with a great cast and by a young director who deserves to go a long way. We were all delighted by the reception we had and I was in no doubt that, from my own point of view, it had all been well worth the time and the effort, and I hope that Ludow goes on producing fine Shakespeare far into the future.

The thirtieth anniversary of the first broadcast of *Only Fools & Horses* fell on 8 September 2011. Although we'd been anticipating this milestone for the previous year or so, it still seemed incredible that it had all started so long ago. There was still terrific public interest and affection for the show and its characters, and much was made of the anniversary, as well as the sad coincidence of John Sullivan having died just before it was reached.

Two weeks later, the first volume of my autobiography, *Being Boycie* was launched at an ebullient, crowded party at Kettner's in Romilly Street, Soho. I could hardly believe that we had finally got there, and we'd still only reached 1985! After that it was a matter of waiting to see what anyone had to say about it, and if anyone would want it.

A year on, I am grateful to the great many of you who bought and read *Being Boycie*. Thank you very much for giving me the confidence to write *Boycie & Beyond*, which, if you've got this far, I hope you've enjoyed.

In both books I've set out to give an honest account of how a committed, lifelong actor can find himself an almost iconic figure, not necessarily through any fault of his own. Against this backdrop, I've tried to depict the colossal temptations and problems involved in being an actor, and to express my gratitude that I've survived them and, with the guidance and thoughtfulness of my wife, Carol, I've been able to reach a place of happy equilibrium.

If I have any advice to pass on to aspiring young actors, it would be go for it, but watch out and be ready for the rough bits. If you're not careful, they can hurt but when it's good, it's very, very good.

Boycie & Beyond

Index

Index